THE CLOSING CIRCLE

by Barry Commoner

"One of the best and most provocative environment books since Rachel Carson's *Silent Spring*—and it may become as controversial."

—*Business Week*

"Poetic in its power . . . Explodes fashionable myths concerning pollution. It is more than a singular man's warning; it is an optimistic testament to the human race's possibilities."

—*Studs Terkel*

"It is certainly the most sober, rigorous, well-organized statement of what our environmental problems are, how we got them, and what we should do about them."

—*The New York Times Book Review*

"We must not be deceived by Commoner's tone of sweet reasonableness. Underneath the gentle exposition can be heard the urgent scream."

—*Newsweek*

D1247626

Barry Commoner

The Closing Circle
Nature, Man & Technology

For LUCY and FRED

RL 9, IL 6-up

THE CLOSING CIRCLE
*A Bantam Book | published by arrangement with
Alfred A. Knopf, Inc.*

PRINTING HISTORY
*Knopf edition published October 1971
2nd printing .... January 1972*
Book-of-the-Month Club edition published August 1971
Saturday Review Book Club edition published November 1971
Ecological Book Club edition published January 1972
A substantial portion of this book appeared in following maga-
zines: THE NEW YORKER, SATURDAY REVIEW, BUSINESS & SOCIETY
REVIEW, DES MOINES REGISTER & TRIBUNE, CHICAGO TRIBUNE, ENVI-
RONMENT, ARCHIVES OF ENVIRONMENTAL HEALTH, PROGRESSIVE,
TODAY'S EDUCATION, NO DEPOSIT—NO RETURN, THE BALANCE OF
NATURE.

*Bantam edition | November 1972
9 printings through April 1979*

The chapter on Lake Erie is adapted from an article written for
The World Book Year Book, *copyright © 1968, Field Enterprises Education Corporation.*

PRINTED IN THE UNITED STATES OF AMERICA

CONTENTS

Preface for the
Second Bantam Edition

History *does* repeat itself. In 1970 the environmental crisis burst upon a surprised world; four years later, still struggling to clean up the environment, we find ourselves in the grip of an equally unexpected enegry crisis. And once more, as in the early days of the environmental crisis, confusion reigns. In rapid succession, theories about the reason for the energy crisis are shot from the publicity guns like puffed cereal, only to turn soggy when immersed in facts.

Oil companies blame environmentalist opposition for their failure to drill for still-plentiful domestic oil; but the fact is that since 1957—long before environmentalism —oil companies have steadily reduced domestic exploration in favor of more profitable areas abroad. Automobile manufacturers blame gasoline shortages on antipollution devices that have cut down gasoline mileage; but the fact is that before these devices were installed the wizards of Detroit had already managed to reduce the gasoline mileage of the average American passenger car more than 10 percent, compared to 1946, by building big, high-powered cars, and that environmentalists opposed the new exhaust devices because they fail to control the key pollutant that triggers the smog reaction—nitrogen oxides (see Chapter 4).

Much of this kind of confusion about the energy crisis could have been eliminated if the lessons of the environmental crisis had been learned. The basic reasons for environmental degradation in the United States and all other industrialized countries since World War II are drastic changes in the technology of agricultural and industrial production and transportation: we now wash our clothes in detergents instead of soap; we drink beer out of throwaway bottles instead of returnable ones; we use man-made nitrogen fertilizer to grow food, instead of manure or crop rotation; we wear clothes made of synthetic fibers instead of cotton or wool; we drive heavy cars with high-powered, high-compression engines instead of the lighter, low-powered low-compression prewar types; we travel in airplanes and private cars and ship our freight by truck instead of using the railroads for both.

All of these changes have worsened environmental degradation: when a washerful of detergent goes down the drain it causes much more pollution than the same amount of soap; a throwaway beer bottle delivers the same amount of beer as a returnable one, but at a much higher cost in pollution and trash, since the returnable bottle is used dozens of times before it is discarded; the heavy use of chemical nitrogen fertilizer pollutes rivers and lakes, while the older agricultural methods did not; synthetic fibers, unlike natural ones, are not biodegradable, so that when discarded they are either burned—causing air pollution—or clutter up the environment forever; the modern car pollutes the air with smog and lead, while the prewar car was smog-free and could run on unleaded gasoline; airlines and private cars produce much more air pollution per passenger mile, and trucks more pollution per ton mile, than the railroads (see Chapter 9).

In every one of these cases the new, more polluting technology is also more wasteful of energy than the one it has displaced. Detergents and synthetic fibers are made out of petroleum, while natural fibers and the fat needed for soap are produced, by plants, from carbon dioxide, water and solar energy, all freely available in the environment; it takes more energy to make a throwaway bottle than it does to wash a returnable one and use it again; the modern high compression engine delivers fewer miles to the gallon than the prewar engines; nitrogen fertilizer is made out of natural gas, an energy cost not incurred when manure or crop rotation is used; railroads use much less fuel per passenger mile than passenger cars or airplanes, and much less fuel per ton mile than trucks.

The record is clear: The same technological changes that have created the environmental crisis have reduced the efficiency with which we use fuel. No one who understands why detergents, synthetic fibers and plastics, throwaway bottles, fertilizer, high-powered automobiles and trucks pollute the environment need be surprised to discover that they also waste energy.

The reason why the new technologies that waste energy and pollute the environment have been introduced is one that every businessman will understand: they are more profitable than the technologies that they have displaced (see Chapter 12). The new technologies are more profitable because they use cheap energy in place of expensive labor. However, for that very reason they are economically vulnerable to real or threatened disruptions in the energy supply and to an increase in its price. As a result, energy problems automatically become production problems: automobile assembly lines are halted by the lack of electric wire, in short supply because the plastic insulation is made of petroleum products, which have been rapidly rising in price (dealers are likely to hold goods back from the market if they expect to get a better price a little later); thousands of auto workers are laid off because the manufacturers did not anticipate that, faced with rising gasoline prices, their customers would prefer small fuel-efficient cars to big gasoline-gulping ones; food production is threatened because the price of propane has increased so much (under the pressure of intense demand for propane from plastics manufacturers) that farmers may be hard pressed to find propane when they need it to dry their grain crop. Because of the energy crisis, we may have to choose between food and plastic olive-stabbers.

In sum, what has been signalized by the environmental crisis, and demonstrated by the energy crisis, is that in adopting the new postwar production technologies the economic system has gained in short-term profitability, at the expense of a polluted environment and a productive system that is highly vulnerable to disruption.

The issues raised by the environmental and energy crises are too deep and pervasive to be solved by technical sleight-of-hand, clever tax schemes, or patchwork legislation. They call for a great national debate, to discover how the resources of the United States can best be used to serve long-term social need rather than short-term private profit.

Barry Commoner
January 15, 1974

1

THE ENVIRONMENTAL CRISIS

The environment has just been rediscovered by the people who live in it. In the United States the event was celebrated in April 1970, during Earth Week. It was a sudden, noisy awakening. School children cleaned up rubbish; college students organized huge demonstrations; determined citizens recaptured the streets from the automobile, at least for a day. Everyone seemed to be aroused to the environmental danger and eager to do something about it.

They were offered lots of advice. Almost every writer, almost every speaker, on the college campuses, in the streets and on television and radio broadcasts, was ready to fix the blame and pronounce a cure for the environmental crisis.

Some regarded the environmental issue as politically innocuous:

Ecology has become the political substitute for the

word "motherhood."—Jesse Unruh, Democratic Leader of the State of California Assembly*

But the FBI took it more seriously:

On April 22, 1970, representatives of the FBI observed about two hundred persons on the Playing Fields shortly after 1:30 p.m. They were joined a few minutes later by a contingent of George Washington University students who arrived chanting "Save Our Earth." . . . A sign was noted which read "God Is Not Dead; He Is Polluted on Earth." . . . Shortly after 8:00 p.m. Senator Edmund Muskie (D), Maine, arrived and gave a short anti-pollution speech. Senator Muskie was followed by journalist I. F. Stone, who spoke for twenty minutes on the themes of anti-pollution, anti-military, and anti-administration.—FBI report entered into Congressional Record by Senator Muskie on April 14, 1971

Some blamed pollution on the rising population:

The pollution problem is a consequence of population. It did not much matter how a lonely American frontiersman disposed of his waste. . . . But as population became denser, the natural chemical and biological recycling processes became overloaded. . . . Freedom to breed will bring ruin to all.—Garrett Hardin, biologist

The causal chain of the deterioration [of the environment] is easily followed to its source. Too many cars, too many factories, too much detergent, too much pesticide, multiplying contrails, inadequate sewage treatment plants, too little water, too much car-

---

*Quotations and factual information are referenced, and often amplified, in the Notes section beginning on p. 303.

bon dioxide—all can be traced easily to *too many people*.—Paul R. Ehrlich, biologist

Some blamed affluence:

> The affluent society has become an effluent society. The 6 percent of the world's population in the United States produces 70 percent or more of the world's solid wastes.—Walter S. Howard, biologist

And praised poverty:

> Blessed be the starving blacks of Mississippi with their outdoor privies, for they are ecologically sound, and they shall inherit a nation.—Wayne H. Davis, biologist

But not without rebuttal from the poor:

> You must not embark on programs to curb economic growth without placing a priority on maintaining income, so that the poorest people won't simply be further depressed in their condition but will have a share, and be able to live decently.—George Wiley, chemist and chairman, National Welfare Rights Organization

And encouragement from industry:

> It is not industry *per se*, but the demands of the public. And the public's demands are increasing at a geometric rate, because of the increasing standard of living and the increasing growth of population. . . . If we can convince the national and local leaders in the environmental crusade of this basic logic, that population causes pollution, then we can help them

3

focus their attention on the major aspect of the problem.—Sherman R. Knapp, chairman of the board, Northeast Utilities

Some blamed man's innate aggressiveness:

The first problem, then, is people. . . . The second problem, a most fundamental one, lies within us—our basic aggressions. . . . As Anthony Storr has said: "The sombre fact is that we are the cruelest and most ruthless species that has ever walked the earth."—William Roth, director, Pacific Life Assurance Company

While others blamed what man had learned:

People are afraid of their humanity because systematically they have been taught to become inhuman. . . . They have no understanding of what it is to love nature. And so our airs are being polluted, our rivers are being poisoned, and our land is being cut up. —Arturo Sandoval, student, Environmental Action

A minister blamed profits:

Environmental rape is a fact of our national life only because it is more profitable than responsible stewardship of earth's limited resources.—Channing E. Phillips, Congregationalist minister

While a historian blamed religion:

Christianity bears a huge burden of guilt. . . . We shall continue to have a worsening ecologic crisis until we reject the Christian axiom that nature has no reason for existence save to serve man.—Lynn White, historian

A politician blamed technology:

> A runaway technology, whose only law is profit, has for years poisoned our air, ravaged our soil, stripped our forests bare, and corrupted our water resources.—Vance Hartke, senator from Indiana

While an environmentalist blamed politicians:

> There is a peculiar paralysis in our political branches of government, which are primarily responsible for legislating and executing the policies environmentalists are urging. . . . Industries who profit by the rape of our environment see to it that legislators friendly to their attitudes are elected, and that bureaucrats of similar attitude are appointed.— Roderick A. Cameron, of the Environmental Defense Fund

Some blamed capitalism:

> Yes, it's official—the conspiracy against pollution. And we have a simple program—arrest Agnew and smash capitalism. We make only one exception to our pollution stand—everyone should light up a joint and get stoned. . . . We say to Agnew country that Earth Day is for the sons and daughters of the American Revolution who are going to tear this capitalism down and set us free.—Rennie Davis, a member of the "Chicago Seven"

While capitalists counterattacked:

> The point I am trying to make is that we are solving most of our problems . . . that conditions are

5

getting better not worse . . . that American industry is spending over three billion dollars a year to clean up the environment and additional billions to develop products that will *keep* it clean . . . and that the real danger is *not* from the free-enterprise Establishment that has made ours the most prosperous, most powerful and most charitable nation on earth. No, the danger today resides in the Disaster Lobby—those crepe-hangers who, for personal gain or out of sheer ignorance, are undermining the American system and threatening the lives and fortunes of the American people. Some people have let the gloom-mongers scare them beyond rational response with talk about atomic annihilation. . . . Since World War II over one *billion* human beings who worried about A-bombs and H-bombs died of other causes. They worried for nothing.—Thomas R. Shepard, Jr., publisher, *Look* Magazine

And one keen observer blamed everyone:

We have met the enemy and he is us.—Pogo

Earth Week and the accompanying outburst of publicity, preaching, and prognostication surprised most people, including those of us who had worked for years to generate public recognition of the environmental crisis. What surprised me most were the numerous, confident explanations of the cause and cure of the crisis. For having spent some years in the effort simply to detect and describe the growing list of environmental problems—radioactive fallout, air and water pollution, the deterioration of the soil—and in tracing some of their links to social and political processes, the identification of a single cause and cure seemed a

6

rather bold step. During Earth Week, I discovered that such reticence was far behind the times.

After the excitement of Earth Week, I tried to find some meaning in the welter of contradictory advice that it produced. It seemed to me that the confusion of Earth Week was a sign that the situation was so complex and ambiguous that people could read into it whatever conclusion their own beliefs—about human nature, economics, and politics—suggested. Like a Rorschach ink blot, Earth Week mirrored personal convictions more than objective knowledge.

Earth Week convinced me of the urgency of a deeper public understanding of the origins of the environmental crisis and its possible cures. That is what this book is about. It is an effort to find out what the environmental crisis *means*.

Such an understanding must begin at the source of life itself: the earth's thin skin of air, water, and soil, and the radiant solar fire that bathes it. Here, several billion years ago, life appeared and was nourished by the earth's substance. As it grew, life evolved, its old forms transforming the earth's skin and new ones adapting to these changes. Living things multiplied in number, variety, and habitat until they formed a global network, becoming deftly enmeshed in the surroundings they had themselves created. This is the *ecosphere,* the home that life has built for itself on the planet's outer surface.

Any living thing that hopes to live on the earth must fit into the ecosphere or perish. The environmental crisis is a sign that the finely sculptured fit between life and its surroundings has begun to corrode. As the links between one living thing and another, and between all of them and their surroundings, begin to break down, the dynamic interactions that sustain the whole have begun to falter and, in some places, stop.

Why, after millions of years of harmonious co-existance, have the relationships between living things and their earthly surroundings begun to collapse? Where did the fabric of the ecosphere begin to unravel? How far will the process go? How can we stop it and restore the broken links?

Understanding the ecosphere comes hard because, to the modern mind, it is a curiously foreign place. We have become accustomed to think of separate, singular events, each dependent upon a unique, singular cause. But in the ecosphere every effect is also a cause: an animal's waste becomes food for soil bacteria; what bacteria excrete nourishes plants; animals eat the plants. Such ecological cycles are hard to fit into human experience in the age of technology, where machine A always yields product B, and product B, once used, is cast away, having no further meaning for the machine, the product, or the user.

Here is the first great fault in the life of man in the ecosphere. We have broken out of the circle of life, converting its endless cycles into man-made, linear events: oil is taken from the ground, distilled into fuel, burned in an engine, converted thereby into noxious fumes, which are emitted into the air. At the end of the line is smog. Other man-made breaks in the ecosphere's cycles spew out toxic chemicals, sewage, heaps of rubbish—the testimony to our power to tear the ecological fabric that has, for millions of years, sustained the planet's life.

Suddenly we have discovered what we should have known long before: that the ecosphere sustains people and everything that they do; that anything that fails to fit into the ecosphere is a threat to its finely balanced cycles; that wastes are not only unpleasant, not only toxic, but, more meaningfully, evidence that the ecosphere is being driven towards collapse.

If we are to survive, we must understand *why* this collapse now threatens. Here, the issues become far more complex than even the ecosphere. Our assaults on the ecosystem are so powerful, so numerous, so finely interconnected, that although the damage they do is clear, it is very difficult to discover how it was done. By which weapon? In whose hand? Are we driving the ecosphere to destruction simply by our growing numbers? By our greedy accumulation of wealth? Or are the machines which we have built to gain this wealth —the magnificent technology that now feeds us out of neat packages, that clothes us in man-made fibers, that surrounds us with new chemical creations—at fault?

This book is concerned with these questions. It begins with the ecosphere, the setting in which civilization has done its great—and terrible—deeds. Then it moves to a description of some of the damage we have done to the ecosphere—to the air, the water, the soil. However, by now such horror stories of environmental destruction are familiar, even tiresome. Much less clear is what we need to learn from them, and so I have chosen less to shed tears of our past mistakes than to try to understand them. Most of this book is an effort to discover which human acts have broken the circle of life, and why. I trace the environmental crisis from its overt manifestations in the ecosphere to the ecological stresses which they reflect, to the faults in productive technology—and in its scientific background—that generate these stresses, and finally to the economic, social, and political forces which have driven us down this self-destructive course. All this in the hope—and expectation—that once we understand the origins of the environmental crisis, we can begin to manage the huge undertaking of surviving it.

2

THE
ECOSPHERE

To survive on the earth, human beings require the stable, continuing existence of a suitable environment. Yet the evidence is overwhelming that the way in which we now live on the earth is driving its thin, life-supporting skin, and ourselves with it, to destruction. To understand this calamity, we need to begin with a close look at the nature of the environment itself. Most of us find this a difficult thing to do, for there is a kind of ambiguity in our relation to the environment. Biologically, human beings *participate* in the environmental system as subsidiary parts of the whole. Yet, human society is designed to *exploit* the environment as a whole, to produce wealth. The paradoxical role we play in the natural environment—at once participant and exploiter—distorts our perception of it.

Among primitive people, a person is seen as a dependent part of nature, a frail reed in a harsh world governed by natural laws that must be obeyed if he is to survive. Pressed by this need, primitive peoples can achieve a remarkable knowledge of their environment. The African Bushman lives in one of the most stringent habitats on earth; food and water are scarce, and the weather is extreme. The Bushman survives because he has an incredibly intimate understanding of this environment. A Bushman can, for example, return after many months and miles of travel to find a single underground tuber, noted in his previous wanderings, when he needs it for his water supply in the dry season.

We who call ourselves advanced seem to have escaped from this kind of dependence on the environment. The Bushman must squeeze water from a searched-out tuber; we get ours by the turn of a tap. Instead of trackless terrain, we have the grid of city streets. Instead of seeking the sun's heat when we need it, or shunning it when it is too strong, we warm and cool ourselves with man-made machines. All this leads us to believe that we have made our own environment and no longer depend on the one provided by nature. In the eager search for the benefits of modern science and technology we have become enticed into a nearly fatal illusion: that through our machines we have at last escaped from dependence on the natural environment.

A good place to experience this illusion is a jet airplane. Safely seated on a plastic cushion, carried in a winged aluminum tube, streaking miles above the earth, through air nearly thin enough to boil the blood, at a speed that seems to make the sun stand still, it is easy to believe that we have conquered nature and have escaped from the ancient bondage to air, water, and soil.

But the illusion is easily shattered, for like the people it carries, the airplane is itself a creature of the earth's environment. Its engines burn fuel and oxygen produced by the earth's green plants. Traced a few steps back, every part of the craft is equally dependent on the environment. The steel came from smelters fed with coal, water, and oxygen—all nature's products. The aluminum was refined from ore using electricity, again produced by combustion of fuel and oxygen or generated by falling water. For every pound of plastic in the plane's interior, we must reckon that some amount of coal was needed to produce the power used to manufacture it. For every manufactured part, gallons of pure water were used. Without the earth's natural environmental constituents—oxygen, water, fuel—the airplane, like man, could not exist.

The environment makes up a huge, enormously complex living machine that forms a thin dynamic layer on the earth's surface, and every human activity depends on the integrity and the proper functioning of this machine. Without the photosynthetic activity of green plants, there would be no oxygen for our engines, smelters, and furnaces, let alone support for human and animal life. Without the action of the plants, animals, and microorganisms that live in them, we could have no pure water in our lakes and rivers. Without the biological processes that have gone on in the soil for thousands of years, we would have neither food crops, oil, nor coal. This machine is our biological capital, the basic apparatus on which our total productivity depends. If we destroy it, our most advanced technology will become useless and any economic and political system that depends on it will founder. The environmental crisis is a signal of this approaching catastrophe.

The global ecosystem is the product of several billion years of evolutionary change in the composition of the planet's skin. The earth is about 5.0 billion years old.

How it was formed from the cloud of cosmic dust that produced the solar system is not yet clear. But we do know that the earth was at first a lifeless, rocky mass, bathed in an atmosphere consisting largely of water vapor, hydrogen gas, ammonia, and methane.

The basic events that, from this simple beginning, generated the complex skin of the earth, including its living inhabitants, are now fairly well known. A fundamental question concerns the origin of life. Living things are made up nearly exclusively of the same four elements—hydrogen, oxygen, carbon, and nitrogen—that comprised the earth's early atmosphere. But in living things these elements take on enormously complex molecular forms, constituting the class of *organic* compounds. The basic feature of an organic compound is a connected array of carbon atoms, arranged in a straight or branched chain, or in rings. Built into this basic structure are the other major atoms—hydrogen, oxygen, and nitrogen (and less frequently, additional ones such as sulfur, phosphorus, and various metals) in proportions and spatial arrangements that are characteristic of each specific organic compound. The resulting variety and complexity is staggering.

What process could convert the few simple molecules in the earth's early atmosphere into the monumentally complex, yet highly selected, assemblage of organic compounds that we now find in living things? For a long time it was believed that this accomplishment was the unique capability of living things. This would mean that life, in its full chemical competence, somehow appeared in a single, spontaneous event on the earth or came to the earth through space from some other source. According to this view, the origin of life must have preceded the appearance of organic chemicals on the earth.

We now know that the reverse is true and that organic compounds were derived from the simple ingredients of the earth's early atmosphere by nonliving, geochemical processes—and themselves later gave rise to life. The geochemical origin of organic compounds has been imitated in the laboratory; a mixture of water, ammonia, and methane, exposed to ultraviolet light, an electric spark, or just heat, produces detectable amounts of such organic compounds as amino acids—which linked together become proteins. Ultraviolet light was readily available from solar radiation on the primitive earth's surface. There is now good reason to believe that under this influence the simple compounds of the earth's early atmosphere were gradually converted into a mixture of organic compounds. Thus, to use an image favored by the originator of this theory, Professor A. I. Oparin, there appeared on the earth a kind of "organic soup."

It was within this soup that the first living things developed, two to three billion years ago. How that happened is a fascinating but poorly understood problem; fortunately we do know enough about the characteristics of the first forms of life to establish their dependence—and their effects—on the environment.

It now seems quite clear that the first forms of life were nourished by the ancient earth's organic soup. All living things require organic substances as food, which is the source of both the energy that drives them and their own substance. Oxygen was lacking in the early earth's atmosphere, so that the first living things must have derived energy from organic foods without combusting them with oxygen. This type of metabolism—fermentation—is the most primitive energy-yielding process in living things; it always produces carbon dioxide.

Themselves the products of several billion years of slow geochemical processes, the first living things became, in turn, powerful agents of geochemical change. To begin with, they rapidly depleted the earth's previously accumulated store of the organic products of geochemical evolution, for this was their food. Later the first photosynthetic organisms reconverted carbon dioxide into organic substances. Then, the rapid proliferation of green plants in the tropical temperature of the early earth deposited a huge mass of organic carbon, which became in time coal, oil, and natural gas. And with the photosynthetic cleavage of the oxygen-containing water molecule, the air acquired free oxygen in its atmosphere. Some of the oxygen was converted to ozone, an avid absorber of ultraviolet radiation. Now, for the first time, the earth's surface was shielded from solar ultraviolet radiation, a serious hazard to life. This event enabled life to emerge from the protection of its original underwater habitat. With free oxygen now available, more efficient forms of living metabolism became possible and the great evolutionary outburst of plants and animals began to populate the planet. Meanwhile terrestrial plants and microorganisms helped to convert the earth's early rocks into soil and developed within it a remarkably complex system of interdependent living things. A similar system developed in surface waters. These systems control the composition of the soil, of surface waters, and the air, and consequently regulate the weather.

There is an important lesson here. In the form in which it first appeared, the earth's life system had an inherently fatal fault: the energy it required was derived from the consumption of a *nonrenewable* resource, the geochemical store of organic matter. Had this fault not been remedied, the rapid self-propagated growth of life would have consumed the earth's original "organic soup." Life would have destroyed the condition for its own survival. Survival—a property now so deeply associated with life—became possible because of a timely evolutionary development: the emergence of the first photosynthetic organisms. These new organisms used sunlight to convert carbon dioxide and inorganic materials to fresh organic matter. This crucial event reconverted the first life-form's waste, carbon dioxide, into its food, organic compounds. It closed the loop and transformed what was a fatally linear process into a circular, self-perpetuating one. Since then the perpetuation of life on the earth has been linked to an essentially perpetual source of energy—the sun.

Here in its primitive form we see the grand scheme which has since been the basis of the remarkable continuity of life: the reciprocal interdependence of one life process on another; the mutual, interconnected development of the earth's life system and the nonliving constituents of the environment; the repeated transformation of the materials of life in great cycles, driven by the energy of the sun.

The result of this evolutionary history can be summarized in a series of propositions about the nature of life and its relation to the environment:

Living things, as a whole, emerged from the nonliving skin of the earth. Life is a very powerful form of chemistry, which, once on the earth, rapidly changed its surface. Every living thing is intimately dependent on its physical and chemical surroundings, so that as these changed, new forms of life suited to new surroundings could emerge. Life begets life, so that once new forms appeared in a favorable environment, they could proliferate and spread until they occupied every suitable environmental niche within physical reach. Every living thing is dependent on many others, either indirectly through the physical and chemical features of the environment or directly for food or a sheltering place. Within every living thing on the earth, indeed within each of its individual cells, is contained another network —on its own scale, as complex as the environmental system—made up of numerous, intricate molecules, elaborately interconnected by chemical reactions, on which the life-properties of the whole organism depend.

Few of us in the scientific community are well prepared to deal with this degree of complexity. We have been trained by modern science to think about events that are vastly more simple—how one particle bounces off another, or how molecule A reacts with molecule B. Confronted by a situation as complex as the environment and its vast array of living inhabitants, we are likely—some more than others—to attempt to reduce it in our minds to a set of separate, simple events, in the hope that their sum will somehow picture the whole. The existence of the environmental crisis warns us that this is an illusory hope. For some time now, biologists have studied isolated animals and plants, and biochemists have studied molecules isolated in test tubes, accumulating the vast, detailed literature of modern biological science. Yet these separate data have yielded no sums that explain the ecology of a lake, for instance, and its vulnerability.

I make this confession as a preliminary to my own effort, in what follows, to describe the environmental system in a way that may help us understand the present crisis. The confession is intended as a reminder that any such description rests on clumsy intellectual crutches. We have so long neglected the task of understanding natural, complex processes, such as those in the environment, that our methods are still crude and uncertain.

Consider the numerous ways of thinking about the environment. First there is its spatial complexity: how can we encompass in a unifying idea the existence, as a stable, continuing entity, of the richly populated, kaleidoscopic ambiance of a tropical jungle and the seemingly dead, unchanging desert? Then there is the multiplicity of living things in the environment: what common features can explain the environmental behavior of a mouse, a hawk, a trout, an earthworm, an ant, the bacteria of the human intestine, or the algae that color Lake Erie green? Then there is the variety of biochemical processes that are not only internal to every living thing, but that also mediate its interactions with other living things and the environment: how can we hold within a single set of ideas photosynthesis, the fermentative decay of organic matter, oxygen-requiring combustion, or the intricate chemical dependence of one organism on another which leads to parasitism?

Each of these separate views of the environmental system is only a narrow slice through the complex whole. While each can illuminate some features of the whole system, the picture it yields is necessarily false to a degree. For in looking at one set of relationships we inevitably ignore a good deal of the rest; yet in the real world everything in the environment is connected to everything else.

One interesting slice through the environment can be taken by tracing the movement of the chemical elements that make up the environmental system. A good choice is the element nitrogen—a crucial constituent of both life and the nonliving environment. The four chemical elements that make up the bulk of living matter—carbon, hydrogen, oxygen, and nitrogen—move in great, interwoven cycles through the ecosphere: now a component of the air, now a constituent of a living organism, now part of some waste product in water, after a time perhaps built into mineral deposits or fossil remains.

Among these four elements of life, nitrogen is particularly important because it is so sensitive an indicator of the quality of life. A first sign of human poverty is a reduced intake of nitrogenous food. A certain outcome is poor health, for so much of the body's vital machinery is made of nitrogen-bearing molecules: proteins, nucleic acids, enzymes, vitamins, and hormones. Nitrogen is, therefore, closely coupled to human needs, and, as we shall see, the global processes that govern the movement of nitrogen are in a particularly delicate balance.

In the ecosphere, nitrogen is found in relatively few basic chemical forms. A striking feature of nitrogen chemistry is that molecules that contain nitrogen linked to oxygen are rather rare. About 80 per cent of the earth's nitrogen is in the air as chemically inert nitrogen gas. Of the remaining 20 per cent, a good deal is a part of the soil's humus, a very complex organic substance. Another significant fraction is contained in living things —almost entirely as organic compounds.

With these facts as a guide, let us look at some features of the nitrogen cycle in the natural environment. The soil is a useful place to begin, for it is, of course, the initial source of nearly all food and many industrial raw materials. The soil is a vastly complex ecosystem, the result of an intricate balance among a wide variety of microorganisms, animals, and plants, acting on a long-established physical substrate.

Nitrogen can enter the soil through nitrogen fixation, a process carried out by various bacteria and algae, some of them living free in the soil and others associated with the roots of legumes such as clover or with the leaves of some tropical plants. Nitrogen also enters the soil from the decay of plant matter and of animal wastes. Much of it eventually becomes incorporated into the soil's humus. Humus slowly releases nitrogen through the action of soil microorganisms, which finally convert it into nitrate. In turn, the nitrate is taken up by the roots of plants and is made into protein and other vital parts of the crop. In nature the plants become food for animals, animal wastes are returned to the soil, and the cycle is complete.

By far the slowest step in this cycle is the release of nitrate from humus. As a result, the natural concentration of nitrate in the soil water is very low and the roots need to work to pull it into the plant. For this work the plant must expend energy, which is released by biological oxidation processes in the roots. The required oxygen must reach the roots from the air, a process that is efficient only if the soil is sufficiently porous. Soil porosity is very dependent on its humus content, for humus has a very spongy structure. Thus, soil porosity, therefore its oxygen content, and hence the efficiency of nutrient absorption by plant roots are closely related to the humus content of the soil. The efficient growth of the plant reconverts inorganic nutrients into organic matter (the plant substance), which when decayed in the soil contributes to its humus content, thus enhancing the soil's porosity and thereby supporting efficient plant growth.

It is useful to pause at this point and consider the implications of the two sets of relationships that have just been described: one the over-all movement of nitrogen atoms through the soil cycle, the other the interdependence of the plant's efficient growth and the structure of the soil. Note that the two cycles are not of the same sort. One describes the literal movement of a physical entity, the nitrogen atom; the other is more abstract, involving a set of dependencies of one process on another. The two cycles are strongly connected at a crucial point—humus. In one cycle, humus is the major store of soil nitrogen for plant growth; in the other, it is responsible for the physical condition of the soil that enables the efficient use of nutrients, including nitrogen released from the humus.

This duality in the role of humus in the soil amplifies the effects of changes in soil condition. Thus, if the soil's humus content declines, the availability of nitrate for plant growth is reduced. Since at the same time the efficiency of nitrate absorption by the roots also falls, the effect of humus on plant growth is self-accelerating. Or, viewed in the opposite sense, adequate soil humus ensures not only a good supply of nutrient nitrogen, but also its thrifty use by the plant. Any environmental agent, such as humus, that links two or more cycles is likely to play a powerful role in the system as a whole. Such a link enhances the complexity of the system, the fineness of its network, and thereby contributes to its stability. For this very reason, when such a link is weakened, the ecological fabric is likely to unravel.

Obviously, to appreciate the crucial significance of a link such as humus, we must see it, simultaneously, in *both* its roles. Unfortunately this type of vision is not fostered by the kind of specialization that isolates biologists into separate camps: experts on soil structure *or* on plant nutrition. As we shall see a little later on, the natural tendency to think of only one thing at a time is a chief reason why we have failed to understand the environment and have blundered into destroying it.

In natural waters a similar nitrogen cycle prevails, except that the large reserve of organic nitrogen, represented in the soil by humus, is lacking. In aquatic ecosystems, nitrogen moves cyclically through the following closed sequence: fish produce organic wastes; decaying microorganisms release nitrogen from organic forms and combine it with oxygen to form nitrate; this is reconverted to organic forms by algae; algal organic matter nourishes small aquatic animals; these in turn are eaten by the fish. The balance between the rate of decay of organic materials and the rate of algal growth determines the concentrations of nitrate in the water. In nature, little nitrate reaches the water from the soil because of its thrifty use in the soil cycle. As a result, the nitrate content of natural surface water is very low, of the order of one part per million, and the algal population is correspondingly low; the water is clear and largely free of noxious organic debris.

Compared with the other ecological arenas—soil and water—the air is the largest, most uniform around the globe and affected least directly by biological action. In nature, air is remarkably uniform in composition: about 80 per cent nitrogen gas, nearly 20 per cent oxygen gas, with a very low concentration of carbon dioxide (about .03 per cent), very much lower concentrations of a few rare gases such as helium, neon, and argon, and variable amounts of water vapor. Like everything else on earth, the behavior of the global sea of air is governed by cycles, but these involve largely physical phenomena rather than chemical or biological ones.

On a short time-scale, the air cycle is simply what we call "weather." The weather cycle is driven by the sun's energy, which bathes the earth incessantly. Any substance on the earth's surface that absorbs solar energy— for example, soil—is warmed by it unless the energy causes a change in state. Energy absorbed by ice, a solid, instead of warming it, can convert it to the liquid state—water. Energy absorbed by water either warms it or converts it to the gaseous state—water vapor. If the energy-absorbing material is readily changed in state—for example, the water in the ocean —a good part of the absorbed solar energy does not raise the temperature. So after a sunny day, the sand is hot and the water relatively cool. Before sundown, air above the hot sand, being warm and light, rises; the cooler air over the water flows in to take its place— there is a cool on-shore breeze.

Absorbed by the oceans, which cover two-thirds of the earth's surface, a good deal of the solar energy is taken up by the conversion of liquid water to water vapor—the process of evaporation. Every gram of water vapor carried in the air embodies a fixed amount of solar energy (about 536 calories per gram). When the reverse process—condensation of water vapor into liquid—occurs, this same quantity of energy is released. So, energy absorbed from the sun, say, during hot summer days in the Caribbean Sea fills the air with water vapor. As the water vapor rises from the earth's surface, it strikes the very cold air of the stratosphere and begins to condense, to form rain. For every gram of water vapor that condenses to rain, 536 calories of energy are released. This heats the air, causing it to rise; cool air rushes in near the surface to replace the rising hot air —winds are created. This is the origin of Caribbean hurricanes.

These are only small examples of weather—the daily changes in the air that bathes each place on the earth. For our purpose, the main thing to keep in mind is that the weather is a means of moving the air mass that covers a particular locale, such as a city, and a way of washing airborne materials—such as pollutants—out of it. The weather keeps the air clean. Anything that becomes airborne, caught by the weather, is eventually brought to earth where it enters the environmental cycles that operate in the water and the soil.

If there is little air movement, whatever is introduced into the air by local activities—for example, smog— tends to accumulate in the air. Still-air conditions have a way of perpetuating themselves. When air is still, it tends to develop into an upper zone of warm air and a lower zone of cold air. This reverses the usual situation, in which the lower layers of air are warmer than the upper ones; it is therefore called an *inversion*. Since cold air is denser than warm air, vertical circulation is prevented under inversion conditions. An inversion may hold the air mass over a city in place for some days. When that happens, as it did in New York City in November 1966, pollutants may accumulate to the point of an emergency.

These weather changes are chiefly in the lower reaches of the atmosphere—the layer between the earth's surface and about 40,000 to 50,000 feet above it. Above that point is the stratosphere, where there is nearly no moisture, no clouds, no rain or snow. Some things that enter the air are so light as to escape into the stratosphere, where they may remain for a long time. Some of the radioactive debris produced by nuclear explosions is associated with such small particles, and they may remain in the stratosphere for months.

On a much longer time-scale, changes in the composition of the air can have strong effects on the amount and kind of solar radiation that reach the earth's surface. These effects are influenced by the amounts of airborne dust particles, water vapor, clouds, carbon dioxide, and ozone. Generally, water vapor and clouds have a shielding effect; radiation directed toward the earth from the sun is scattered by water droplets and much of it may then fail to reach the earth. Therefore cloudy conditions tend to reduce the earth's temperature.

Carbon dioxide has a special effect because it is transparent to most of the sun's radiation except that in the infrared region of the spectrum. In this respect, carbon dioxide is like glass, which readily transmits visible light, but reflects infrared. This is what makes glass so useful in a greenhouse in the winter. Visible energy enters through the glass, is absorbed by the soil in the greenhouse, and then is converted to heat, which is reradiated from the soil as infrared energy. But this infrared energy, reaching the greenhouse glass, is bounced back and held within the greenhouse as heat. This explains the warmth of an otherwise unheated greenhouse on a sunny winter day. Like glass, the carbon dioxide in the air that blankets the earth acts like a giant energy valve. Visible solar energy easily passes through it; reaching the earth, much of this energy is converted to heat, but the resultant infrared radiation is kept within the earth's air blanket by the heat reflection due to carbon dioxide.

Thus, the higher the carbon dioxide concentration in the air, the larger the proportion of solar radiation that is retained by the earth as heat. This explains why on the early earth, when the carbon dioxide concentration was high, the average temperature of the earth approached the tropical. Then, as great masses of plants converted much of the carbon dioxide to vegetation—which became fossilized to coal, oil, and gas—the earth became cooler. Now that we have been burning these fossil fuels and reconverting them to carbon dioxide, the carbon dioxide concentration of the atmosphere has been rising; what effect this may be having on the earth's temperature is now under intense scientific discussion.

Another constituent of the air, ozone, plays a special role in governing the radiation that is received at the earth's surface. Ozone is a chemically reactive molecule composed of three atoms of oxygen joined in a triangle. It is a good absorber of ultraviolet radiation. Ozone is formed from oxygen, but since it reacts vigorously with substances near the earth's surface, it is present, as such, only in the upper reaches of the stratosphere. So, when the earth's atmosphere acquired its oxygen from the photosynthetic activity of green plants, the planet also acquired a high-altitude blanket of ozone. Until then the earth's surface was bathed in intense ultraviolet radiation, which was, in fact, the energy source that converted the early earth's blanket of methane, water, and ammonia into the soup of organic compounds in which the first living things originated. However, ultraviolet radiation is very damaging to the delicate balance of chemical reactions in living cells, and it is likely that the first living things survived only by growing under a layer of water sufficiently thick to protect them from

27

the ultraviolet radiation that reached the earth's surface.

Only when oxygen was formed, and with it the protective layer of ozone, was the intensity of ultraviolet radiation on the earth's surface reduced sufficiently to allow living things to emerge from the protection of water and begin to inhabit the earth's surface. The continued existence of terrestrial life is dependent on the layer of ozone in the stratosphere—a protective device that itself is the product of life. Should the ozone in the stratosphere be reduced, terrestrial life would be seriously threatened by solar ultraviolet radiation. It is unfortunate that some human activities raise this threat. An example is the supersonic transport (the SST).

In broad outline, these are the environmental cycles which govern the behavior of the three great global systems: the air, the water, and the soil. Within each of them live many thousands of different species of living things. Each species is suited to its particular environmental niche, and each, through its life processes, affects the physical and chemical properties of its immediate environment.

Each living species is also linked to many others. These links are bewildering in their variety and marvelous in their intricate detail. An animal, such as a deer, may depend on plants for food; the plants depend on the action of soil bacteria for their nutrients; the bacteria in turn live on the organic wastes dropped by the animals on the soil. At the same time, the deer is food for the mountain lion. Insects may live on the juices of plants or gather pollen from their flowers. Other insects suck blood from animals. Bacteria may live on the internal tissues of animals and plants. Fungi degrade the bodies of dead plants and animals. All this, many times multiplied and organized species by species in intricate, precise relationships, makes up the vast network of life on the earth.

The science that studies these relationships and the processes linking each living thing to the physical and chemical environment is *ecology*. It is the science of planetary housekeeping. For the environment is, so to speak, the house created on the earth *by* living things *for* living things. It is a young science and much of what it teaches has been learned from only small segments of the whole network of life on the earth. Ecology has not yet explicitly developed the kind of cohesive, simplifying generalizations exemplified by, say, the laws of physics. Nevertheless there are a number of generalizations that are already evident in what we now know about the ecosphere and that can be organized into a kind of informal set of "laws of ecology." These are described in what follows.

The First Law of Ecology:
Everything Is Connected to Everything Else

Some of the evidence that leads to this generalization has already been discussed. It reflects the existence of the elaborate network of interconnections in the ecosphere: among different living organisms, and between populations, species, and individual organisms and their physicochemical surroundings.

The single fact that an ecosystem consists of multiple interconnected parts, which act on one another, has some surprising consequences. Our ability to picture the behavior of such systems has been helped considerably by the development, even more recent than ecology, of the science of cybernetics. We owe the basic concept, and the word itself, to the inventive mind of the late Norbert Wiener.

The word "cybernetics" derives from the Greek word for helmsman; it is concerned with cycles of events that steer, or govern, the behavior of a system. The helmsman is part of a system that also includes the compass, the rudder, and the ship. If the ship veers off the chosen compass course, the change shows up in the movement of the compass needle. Observed and interpreted by the helmsman this event determines a subsequent one: the helmsman turns the rudder, which swings the ship back to its original course. When this happens, the compass needle returns to its original, on-course position and the cycle is complete. If the helmsman turns the rudder too far in response to a small deflection of the compass needle, the excess swing of the ship shows up in the compass—which signals the helmsman to correct his overreaction by an opposite movement. Thus the operation of this cycle stabilizes the course of the ship.

In quite a similar way, stabilizing cybernetic relations are built into an ecological cycle. Consider, for example, the fresh-water ecological cycle: fish—organic waste—bacteria of decay—inorganic products—algae—fish. Suppose that due to unusually warm summer weather there is a rapid growth of algae. This depletes the supply of inorganic nutrients so that two sectors of the cycle, algae and nutrients, are out of balance, but in opposite directions. The operation of the ecological cycle, like that of the ship, soon brings the situation back into balance. For the excess in algae increases the ease with which fish can feed on them; this reduces the algal population, increases fish waste production, and eventually leads to an increased level of nutrients when the waste decays. Thus, the levels of algae and nutrients tend to return to their original balanced position.

In such cybernetic systems the course is not maintained by rigid control, but flexibly. Thus the ship does not move unwaveringly on its path, but actually follows it in a wavelike motion that swings equally to both sides of the true course. The frequency of these swings depends on the relative speeds of the various steps in the cycle, such as the rate at which the ship responds to the rudder.

Ecological systems exhibit similar cycles, although these are often obscured by the effects of daily or seasonal variations in weather and environmental agents. The most famous examples of such ecological oscillations are the periodic fluctuations of the size of fur-bearing animal populations. For example, from trapping records in Canada it is known that the populations of rabbits and lynx follow ten-year fluctuations. When there are many rabbits the lynx prosper; the rising population of lynx increasingly ravages the rabbit population, reducing it; as the latter become scarce, there is insufficient food to support the now numerous lynx; as the lynx begin to die off, the rabbits are less fiercely hunted and increase in number. And so on. These oscillations are built into the operation of the simple cycle, in which the lynx population is positively related to the number of rabbits and the rabbit population is negatively related to the number of lynx.

In such an oscillating system there is always the danger that the whole system will collapse when an oscillation swings so wide of the balance point that the system can no longer compensate for it. Suppose, for example, in one particular swing of the rabbit—lynx cycle, the lynx manage to eat *all* the rabbits (or, for that matter, all but one). Now the rabbit population can no longer reproduce. As usual, the lynx begin to starve as the rabbits are consumed; but this time the drop in the lynx population is not followed by an increase in rabbits. The lynx then die off. The entire rabbit—lynx system collapses.

This is similar to the ecological collapse which accompanies what is called "eutrophication." If the nutrient level of the water becomes so high as to stimulate the rapid growth of algae, the dense algal population cannot be long sustained because of the intrinsic limitations of photosynthetic efficiency. As the thickness of the algal layer in the water increases, the light required for photosynthesis that can reach the lower parts of the algal layer becomes sharply diminished, so that any strong overgrowth of algae very quickly dies back, releasing organic debris. The organic matter level may then become so great that its decay totally depletes the oxygen content of the water. The bacteria of decay then die off, for they must have oxygen to survive. The entire aquatic cycle collapses.

The dynamic behavior of a cybernetic system—for example, the frequency of its natural oscillations, the speed with which it responds to external changes, and its over-all rate of operation—depends on the relative rates of its constituent steps. In the ship system, the compass needle swings in fractions of a second; the helmsman's reaction takes some seconds; the ship responds over a time of minutes. These different reaction times interact to produce, for example, the ship's characteristic oscillation frequency around its true course.

In the aquatic ecosystem, each biological step also has a characteristic reaction time, which depends on the metabolic and reproductive rates of the organisms involved. The time to produce a new generation of fish may be some months; of algae, a matter of days; decay bacteria can reproduce in a few hours. The metabolic rates of these organisms—that is, the rates at which they use nutrients, consume oxygen, or produce waste —is inversely related to their size. If the metabolic rate of a fish is 1, the algal rate is about 100, and the bacterial rate about 10,000.

If the entire cyclical system is to remain in balance, the over-all rate of turnover must be governed by the slowest step—in this case, the growth and metabolism of the fish. Any external effect that forces part of the cycle to operate faster than the over-all rate leads to trouble. So, for example, the rate of waste production by fish determines the rate of bacterial decay and the rate of oxygen consumption due to that decay. In a balanced situation, enough oxygen is produced by the algae and enters from the air to support the decay bacteria. Suppose that the rate at which organic waste enters the cycle is increased artificially, for example, by dumping sewage into the water. Now the decay bacteria are supplied with organic waste at a much higher level than usual; because of their rapid metabolism they are able to act quickly on the increased organic load. As a result, the rate of oxygen consumption by the decay bacteria can easily exceed the rate of oxygen production by the algae (and its rate of entry from the air) so that the oxygen level goes to zero and the system collapses. Thus, the rates of the separate processes in the cycle are in a natural state of balance which is maintained only so long as there are no external intrusions on the system. When such an effect originates outside the cycle, it is not controlled by the self-governing cyclical relations and is a threat to the stability of the whole system.

33

Ecosystems differ considerably in their rate characteristics and therefore vary a great deal in the speed with which they react to changed situations or approach the point of collapse. For example, aquatic ecosystems turn over much faster than soil ecosystems. Thus, an acre of richly populated marine shoreline or an acre of fish pond produces about seven times as much organic material as an acre of alfalfa annually. The slow turnover of the soil cycle is due to the rather low rate of one of its many steps—the release of nutrient from the soil's organic store, which is very much slower than the comparable step in aquatic systems.

The amount of stress which an ecosystem can absorb before it is driven to collapse is also a result of its various interconnections and their relative speeds of response. The more complex the ecosystem, the more successfully it can resist a stress. For example, in the rabbit—lynx system, if the lynx had an alternative source of food they might survive the sudden depletion of rabbits. In this way, branching—which establishes alternative pathways—increases the resistance of an ecosystem to stress. Most ecosystems are so complex that the cycles are not simple circular paths, but are crisscrossed with branches to form a network or a fabric of interconnections. Like a net, in which each knot is connected to others by several strands, such a fabric can resist collapse better than a simple, unbranched circle of threads—which if cut anywhere breaks down as a whole. Environmental pollution is often a sign that ecological links have been cut and that the ecosystem has been artificially simplified and made more vulnerable to stress and to final collapse.

The feedback characteristics of ecosystems result in amplification and intensification processes of considerable magnitude. For example, the fact that in food chains small organisms are eaten by bigger ones and the latter by still bigger ones inevitably results in the concentration of certain environmental constituents in the bodies of the largest organisms at the top of the food chain. Smaller organisms always exhibit much higher metabolic rates than larger ones, so that the amount of their food which is oxidized relative to the amount incorporated into the body of the organism is thereby greater. Consequently, an animal at the top of the food chain depends on the consumption of an enormously greater mass of the bodies of organisms lower down in the food chain. Therefore, any *non*metabolized material present in the lower organisms of this chain will become concentrated in the body of the top one. Thus, if the concentration of DDT (which is not readily metabolized) in the soil is 1 unit, earthworms living in the soil will achieve a concentration of from 10 to 40 units, and in woodcocks feeding on the earthworms the DDT level will rise to about 200 units.

All this results from a simple fact about ecosystems—everything is connected to everything else: the system is stabilized by its dynamic self-compensating properties; these same properties, if overstressed, can lead to a dramatic collapse; the complexity of the ecological network and its intrinsic rate of turnover determine how much it can be stressed, and for how long, without collapsing; the ecological network is an amplifier, so that a small perturbation in one place may have large, distant, long-delayed effects.

The Second Law of Ecology:
Everything Must Go Somewhere

This is, of course, simply a somewhat informal restatement of a basic law of physics—that matter is indestructible. Applied to ecology, the law emphasizes that in nature there is no such thing as "waste." In every natural system, what is excreted by one organism as waste is taken up by another as food. Animals release carbon dioxide as a respiratory waste; this is an essential nutrient for green plants. Plants excrete oxygen, which is used by animals. Animal organic wastes nourish the bacteria of decay. Their wastes, inorganic materials such as nitrate, phosphate, and carbon dioxide, become algal nutrients.

A persistent effort to answer the question "Where does it go?" can yield a surprising amount of valuable information about an ecosystem. Consider, for example, the fate of a household item which contains mercury—a substance with environmental effects that have just recently surfaced. A dry-cell battery containing mercury is purchased, used to the point of exhaustion, and then "thrown out." But where does it really go? First it is placed in a container of rubbish; this is collected and taken to an incinerator. Here the mercury is heated; this produces mercury vapor which is emitted by the incinerator stack, and mercury *vapor* is toxic. Mercury vapor is carried by the wind, eventually brought to earth in rain or snow. Entering a mountain lake, let us say, the mercury condenses and sinks to the bottom. Here it is acted on by bacteria which convert it to methyl mercury. This is soluble and taken up by fish; since it is not metabolized, the mercury accumulates in the organs and flesh of the fish. The fish is caught and eaten by a man and the mercury becomes deposited in his organs, where it might be harmful. And so on.

This is an effective way to trace out an ecological path. It is also an excellent way to counteract the prevalent notion that something which is regarded as useless simply "goes away" when it is discarded. Nothing "goes away"; it is simply transferred from place to place, converted from one molecular form to another, acting on the life processes of any organism in which it becomes, for a time, lodged. One of the chief reasons for the present environmental crisis is that great amounts of materials have been extracted from the earth, converted into new forms, and discharged into the environment without taking into account that "everything has to go somewhere." The result, too often, is the accumulation of harmful amounts of material in places where, in nature, they do not belong.

The Third Law of Ecology:
Nature Knows Best

In my experience this principle is likely to encounter considerable resistance, for it appears to contradict a deeply held idea about the unique competence of human beings. One of the most pervasive features of modern technology is the notion that it is intended to "improve on nature"—to provide food, clothing, shelter, and means of communication and expression which are superior to those available to man in nature. Stated baldly, the third law of ecology holds that any major man-made change in a natural system is likely to be *detrimental* to that system. This is a rather extreme claim; nevertheless I believe it has a good deal of merit if understood in a properly defined context.

I have found it useful to explain this principle by means of an analogy. Suppose you were to open the back of your watch, close your eyes, and poke a pencil into the exposed works. The almost certain result would be damage to the watch. Nevertheless, this result is not *absolutely* certain. There is some finite possibility that the watch was out of adjustment and that the random thrust of the pencil happened to make the precise change needed to improve it. However, this outcome is exceedingly improbable. The question at issue is: why? The answer is self-evident: there is a very considerable amount of what technologists now call "research and development" (or, more familiarly, "R & D") behind the watch. This means that over the years numerous watchmakers, each taught by a predecessor, have tried out a huge variety of detailed arrangements of watch works, have discarded those that are not compatible with the over-all operation of the system and retained the better features. In effect, the watch mechanism, as it now exists, represents a very restricted selection, from among an enormous variety of possible arrangements of component parts, of a singular organization of the watch works. Any random change made in the watch is likely to fall into the very large class of inconsistent, or harmful, arrangements which have been tried out in past watch-making experience and discarded. One might say, as a law of watches, that "the watchmaker knows best."

There is a close, and very meaningful, analogy in biological systems. It is possible to induce a certain range of random, inherited changes in a living thing by treating it with an agent, such as x-irradiation, that increases the frequency of mutations. Generally, exposure to x-rays increases the frequency of all mutations which have been observed, albeit very infrequently, in nature and can therefore be regarded as *possible* changes. What is significant, for our purpose, is the universal observation that when mutation frequency is enhanced by x-rays or other means, nearly all the mutations are harmful to the organisms and the great majority so damaging as to kill the organism before it is fully formed.

In other words, like the watch, a living organism that is forced to sustain a random change in its organization is almost certain to be damaged rather than improved. And in both cases, the explanation is the same—a great deal of "R & D." In effect there are some two to three billion years of "R & D" behind every living thing. In that time, a staggering number of new individual living things have been produced, affording in each case the opportunity to try out the suitability of some random genetic change. If the change damages the viability of the organism, it is likely to kill it before the change can be passed on to future generations. In this way, living things accumulate a complex organization of compatible parts; those possible arrangements that are not compatible with the whole are screened out over the long course of evolution. Thus, the structure of a present living thing or the organization of a current natural ecosystem is likely to be "best" in the sense that it has been so heavily screened for disadvantageous components that any new one is very likely to be worse than the present ones.

This principle is particularly relevant to the field of organic chemistry. Living things are composed of many thousands of different organic compounds, and it is sometimes imagined that at least some of these might be improved upon if they were replaced by some man-made variant of the natural substance. The third law of ecology suggests that the artificial introduction of an organic compound that does not occur in nature, but is man-made and is nevertheless active in a living system, is very likely to be harmful.

This is due to the fact that the varieties of chemical substances actually found in living things are vastly more restricted than the *possible* varieties. A striking illustration is that if one molecule each of all the possible types of proteins were made, they would together weigh more than the observable universe. Obviously there are a fantastically large number of protein types that are *not* made by living cells. And on the basis of the foregoing, one would reason that many of these possible protein types were once formed in some particular living things, found to be harmful, and rejected through the death of the experiment. In the same way, living cells synthesize fatty acids (a type of organic molecule that contains carbon chains of various lengths) with even-numbered carbon chain lengths (i.e., 4, 6, 8, etc., carbons), but no fatty acids with odd-numbered carbon chain lengths. This suggests that the latter have once been tried out and found wanting. Similarly, organic compounds that contain attached nitrogen and oxygen atoms are singularly rare in living things. This should warn us that the artificial introduction of substances of this type would be dangerous. This is indeed the case, for such substances are usually toxic and frequently carcinogenic. And, I would suppose from the fact that DDT is nowhere found in nature, that somewhere, at some time in the past, some unfortunate cell synthesized this molecule—and died.

One of the striking facts about the chemistry of living systems is that for every organic substance produced by a living organism, there exists, somewhere in nature, an enzyme capable of breaking that substance down. In effect, no organic substance is synthesized unless there is provision for its degradation; recycling is thus enforced. Thus, when a new man-made organic substance is synthesized with a molecular structure that departs significantly from the types which occur in nature, it is probable that no degradative enzyme exists, and the material tends to accumulate.

Given these considerations, it would be prudent, I believe, to regard every man-made organic chemical *not* found in nature which has a strong action on any one organism as potentially dangerous to other forms of life. Operationally, this view means that all man-made organic compounds that are at all active biologically ought to be treated as we do drugs, or rather as we *should* treat them—prudently, cautiously. Such caution or prudence is, of course, impossible when billions of pounds of the substance are produced and broadly disseminated into the ecosystem where it can reach and affect numerous organisms not under our observation. Yet this is precisely what we have done with detergents, insecticides, and herbicides. The often catastrophic results lend considerable force to the view that "Nature knows best."

The Fourth Law of Ecology:
There Is No Such Thing as a Free Lunch

In my experience, this idea has proven so illuminating for environmental problems that I have borrowed it from its original source, economics. The "law" derives from a story that economists like to tell about an oil-rich potentate who decided that his new wealth needed the guidance of economic science. Accordingly he ordered his advisers, on pain of death, to produce a set of volumes containing all the wisdom of economics. When the tomes arrived, the potentate was impatient and again issued an order—to reduce all the knowledge of economics to a single volume. The story goes on in this vein, as such stories will, until the advisers are required, if they are to survive, to reduce the totality of economic science to a single sentence. This is the origin of the "free lunch" law.

In ecology, as in economics, the law is intended to warn that every gain is won at some cost. In a way, this ecological law embodies the previous three laws. Because the global ecosystem is a connected whole, in which nothing can be gained or lost and which is not subject to over-all improvement, anything extracted from it by human effort must be replaced. Payment of this price cannot be avoided; it can only be delayed. The present environmental crisis is a warning that we have delayed nearly too long.

The preceding pages provide a view of the web of life on the earth. An effort has been made to develop this view from available facts, through logical relations, into a set of comprehensive generalizations. In other words, the effort has been scientific.

Nevertheless, it is difficult to ignore the embarrassing fact that the final generalizations which emerge from all this—the four laws of ecology—are ideas that have been widely held by many people without any scientific analysis or professional authorization. The complex web in which all life is enmeshed, and man's place in it, are clearly—and beautifully—described in the poems of Walt Whitman. A great deal about the interplay of the physical features of the environment and the creatures that inhabit it can be learned from *Moby Dick*. Mark Twain is not only a marvelous source of wisdom about the nature of the environment of the United States from the Mississippi westward, but also a rather incisive critic of the irrelevance of science which loses connection to the realities of life. As the critic Leo Marx reminds us, "Anyone familiar with the work of the classic American writers (I am thinking of men like Cooper, Emerson, Thoreau, Melville, Whitman, and Mark Twain) is likely to have developed an interest in what we recently have learned to call ecology."

Unfortunately, this literary heritage has not been enough to save us from ecological disaster. After all, every American technician, industrialist, agriculturalist, or public official who has condoned or participated in the assault on the environment has read at least some of Cooper, Emerson, Thoreau, Melville, Whitman, and Mark Twain. Many of them are campers, bird-watchers, or avid fishermen, and therefore to some degree personally aware of the natural processes that the science of ecology hopes to elucidate. Nevertheless, most of them were taken unawares by the environmental crisis, failing to understand, apparently, that Thoreau's woods, Mark Twain's rivers, and Melville's oceans are *today* under attack.

The rising miasma of pollution has helped us to achieve this understanding. For, in Leo Marx's words, "The current environmental crisis has in a sense put a literal, factual, often quantifiable base under this poetic idea [i.e., the need for human harmony with nature]." This is perhaps the major value of the effort to show that the simple generalizations which have already emerged from perceptive human contact with the natural world have a valid base in the facts and principles of a science, ecology. Thus linked to science, these ideas become tools for restoring the damage inflicted on nature by the environmental crisis.

In the woods around Walden Pond or on the reaches of the Mississippi, most of the information needed to understand the natural world can be gained by personal experience. In the world of nuclear bombs, smog, and foul water, environmental understanding needs help from the scientist.

3

NUCLEAR
FIRE

I learned about the environment from the United States Atomic Energy Commission in 1953. Until then, like most people, I had taken the air, water, soil, and our natural surroundings more or less for granted. Although I was a scientist working on the fundamental properties of living things, I had received hardly any training in the special branch of biology that deals with environmental relations—ecology. However, like most of the scientists who had worked for the U.S. war program during World War II, I was overwhelmingly concerned with the new, enormously destructive force of nuclear energy born during the war.

In 1946 the Atomic Energy Commission (AEC) was created, to take charge of a massive U.S. program to develop the military, scientific, and industrial potential of atomic and nuclear energy. By 1951 the United States had exploded sixteen test bombs and the Soviet Union, thirteen, and the following year Great Britain joined in with its first test.

These explosions took place in remote, uninhabited areas of the world and their results were blanketed in military secrecy. The AEC normally issued only a terse announcement that a test had taken place, that a bomb's radiation had been confined to a local area, and in any case was "harmless" to the public. Public discussion of the nuclear arms race was muzzled by Cold War hysteria and McCarthyism. But nature broke through these barriers.

On April 26, 1953, the city of Troy, New York, was drenched with a sudden cloud burst. As the rain fell, physicists in nearby university laboratories who were experimenting with radioactivity noticed a sudden surge in their "background" radiation counts. They soon discovered that the rain was highly radioactive and surmised that radio active debris—fallout—from nuclear tests in Nevada had been carried by winds across the country and brought to earth by the heavy rain. Some of the physicists warned their wives to bring the children inside; but they made no public report, for that would violate the secrecy rules. However, scientists have a strong tendency to communicate among themselves, and soon physicists in laboratories throughout the United States were privately testing the radioactivity in rainfall and in dust wiped off their cars. It was everywhere: air, rain, soil, food, and water were contaminated by the radioactivity from nuclear explosions. Despite official secrecy, atomic energy had made its environmental debut.

All atomic radiation is destructive to living things, and many biologists regarded fallout as a potential hazard to everything alive. But, as the AEC was quick to point out, the fallout radiation reaching a person from the air, dust, or soil was low—not much higher than the in-

tensity of radiation naturally emanated in the external
environment from radium in rocks and by cosmic rays
from outer space. And much of it was incapable of
penetrating very deeply into the body. The hazard of
such radiation, from outside the body, was slight—or so
it seemed.

Then a new fallout term turned up in private conver-
sations among scientists—strontium 90. My own experience is probably typical of most nonphysicists who had
no professional interest in environmental radioactivity.
I recall several cryptic remarks by physicist friends that
radioactive strontium—strontium 90—had been detected in fallout. More meaningful was the worried look
that accompanied the information; for some reason,
which was never stated, strontium 90 appeared to be a
particularly dangerous form of radioactivity.

As it happens, strontium, a natural, harmless element,
and its radioactive isotope, strontium 90, both move
through the environment in concert with calcium, a
chemically similar element. And calcium is avidly withdrawn from the soil by plants, becoming incorporated
into food and then taken up in the human body. Once
fallout appeared on the earth, inevitably strontium 90
would accompany calcium as it moved through the food
chain, ultimately becoming concentrated, along with
calcium, in vegetables, in milk, in the bones of people.

Radiation from strontium 90 cannot penetrate
through more than a small fraction of an inch of living
tissue. However, once it is incorporated into the body,
the isotope becomes closely packed around the living
cells of the bone. These cells then lie within easy reach
of strontium 90 radiation, and the risk to them—for
example, from cancer—becomes enormously more
severe than the risk from the same amount of strontium

90 outside the body. Suddenly, many of us in the scientific community began to worry about the fallout, and by the end of 1953 this concern broke through the screen of secrecy, and the fallout problem became public. Then a serious accident during an AEC test in the Pacific Ocean in March 1954 helped to dramatize the fallout problem—the unexpected exposure to fallout of the crew of the Japanese fishing boat *The Lucky Dragon*. A number of sailors suffered serious radiation sickness; several later died of it.

In 1953 the AEC had claimed that the hazard of strontium 90 was limited to "the ingestion of bone splinters which might be intermingled with muscle tissue during butchering and cutting of meat." By 1954 open scientific discussion of the biology of strontium 90 absorption had reminded the AEC that most people ingest far more calcium—and with it, strontium 90—from milk than from splinters of bone in their hamburgers. In that year the AEC initiated an urgent project to find ways of removing strontium 90 from contaminated milk.

Before long, strontium 90 data from all parts of the world began to appear in scientific journals, and it became clear that tests of nuclear weapons had unwittingly set off the first global environmental experiment in human history. Fallout had spread strontium 90—and several other radioactive elements—into the huge planetary network of living things; man-made radioactivity had accumulated in every plant, animal, and microorganism on the earth.

For many of us, the meaning of the environment and its importance to human life was suddenly brought to light. With elaborate skill and enormous resources, the AEC—and its Soviet and British counterparts—had accomplished what they thought to be a specific, technological feat for the single purpose of producing huge, destructive explosions. No one had *intended* to poison the earth with radioactivity or to threaten the health of human beings. But now, for the first time in the history of man, children grew up with strontium 90 built into their bones and iodine 131 embedded in their thyroid glands.

What linked the secret, supposedly isolated, nuclear exposions to the children was the environment. Winds carried fallout debris from the test site across the face of the globe; rain and snow brought it to earth; the growth of grass and food crops drew it from the soil; foods carried fallout radioactivity into children's bodies; natural biological processes in their bones and glands intensely concentrated the radioactive elements and amplified the risk to the children's health. Each nuclear explosion thrust radioactivity into the environment, the elaborate communication network in which every living thing is emmeshed. Unwittingly, the military technicians had tied their bombs into the network, with results that no one wanted—or could have predicted.

The nuclear tests revealed how little we knew about the environmental network. When the test program began, it was assumed that fallout driven into the stratosphere by the force of a nuclear explosion would remain there for years, allowing time for much of the initial radioactivity to decay harmlessly. Only later was it learned that there are currents in the stratosphere that carry fallout to the earth in a matter of months and which, rather than allowing it to spread evenly over the globe, dump most of it in the North Temperate Zone. About 80 per cent of the world's people live there. Contrary to AEC expectations, Arctic Eskimos and

Laplanders had much more fallout radioactivity in their bodies than did people in the temperate zones of the world, although the amount of fallout reaching the ground in the arctic was less than a tenth of that in the North Temperate Zone. The reason: the distinctive biological chain of the Arctic, where lichens, unlike grass, take up fallout directly from the air rather than through the soil, which can dilute it. Thus, lichens introduce intense radioactivity into the caribou and reindeer which eat them, and into the Eskimos and Laplanders who live on caribou and reindeer. We are still unable to explain large variations in fallout uptake in local regions of the North Temperate Zone—why milk in Mandan, North Dakota, or New Orleans, Louisiana, has exceeded all other United States milk supplies in strontium 90 level, or why the world's record for strontium 90 in milk is held by the area of Milan, Italy.

We also learned, from fallout, how little was known about the risks incurred by large populations exposed to radiation or toxic substances. Before the advent of nuclear energy, medical experience with the internal effects of radiation was very limited, based largely on the fate of several hundred unfortunate women who in the 1920's had used their lips to point up brushes for applying radium-containing luminous paint on watch dials. Standards of radiation exposure were set on the assumption that, at some minimal level, the body would experience no harm at all from radiation, and the AEC used these standards in order to support their claim that fallout was "harmless" to the population as a whole. Later, when it was realized that unlike industrial workers, the general population is unable to escape exposure (for example, by quitting a job) and includes especially susceptible individuals such as children and the aged, the "acceptable" limits were reduced to about 3 per cent of their original value. Finally, experiments showed that *every* exposure to radiation, however small, carries with it *some* risk, in the form of genetic damage or cancer; that there is no absolutely "harmless" exposure to radiation. So that in the end, despite its complex scientific features, the problem of exposure to radiation becomes not a scientific matter, but one of public morality. For no one can say, on scientific grounds, how many children ought to risk thyroid cancer or genetic defects from fallout for the sake of developing a new nuclear weapon, which itself is only a step toward world catastrophe. This becomes not a matter for "expert" decision, but for public judgment —a political question, and a moral one.

Fallout made its political debut in the 1956 U.S. presidential contest between Adlai E. Stevenson and Dwight D. Eisenhower. During the campaign, Dr. Evarts Graham of Washington University, a pioneer in lung surgery and the effects of smoking on lung cancer, asked several of us in the university's science faculty to prepare factual material on fallout, which Dr. Graham incorporated into a letter to Mr. Stevenson. When the letter was read in the course of a campaign speech by Mr. Stevenson, a central issue of the campaign was joined.

Mr. Stevenson lost the election, but his defeat convinced many scientists of the vital need to get the facts about nuclear weapons to the public.

In 1958 some of us at Washington University in St. Louis, together with a group of civic leaders, organized the St. Louis Committee for Nuclear Information, which through its magazine and speakers' bureau pioneered the development of what has since become the scientists' information movement, now largely devoted to public education about all environmental problems. Many of us went out into the community, to PTA meetings, to church and civic groups and tried to explain what the fallout hassle was about. We talked about the origin of strontium 90 and iodine 131 in nuclear explosions and their movement through the environment into human bodies. We discussed the potential human cost of the supposed benefits of new nuclear weapons. We emphasized that the balancing of social judgment against cost should be made by every citizen and not left to the experts. And similar efforts were being made in many parts of the country.

In 1963, much to the surprise of political observers, the United States Senate overwhelmingly confirmed the United States-USSR Limited Nuclear Test Ban Treaty ending the testing of nuclear weapons in the atmosphere by the two great nuclear powers. This unexpected event was a tribute to the political effectiveness of the scientists' campaign to inform the public about fallout.

The Nuclear Test Ban Treaty should be regarded, I believe, as the first victorious battle in the campaign to save the environment—and its human inhabitants—from the blind assaults of modern technology. It was only a small victory, for U.S. and Soviet nuclear tests continue in underground vaults, and China and France, which are not bound by the Treaty, continue atmospheric testing. But although the Nuclear Test Ban Treaty has failed to stop the nuclear arms race, it has had two important results. The first is that it has saved lives.

The human cost of fallout is not exactly known. What is known, and widely acknowledged, is that a number of serious hazards to human health—cancer, genetic defects, general life-shortening—are instigated by radiation. A good part of the natural incidence of cancer and genetic defects must be due to the "natural" (i.e., pre-fallout) level of radiation from radioactive rocks and cosmic rays. From a comparison of the natural rate of radiation-induced genetic defects with the rate of defects following the extra radiation due to fallout, it can be estimated that fallout had probably caused about 5,000 defective births in the U.S. population and about 86,000 in the world population up to 1963. The United Nations Scientific Committee on the Effects of Atomic Radiation has made a similar estimate: between 2,500 and 100,000 serious genetic defects, world-wide, due to tests up to 1958. On the other hand, Dr. Ernest Sternglass estimates that fallout may be responsible for 400,000 infant and fetal deaths in the United States alone. Dr. Arthur R. Tamplin of the AEC's Livermore (California) Laboratory believes that a better estimate of the number of such deaths due to fallout is 4,000. Obviously the exact estimate of the human cost of fallout radiation is a matter of dispute. But the crucial scientific fact, which none of the contending parties now denies, is that fallout has exacted *some* cost in human disease and death. And the effect of the Nuclear Test Ban Treaty on that cost is equally clear. Had nuclear testing continued until 1970 at the 1962 rate, the fallout radiation burden borne by human beings would now be much greater than it is—in the case of strontium 90, about eight to ten times greater.

The second important result of the treaty is that it established that nuclear weaponry is a *scientific* failure. We now know that nuclear weapons are, in fact, incapable of defending the nation: regardless of the outcome of a nuclear war between the two major powers, neither society would survive the holocaust. In this sense, the nuclear bomb is a useless weapon—a fact of which the government was apparently unaware when the decision to "go nuclear" was made sometime after 1945. No elaborate proof is needed for this assertion. It is now widely recognized that the failure of nuclear "defense" lies in the ecological disasters that it would surely set off. To show that the United States military were unaware of this fatal fault of nuclear weapons, it is sufficient to quote the following from a 1961 report of the Rand Corporation to the United States Air Force on the ecological consequences of nuclear war:

> It is a point of view which has been strangely neglected (although many have been vaguely concerned), and detailed research is conspicuously absent. . . . Many of the ecological principles underlying the problems involved are not part of the intellectual equipment of people ordinarily concerned with Civil Defense and postwar recovery.

Like the nuclear test program, the entire system of nuclear weaponry, when subjected to an environmental test, fails.

That the AEC failed to learn a lesson in environmental science from its experience with nuclear weapons is also evident in its later efforts to develop the peaceful uses of nuclear energy. Here, for example, are samples of the efforts of Dr. Gerald W. Johnson, associate director of the Plowshare program (an AEC program to use nuclear explosions for peacetime purposes): April 1964, Columbus, Mississippi—proposal to use nuclear explosives in the construction of a 253-mile canal from the Tennessee River to the Gulf of Mexico. February 1965, St. Louis, Missouri—proposal to use nuclear explosives "inexpensively to blast navigational obstructions" in the Mississippi River. September 1965, Seattle, Washington—proposal to use nuclear explosives to dig a canal from the Columbia River to Puget Sound.

In making these proposals, AEC officials always warned the public that the promised project would have to be preceded by extensive research, designed to work out a few remaining wrinkles in the technology of nuclear excavations. These included minimizing the radiation hazard and finding some way around a provision of the Nuclear Test Ban Treaty against dissemination of radioactive material outside the nation's borders.

The needed research has now been completed in connection with a proposal to blast a new sea-level canal across the Isthmus of Panama. This was so monumental a scheme as to require a six-year study by a presidential commission. The commission's report, issued in December 1970, is illuminating. After spending $17 million studying the possibility of constructing the canal with nuclear explosives, the commission recommended that the canal be constructed by *conventional* methods. The reasons given for rejecting the nuclear approach included "unanswered questions about the safety of nuclear devices" and "possible conflicts with the Nuclear Test Ban Treaty."

In April 1964, Dr. Johnson, speaking at Columbus, Mississippi, was asked by a member of the audience: "Has Project Plowshare ever done anything of practical benefit to us?"

His reply: "The answer is no."

Today the answer is still no. Since it began in 1957,

the Plowshare program has produced stacks of reports, dozens of scientific symposia, numerous press releases—and two wells that yield gas which is probably too radioactive for commercial use. The total cost is about $138 million. In 1970 federal funds were withdrawn from Plowshare, and there is little prospect that they will be restored. Plowshare has been a $138 million exercise in futility. It has foundered in the environment.

The only peacetime use of nuclear energy which is now *operational* is the generation of electric power. Like every other nuclear activity in the United States, this is under the aegis of the AEC. In its enabling legislation, the AEC is charged with promoting the domestic use of nuclear energy. It also sets the safety standards for the construction and operation of nuclear plants, grants the necessary licenses, and checks for violations. With this unprecedented range of administrative powers concentrated in a single agency, along with the AEC's overriding importance in the national military program and its essentially unhindered access to funds, the nuclear power industry has grown rapidly.

The first full-scale nuclear power plant in the United States went into operation in 1957. By 1965 there were eleven operating plants. In 1970 fourteen plants were in operation, and seventy-eight more were under construction or in preparation. By 1975 eighty-four plants are expected to be in operation. Although nuclear plants now account for only about one per cent of the nation's total electric output, this figure is expected to rise to 37 per cent by 1980 and to more than 50 per cent by 2000.

In the light of these statistics, the nuclear power industry in the United States would appear to be a spectacular success story. However, anyone attending the industry's annual meeting, the Atomic Industrial Forum, in 1970, would have received a very different impression. In the past years such meetings were devoted to speeches extolling the undiluted virtues of nuclear power and to more technical expositions on the engineering of nuclear reactors. That year a new subject dominated the talks: ecology. For the first time, the industry had been forced publicly to face the environmental consequences of its operation. And the outlook was not very bright.

Unlike fossil-fuel power plants, nuclear power plants do not produce chemical pollutants such as sulfur dioxide or dust. However they do produce radioactive pollutants. The AEC claims that this is no cause for public concern because nuclear plants release radioactive materials into the environment in amounts which are well below AEC safety standards. Nevertheless, in recent years public concern has been sufficiently intense to delay, and in some cases block, the construction of several projected power plants. In the words of the then chairman of the AEC, Dr. Glenn T. Seaborg, "The public is up-tight about the environment."

But the AEC has been harassed by more than public complaints. In Minnesota the State Water Pollution Control Agency adopted environmental requirements for a proposed nuclear reactor which are appreciably more stringent than those of the AEC. The AEC disputed the state's right to impose these standards, and the power company attacked the action in the courts. Then a new concern about the environmental effects of radiation arose within the AEC's own Livermore Laboratory. There, in 1963—the year of the limited Nuclear Test Ban Treaty—the AEC decided to establish a research group to "plan and conduct studies of environmental contamination due to release of radioactivity from nuclear detonations for peaceful or military purposes." Dr. John W. Gofman, professor of medical physics at the University of California (which operates the Livermore Laboratory for the AEC), was chosen to direct the program. Since 1963 Dr. Gofman, in collaboration with Dr. Tamplin, has produced a long series of reports on radioactive contamination of the environment. A chief outcome of this work is their proposal that the AEC radiation standards be reduced to 1/10 their present level—a proposal which was then intensely opposed by the AEC and the nuclear power industry.

Some sense of the scope of this controversy can be gained from the following: Drs. Gofman and Tamplin concluded that if the radiation dosage "acceptable" under AEC standards were in fact received by the total United States population, the result would be 32,000 extra deaths each year, from cancer and leukemia. In rebuttal, the late Dr. Theos J. Thompson, an AEC commissioner, asserted that radiation exposure to the general population due to the actual operation of the nuclear power industry is less than 1/17,000 of the exposure permitted by the AEC standard. On the other hand, Dr. K. Z. Morgan of the AEC's Oak Ridge National Laboratory has calculated that extra deaths annually due to all types of radiation-induced disease resulting from present nuclear industry operations are about one-half per cent of the deaths expected from exposure at the acceptable standard. This would leave little room for complacency, for the expected expansion of the nuclear power industry might well take radiation exposures beyond even the present "acceptable" standard by the year 2000.

In 1971, after strongly resisting proposals for more stringent reactor emission standards, the AEC gave in to a degree by proposing an appreciable reduction in permissible radioactive release. However, in taking this action, the AEC gave no explanation for its earlier opposition to more rigorous standards or for its continued opposition to the Gofman-Tamplin proposal. Until these discrepancies are cleared up, the controversy over the environmental effects of nuclear power plants will continue. Yet on the outcome of this controversy hangs the entire future of the nuclear power industry. Radioactive emissions from nuclear plants may arise from the development of tiny leaks in the metal sheaths around the reactor's fuel elements. The fabrication of these sheaths is an exacting task; long stretches of thin metal tubing must be made to withstand not only mechanical strains, but also the deteriorating effects of intense radiation. Reducing the present amounts of radioactive emissions will require either the improvement of this already highly advanced and difficult technology or the addition of devices which remove, much more effectively than at present, radioactive materials in liquid and gaseous reactor effluents. Either of these developments would be sufficiently expensive to reduce the present economic position that nucelar power holds, tenuously, against competition from more conventional generators. If the power industry is required to adjust to this change through its own private enterprise, it will be forced, by economic considerations, to choose conventional generators over nuclear ones. On the other hand, if the difference is to be made up by government subsidy, the industry faces the prospect of admitting deeper government penetration into its economic operations.

At the same time, the power industry is confronted by a growing national shortage of electricity. Blackouts and brownouts have become increasingly commonplace in certain areas of the United States. Thus, on one hand, the industry is pressed to construct new power plants as soon as possible; on the other, it faces the need to choose between nuclear generators and conventional ones. The hope that the bonanza of nuclear power would enable the nation to expand power generation without restraint has suddenly been shattered against the same barrier which nuclear technology has, at every turn, confronted—the environment.

When the world learned, on that fateful day in 1945, of the successful construction of an atomic bomb, it was clear that a new period in human history had begun. Those who have marked the day by remembering the Hiroshima dead foresaw an era of deadly peril for humanity and feared an inexorable march toward the holocaust of a Third, and final, World War. Those who sensed, instead, in the brilliant flash of the bomb that man had at last "harnessed the power of the stars," dreamed of an era in which, with unlimited power, mankind—or some lesser portion of it—could achieve all the goals that power commands.

As the atomic era has unfolded since 1945, the contrast between these two visions has sharpened and the gulf between those who follow them has grown wider. On one side are those who fear that humanity will be crushed beneath the ungovernable power of nuclear technology; many of them are the young, who were born with the bomb and have lived a life in which, because of it, doomsday may come tomorrow. On the other side are some of their elders, who possess or hope to possess some of the new power, if need be at the cost of human lives.

Despite this confrontation, there is a widespread conviction that the new knowledge is sound, that the new technology is therefore competent, and that the new power is thereby irresistible. The first 25 years of the atomic age tell us that this belief is deeply, tragically, wrong. Isolated on a Pacific island or confined to the grounds of a power plant, nuclear energy is a success. It works: it vaporizes the island; it sends electricity surging out of the power plant. But neither the island nor the power plant—nor anything else on the earth's surface—exists apart from the thin, dynamic fabric that envelopes the planet: its environment, the ecosphere. And once power from the split atom impinges on the environment, as it must, we discover that our knowledge is incomplete, that the new technology is therefore incompetent and that the new power is thereby something that *must* be governed if we are to survive.

This, it seems to me, is the meaning of the first environmental encounter of the new age of technology. Our experience with nuclear power tells us that modern technology has achieved a scale and intensity that begin to match that of the global system in which we live. It reminds us that we cannot wield this power without deeply intruding on the delicate environmental fabric that supports us. It warns us that our capability to intrude on the environment far outstrips our knowledge of the consequences. It tells us that every environmental incursion, whatever its benefits, has a cost—which, from the still silent testimony of the world's nuclear weapons, may be survival.

Yet this same experience with the first 25 years of

the nuclear age has a more hopeful message: seen in its true, environmental context, the power of nuclear technology is subject less to the control of the technologist than to the governance of the public will.

4

LOS
ANGELES
AIR

For teaching us a good deal of what we now know about modern air pollution, the world owes a great debt to the city of Los Angeles, California. There are few cities in the world with climates so richly endowed by nature and now so disastrously polluted by man. In Los Angeles this contrast was strong enough to motivate early attention to the cause and cure of air pollution. As a result, scientists and public officials in California have produced what is probably the most complete and informative record we have of that complex and still unresolved morass, modern urban air.

The first air pollutant to cause trouble in Los Angeles was an ancient one—dust. Between 1940 and 1946 dust-fall in the city increased from about 100 tons to nearly 400 tons per day. The sources were easily located: industrial smokestacks and incinerators. Beginning in 1947 control measures—the installation of dust-precipitators and prohibition of open burning— were instituted. Within two years dust-fall was down to

200 tons per day and has since declined to its prewar level.

However, in 1943 the residents of Los Angeles noticed something new in the air: a whitish haze, sometimes tinged with yellow-brown that brought with it eye-smarting and tears. This condition rapidly worsened and spread throughout the mountain-ringed basin that comprises Los Angeles County.

The Angelenos came to call the new pollutant "smog," adopting a term invented in England to describe the thick clouds which in five days in 1952 killed 4,000 Londoners—the world's worst air pollution disaster. The dangerous component in London smog was sulfur dioxide, a gas that attacks the cells lining the lungs' air passages, reducing their natural self-protective action against other air pollutants such as dust and bringing on serious respiratory distress. On the basis of the English experience, sulfur dioxide appeared to be the most likely cause of the new pollution problem in Los Angeles. Sulfur dioxide emissions had in fact increased sharply in the area as a result of wartime industrialization (sulfur dioxide is produced by the burning of sulfur-containing coal and fuel oil). An effort was made to control these emissions, through fuel changes. This succeeded, and beginning in 1947 sulfur dioxide emissions were gradually reduced, reaching the prewar levels by 1960.

Nevertheless, smog worsened. The first clue to its real origin came from the California Institute of Technology laboratory of Dr. Arie J. Haagen-Smit who was interested in the effects of light on organic compounds, especially from plants. He discovered that the eye-irritating haze was produced by the action of sunlight on otherwise invisible pollutants in the air.

Later research revealed the whole story. It begins with nitrogen oxides, which are produced whenever air becomes hot enough (as it does in high-temperature power plants and high-powered gasoline engines) to cause its natural nitrogen and oxygen to interact. Activated by sunlight, nitrogen oxides combine with organic compounds such as waste gasoline, producing the material which is the chief visible—and noxious—final product of photochemical smog, peroxyacetylnitrate (PAN). Thus Los Angeles smog is different from London smog (named from *smo*ke plus *fog*), and a strict etymology would forbid its use to describe Los Angeles air. It is some kind of tribute to the growing importance of the Los Angeles type of smog that London's word has now been taken over by this newcomer among air pollutants. As now used, at least in the United States, the word "smog" (more precisely, "photochemical smog") refers to the Los Angeles variety.

With this chemical information in hand, Los Angeles authorities were quick to seek smog-control methods. An obvious approach was to reduce emissions of hydrocarbons into the air. A ready target were the numerous oil fields, refineries, and other activities of the large petroleum industry that had sprung up in the area. Rigid controls were imposed on open venting of oil wells and refineries. Hydrocarbon emissions from the petroleum industry were sharply reduced, from about 2,100 tons per day in 1940 to about 250 tons per day in 1957.

Nevertheless, Los Angeles smog conditions continued to deteriorate. Year by year high smog levels become more frequent. In 1959 eye irritation was reported in Los Angeles County on 187 days of the year; in 1960 there were 198 such days; in 1961, 186 days; in 1962, 212 days. Despite a vigorous and successful effort to control industrial emissions of hydrocarbons, Los Angeles was still in the grip of smog.

In 1953 new evidence made the situation—if not the air—much clearer. A survey showed that while the petroleum industry was emitting about 500 tons of hydrocarbons per day, about 1,300 tons per day were being emitted by automobiles, trucks, and buses. By 1957 motor vehicles were responsible for about 80 per cent of a total emission of about 2,500 tons of hydrocarbons per day. The real culprit had been found: the automobile industry.

This was an adversary worthy of even as extravagant a city as Los Angeles. The United States automobile industry sells about $15 billion of its products each year. It is closely tied to the petroleum industry, which produces about $10 billion worth of goods annually. The automobile industry is a major segment of the nation's military and financial complex. Industry executives have served in high national office. The industry's advertising budget amounts to hundreds of millions of dollars annually, a major part of the support of news media. The industry's technical facilities are enormous; it employs thousands of highly trained engineers and scientists.

Pitted against this formidable power were a few Los Angeles officials. Probably the most single-minded among them in the battle over automotive smog has been Los Angeles County Supervisor, Kenneth Hahn. The record of his long encounter with the giants of Detroit is illuminating.

On February 19, 1953, Mr. Hahn wrote to the president of the Ford Motor Company to ask whether the company "has conducted, or is conducting, research or experimentation designed to eliminate or substantially reduce exhaust vapors." The reply, from a member of the company's News Department, asserted that "the Ford engineering staff, although mindful that automobile engines produce exhaust gases, feels these vapors are dissipated in the atmosphere quickly and do not represent an air pollution problem." In their replies to Mr. Hahn, neither the Ford Motor Company nor the General Motors Corporation indicated an interest, at that time, in developing devices that might control exhaust emissions.

Mr. Hahn persisted, and by the end of 1953 the automobile manufacturers acknowledged that an industry-wide study of the problem was under way. Nineteen months later Mr. Hahn wrote again, asking if an exhaust control had been developed. The reply from one of the Detroit engineering giants: "We will soon be in a position to make recommendations which should point the way to reduction of hydrocarbons in automotive exhaust gases."

Eighteen more months pass. Now Mr. Hahn inquires whether exhaust-control devices will be installed on 1957 model cars. The answer: "We have . . . established the 1958 model year as the goal for the production of deceleration devices."

The correspondence continues, until on October 18, 1960, Mr. Hahn is informed by the president of the General Motors Corporation: "I am gratified to be able to report that positive crankcase ventilation is available on all 1961 General Motors passenger cars being delivered to California. We believe that this relatively uncomplicated, inexpensive device will perform a major job of reducing air pollution." Since such a crankcase device eliminates only 25 per cent of the emitted hydrocarbons (most coming from the engine exhaust), Mr. Hahn replied to express his disappointment in the action. By 1965 no action to control exhaust emissions had been taken and Mr. Hahn's correspondence concludes with an appeal to the president of the United States for congressional action. In 1966 exhaust-control devices appeared on new cars in California and the emissions of hydrocarbons from that source began a downward trend in Los Angeles.

Between 1965 and 1968 emission of waste hydrocarbons from motor vehicles was reduced from 1,950 to 1,720 tons per day (without controls, emissions would have risen to 2,400 tons per day by 1968). Eye irritation was also reduced. At the same time, the levels of another important pollutant emitted by vehicles, carbon monoxide, were also reduced, for the new devices acted on this pollutant as well as on hydrocarbons. Between 1965 and 1968 the number of days on which carbon monoxide exceeded the "serious" level (30 parts per million for eight hours) fell from 58 to 6. The 1968 value was even below the value for 1955 (eleven days).

It might appear, then, that by 1968 Los Angeles would be ready to celebrate the end of a long and frustrating search for a solution to the smog problem. But now the situation took a new and ominous turn: the *improvements* in exhaust emissions had themselves brought on a new problem. For, coincident with the 12 per cent drop in hydrocarbon emissions from 1965 to 1968, the burden of nitrogen oxides in Los Angeles air *increased* by 28 per cent. In 1965 nitrogen dioxide exceeded the "adverse" level on 100 days; in 1968 this level was exceeded on 132 days.

This was cause for serious concern. While nitrogen oxide is relatively innocuous (except as an ingredient of the smog-forming reaction), nitirogen *di*oxide is highly poisonous, with a long history as the cause of serious industrial hazards. The gas destroys the cells of the lung, tends to enlarge lung blood vessels, and at a sufficiently high concentration, causes accumulation of fluid in the lungs, which may lead to death. Such serious effects are observed only at nitrogen dioxide concentrations that are well above the levels encountered in urban air. However, based on the effects of low levels of nitrogen dioxides on laboratory animals and taking into account the presence of especially sensitive individuals in a large population, the acceptable level for brief (one hour) exposure to nitrogen dioxide in urban air has been set at 2 parts per million (ppm). This value is uncomfortably close to the peak values recorded in Los Angeles—1.3 ppm.

Nitrogen dioxide is a colored gas which tinges the air a kind of whisky brown. As the concentration has increased in Los Angeles air, serious visibility problems have arisen—in the air lanes and along the high-speed freeways. In addition, nitrogen dioxide is toxic to plants; at levels less than 1 ppm the growth of tomato plants is reduced about 30 per cent.

There are two reasons why nitrogen dioxide levels would be expected to increase as a result of efforts to control other exhaust pollutants. One is the simple ecological rule that "everything must go somewhere." The nitrogen oxide-nitrogen dioxide mixture, formed in the air by the action of sunlight, combines with waste hydrocarbon to produce PAN. The latter eventually condenses and comes down to earth as a gummy precipitate, which is easily detected on a car windshield after a short time on a Los Angeles freeway. Hence, if hydrocarbon emissions are reduced so that the rate of smog formation declines, nitrogen oxides necessarily accumulate at higher levels.

Another reason for the unexpected rise in nitrogen oxide is that in devising the present pollution controls the automobile manufacturers considered only the demand for reduced emission of hydrocarbons and carbon monoxide. This goal led them to engine modifications designed to increase the extent of fuel combustion in the cylinders by increasing the engine's air intake. This also enhances the combustion of the major constituent of the air, nitrogen, to nitrogen oxides. Thus the engine modification introduced to reduce hydrocarbon emission increases nitrogen oxide emission. In enforcing the new automobile engine modifications, Los Angeles had simply traded one pollution problem for another.

Once more the fight against smog shifted to a new battleground: suppression of the emission of nitrogen oxides. Nitrogen oxides are produced wherever high temperature combustion occurs. In Los Angeles from about 20 to 25 per cent of the total emission is due to electric power plants and from about 75 to 80 per cent is emitted by vehicles. Again, the smog problem was laid at the door of the automotive industry.

The industry has begun to respond to this new—at least to them—problem. Catalytic exhaust devices have been developed for the purpose of converting engine-generated nitrogen oxides to innocuous products. However, it appears that the catalysts are poisoned by the lead which is widely used as a gasoline additive, and here the smog problem reaches to the heart of the automotive industry—the modern high-powered, high-compression gasoline engine, which operates effectively only on high-octane fuels. Such fuels are usually achieved by adding tetraethyl lead. Nonlead high-octane fuels also exist, but their use will require a large-scale change in the petroleum industry—or, alternatively, an equally large change in the design of automotive engines. There is also a serious question about the effectiveness of the increasingly complex exhaust devices under actual conditions of use. For example, California tests show that present exhaust devices lose their effectiveness for controlling hydrocarbon and carbon monoxide emissions and, on the average, exceed the California emission standards after 5,000 to 10,000 miles of use.

It should be remembered, too, that lead is itself poisonous. Since 1923, when tetraethyl lead was introduced as a gasoline additive in the United States, the amount disseminated into the environment has constantly increased. At present, annual use of lead in gasoline in the United States amounts to about 2 pounds per person. Near-toxic levels of lead have been found in traffic policemen and others who are heavily exposed to exhaust fumes. A recent study showed that pigeons living in Philadelphia contained ten times as much lead as pigeons living in rural areas. Lead is a major environmental hazard which is very largely due to the development by the auto industry of the modern high-compression engine.

Dissatisfied by the efforts of the auto industry, California officials brought the industry into court to account for its failure to act in good time to solve the air pollution problem. However, in 1969 litigation was abandoned by the United States Department of Justice and the industry promised to do better and to meet a schedule of emission reduction set up by the United

States National Air Pollution Control Agency. In November 1970 the agency relaxed the emission standards that the industry was supposed to meet in the next year's car models. More stringent standards have been proposed for 1975, but the industry claims that it will probably be unable to meet them.

This is where matters stand at this time. After persistent, intensive efforts to control photochemical smog, Los Angeles has exchanged a small improvement in the level of one noxious agent, PAN, and a larger decrease in carbon monoxide levels, for a serious increase in the level of another toxic agent, nitrogen dioxide. The battleground is now located in Detroit, where the automobile industry is yet to be convinced that air pollution control requires a drastic revision of the engines that drive its vehicles.

One of the early defenses put up by the auto industry was that photochemical smog is unique to Los Angeles, a special effect arising from the area's conformation and intense sunlight. We now know that photochemical smog affects nearly every major city in the United States and a surprising number of smaller ones, such as Phoenix, Arizona. Photochemical smog has appeared in most of the major cities of the world—Tokyo, Sydney, Mexico City, Buenos Aires, to name a few—except those, such as London, that have little sunshine. Through the perverse logic of modern technology, what was once regarded as an unfavorable aspect of a city's climate has become a blessing.

Photochemical smog and its accompaniments, such as nitrogen oxides and hydrocarbons, are only part of a city's total air pollution problem. In addition, modern urban air contains: sulfur dioxide and related products of sulfur oxidation; dust originating in furnace ash, industrial operations, and the wearing down of motor tires and asphalt paving by traffic; asbestos particles from automotive brake linings and building materials; mercury vapor from industrial operations; a variety of organic compounds released into the air by combustion and chemical industrial processes. A United States Public Health Service study of the air in a number of large United States cities in 1963 recorded, on the average, the presence of thirty-nine different identifiable substances not found in "natural" air. This list is certainly incomplete, for it continues to grow; two major urban air pollutants, mercury and asbestos, have been recognized only in the last few years. The chemical composition of urban dust is still poorly known; only about 40 per cent of the mixture of substances that makes up urban dust has thus far been identified.

Moreover many of these air pollutants interact chemically, and their reactions are influenced by temperature, humidity, and light intensity. This leads to the dismal, but I believe realistic, conclusion that the detailed composition of polluted air is not merely unknown, but also unknowable to a considerable degree.

In order to describe the course of a particular chemical reaction, it is necessary to study it in isolation, separate from other processes that might change the reaction under study. However if, for the sake of such an analysis, a few ingredients are isolated from the mixture of polluted air, this artificial change destroys precisely the complex of chemical reactions that needs to be understood. This is the ultimate theoretical limitation; in practice, some information can be gotten out of the study of isolated chemical reactions which are believed to occur in polluted air. Thus, it has been possible to work out, in general terms, the sequence of chemical reactions that leads to the appearance of PAN in Los Angeles smog, largely because this type of pollution dominates in Los Angeles air. However, this knowledge has not provided an effective understanding of smog in New York City—where sulfur dioxide appears to enter into the chemistry of smog in some as yet undefined way. Because complexity and variability are inseparable from air pollution, the problem is one that resists piecemeal analysis and eludes detailed description.

Under these circumstances it becomes very difficult to evaluate the hazard of air pollution to health. The search for a simple cause-and-effect relationship between a given air pollutant and a specific disease breaks down in a hopeless morass of complex interactions.

Consider, for example, the problem of lung cancer arising from chemicals such as benzpyrene which are commonly found in polluted urban air. The general method of evaluating the hazard of benzpyrene is to determine its concentration in the air and to relate this to animal experiments in which a particular concentration of benzpyrene is observed to give rise to a measurable incidence of cancer. On that basis it can be calculated that the risk from lung cancer due to breathing New York air is about equivalent to the risk of smoking two packs of cigarettes a day.

However neat and dramatic this conclusion, it may be far from accurate. One reason is that the biological action of benzpyrene may be greatly influenced by other health effects, which are themselves due to other air pollutants. In animal experiments it has been found that while a low concentration of benzpyrene may by itself fail to cause cancer in mice, it can cause cancer if the animals have also been exposed to infection. In turn, the incidence of infection may be increased by air pollutants such as nitrogen dioxide. Similarly, sulfur dioxide has a more potent effect on the restriction of lung air passages when dust is also present in the air. Sulfur dioxide tends to paralyze the ciliated cells of the lung air passages—which help to remove air pollutants from the lungs. Thus, it hinders the self-protective cleansing process in the lung. For this reason sulfur dioxide intensifies the contact between a carcinogen such as benzpyrene and the lung and can thereby increase the risk of cancer from a particular concentration of the carcinogen.

This is a reminder, then, that it is extremely difficult to blame any single air pollutant for a particular health effect. Nevertheless, "scientific method" is, at present, closely bound to the notion of a singular cause and effect, and most studies of the health effects of air pollution make strong efforts to find them. Such studies show no specific cause-and-effect relationships apart from a few special cases—a particular form of lung cancer due to asbestos fibers and the effect of certain metals, such as cadmium, on heart disease. However, statistical studies do show that people living in urban polluted air experience more disease than people living in less polluted, usually rural, air. The health effects that have been observed to worsen with general exposure to urban air pollution include coughing, frequency of colds and other respiratory disease, increased resistance of respiratory air passages, emphysema, bronchitis, lung cancer, cardiovascular disorders, eye irritation, and asthma. At the same time, it is possible to demonstrate that certain environmental factors are correlated with general disease indicators—such as frequency of hospital admissions. These factors include temperature, humidity, barometric pressure, concentrations of dust, sulfur dioxide and nitrogen oxides, and the metals, cadmium, zinc, tin, and vanadium. But these same disease indicators are also affected by factors not related to air pollution, including age, working conditions, economic level, and cigarette smoking.

These multiple complexities help to explain why it is difficult, if not impossible, to "prove" that any single air pollutant is the specific cause of a particular disease. The conclusion that *can* be firmly reached is scientifically crude, but meaningful: polluted air makes people sicker than they would otherwise be and hastens their death.

One thing that does clearly emerge from nearly all statistical studies of the effects of air pollution on health is that they are most heavily borne by the poor, by children, by the aged and infirm; the most striking effects of air pollution on health seem to occur where the victim's health is already precarious. Certain features of social progress, such as improved nutrition, living conditions, and medical care, are known to improve human resistance to disease and thereby to improve health generally. In a sense, air pollution has a similar—but opposite—effect on human health. It destroys social progress.

The paradigm of the enormous benefits of modern technology to the common man—as distinct from astronauts and generals—is the automobile. The dividing line between its success and failure is the factory door. So long as the automobile is being constructed, technology is admirably successful. However, once the automobile is allowed out of the factory and into the environment, it reveals itself as an agent which has rendered urban air pathogenic, burdened human bodies with nearly toxic levels of carbon monoxide and lead, embedded carcinogenic particles of asbestos in human lungs and killed and maimed many thousands annually. The human value of the automobile is created by technology and diminished by its environmental failure.

Air pollution is not merely a nuisance and a threat to health. It is a reminder that our most celebrated technological achievements—the automobile, the jet plane, the power plant, industry in general, and indeed the modern city itself—are, in the environment, failures.

5

ILLINOIS
EARTH

If one were to search for a city that represented the opposite pole from Los Angeles in pollution problems, one might easily choose Decatur, Illinois—a quiet city of 100,000 population lying in the open farmland of Illinois, about 120 miles from the nearest large city, St. Louis. There are a few local industries, none of them very serious polluters. It would seem to be an unlikely place to find evidence of the environmental crisis.

Yet Decatur now confronts a pollution problem as serious in its potential human hazards, and as far-reaching in its significance for the United States and the world, as air pollution in Los Angeles.

There was no evidence of environmental trouble in Decatur until a few years ago, when the local Health Department received a sample of water for a routine test for nitrate content. The department conducted such tests chiefly as a service to surrounding farms. For a number of years it has been known that shallow wells on farms in the Midwest often contain nitrate above the levels recommended by public health authorities. Nitrate itself appears to be relatively innocuous in the human body. However it can be converted to *nitrite* by the action of certain intestinal bacteria, which are often more active in infants than adults. And nitrite is poisonous, for it combines with hemoglobin in the blood, converting it to methemoglobin and preventing the transport of oxygen by the blood. An infant thus affected turns blue and is in serious danger of asphyxiation and death. The problem was discovered some years ago by physicians in Missouri and since then health officials have been alert to it, warning farmers to use a new water supply when their wells exceed the recommended nitrate level, 45 parts per million. The problem is world-wide; infant methemoglobinemia from excessive nitrate has been reported in France, Germany, Czechoslovakia, and Israel.

The Health Department found that the Decatur sample in question exceeded somewhat the 45 ppm limit, which was not too surprising, since nitrate-polluted wells are fairly common in the area. However, the citizen who had submitted the sample also informed the Health Department that the sample did not come from a farm well, but from the Decatur city water supply.

The city obtains its water from Lake Decatur, an impoundment of the Sangamon River, and tests quickly showed that both the lake and the river water had a nitrate level at about the 45 ppm limit. This was in spring. By summer the values had declined considerably, only to rise again in the winter, so that in the following spring months they had again reached a dangerous nitrate level. Since then the cycle has been repeated, and the city faces a serious, and as yet unsolved, public health problem.

I learned all this through telephone calls from Dr. Leo Michl of the Health Department. At the time I was teaching a course on environmental problems, among them the nitrate pollution found in midwestern rivers. Since students these days are rather concerned with the relevance of science to public affairs, it was perhaps not too surprising that one student, who happened to live in Illinois, telephoned the Decatur newspaper to report the water situation. After the facts were confirmed by the Health Department, the newspaper published the news: that the city's water supply had in recent spring months been polluted with excessive nitrate and that fertilizer used on the surrounding farmlands was a possible source.

The newspaper account agitated a number of people. The intensive use of inorganic nitrogen fertilizer has become the mainstay of farms in the Decatur area, as it has in many other parts of the world. Since 1945 the cost to the U.S. farmer of most of his needed resources —land, labor, machinery, and fuel—has increased considerably relative to the cash value of his crops. On the other hand, the relative cost of fertilizer has declined significantly. As a result, the farmer receives his greatest economic return, per dollar invested, from the use of nitrogen fertilizer. If public health considerations should force a reduction in the use of such fertilizer, the farmer might face economic ruin.

To appreciate how acutely this conflict affects the Illinois farmer, it is necessary to understand the soil situation in that area. Illinois is in the great Corn Belt of the United States, where corn, an avid consumer of soil nitrogen, is the major crop. However, the nitrogen available from the natural fertility of the soil has declined since farming began in the area. Recall that in nature nitrogen is taken up by plant roots largely as nitrate, which is gradually released from nitrogen stored in the soil as part of the humus—a very complex brown-black organic material. This is accomplished by the bacteria in the soil, which gradually convert the organic nitrogen of humus into inorganic nitrate. Under natural conditions, a rather large store of humus nitrogen is maintained in the soil by the addition of the organic remains of plants and of the bodily wastes of animals. Soil organic nitrogen is also formed by the fixation of nitrogen taken from the air and acted upon by certain soil bacteria. When the soil is heavily cropped and the crop is removed from the land and sold, rather than fed to animals, as is the case in most Illinois farms, the supply of humus nitrogen necessarily declines.

Under these circumstances, crop yields can be increased considerably by the addition of artificial inorganic nitrogen to the soil. In Illinois, total annual use of inorganic nitrogen as fertilizer has increased from less than 10,000 tons in 1945 to about 600,000 tons in 1966.

Accordingly, this increasing use of fertilizer nitrogen has markedly improved the yield of corn per acre. From 1945 through 1948, when very little nitrogen was used, the average corn yield was about 50 bushels per acre; in 1958, when about 100,000 tons of nitrogen were used, the average corn yield was about 70 bushels per acre. This represents an increment of 20 bushels per acre in yield, in response to a fertilizer increment of about 100,000 tons per year. In 1965, 400,000 tons of nitrogen were used to obtain an average yield of about 95 bushels per acre—an increase in usage of 300,000 tons to obtain an added 25 bushels per acre yield. Obviously, the law of diminishing returns is at work here; increasing amounts of fertilizer nitrogen must be used to obtain the same increment in yield, as cultivation becomes increasingly intense.

In these figures lies the crux of the issue that confronts Decatur. Local farmers find that if they receive only about an 80 bushel per acre return from their corn crop, they just about meet expenses. To operate at a profit, the yield per acre *must* be increased above that point, and under present conditions this can only be achieved by using fertilizer nitrogen at levels that are utilized very inefficiently by the crop.

Farmers are not concerned by this inefficiency because the cost of fertilizer is very low. But, of course, the inefficient uptake of the last few pounds of nitrogen per acre means that a good deal of it must go somewhere else. The fate of this "lost" nitrogen was suggested by Illinois State Water Survey data which showed that between 1950 and 1965, when fertilizer nitrogen use increased fivefold, there was a significant increase in the nitrate levels of a number of the rivers that drain Illinois farmlands. There was good reason to believe that the intensive use of fertilizer nitrogen was the basic cause of the dangerously high levels of nitrate in the Decatur water supply.

This possibility put the citizens of Decatur in a very difficult position. Clearly there was a hazard to their water supply which needed to be corrected; but if it were corrected by reducing the use of fertilizer nitrogen on the surrounding farms, not only the farmers but Decatur itself would suffer economically, since the economy of the city is largely dependent on the farms.

Indeed, controversy had already broken out following

my presentation of a paper on the relation between fertilizer and nitrate levels in midwestern rivers at the annual meeting of the American Association for the Advancement of Science. Within two weeks after that symposium, the vice president of the National Plant Food Institute, which is the fertilizer trade association in the United States, had addressed a letter enclosing a copy of the AAAS paper to soil experts at nine major universities to alert them to the need for rebutting it.

This attitude on the part of an association concerned with fostering the sale of fertilizer is understandable, given their vested interest in increased use of fertilizer—a two-billion dollar industry in the United States.

However, even within the scientific community itself, "objectivity" is a difficult and perhaps an illusory goal. After all, we are all human beings as well as scientists. Like everyone else, we in the scientific community develop a set of personal values which reflect, among other things, our relations to major segments of society and our vested interest in the significance and validity of our own work. In my own case, for example, because I am deeply concerned about environmental deterioration, I hold more valuable the full public discussion of pollution problems than the peace of mind or economic condition of the fertilizer association or of the farmers. This is not a position that can be defended, or criticized, on *scientific* grounds.

Such personal values exist in each of us, and in a scientist they are powerful factors in determining what he studies and how he views his results. The reason why the scientific enterprise has a well-deserved reputation for unearthing the truth about natural phenomena is not the "objectivity" of its practitioners, but the fact that they abide by a rule long established in science—open discussion and publication. Whatever his personal aims, values, and prejudices, when a scientist speaks and publishes openly—presenting facts, interpretations, and conclusions—he has done his service to the truth. For science gets at the truth not so much by avoiding mistakes or personal bias as by displaying them in public—where they can be corrected.

It is not surprising, then, that not only the officers of the fertilizer trade association, but also some individual university scientists should be irritated to a degree by observations regarding the hazards of fertilizers to water quality. For the farmers who now use so much fertilizer nitrogen do so on the advice of agricultural scientists—men who have devoted their lives to the deeply felt aim of improving the yields of the farmers' crops and their economic well-being. Indeed, the enormous economic value of fertilizer nitrogen to the United States farmer is a tribute to the personal devotion and competence of agricultural scientists. What is at fault in this situation is not the *agricultural* consequence of intensive nitrogen fertilization for farm yields, but its *ecological* consequences for water supplies. And until very recently (indeed, largely as a result of the controversy over pesticides, fertilizers, and other agricultural chemicals), this broader context was usually considered to lie outside the scope of agricultural science.

Now in addition to open discussion, the scientific enterprise has another procedure for getting at the truth —more data. Accordingly, some of us at the Washington University Center for the Biology of Natural Systems decided to study the Decatur situation in detail. Excellent information about the nitrate levels of the Sangamon River were already available from the Illinois State Water Survey, and data regarding fertilizer usage were also at hand. But, despite the evident parallelism between the two sets of data, such results were open to criticism so long as there was no information which literally traced the movement of fertilizer nitrogen from the point of application in the soil to the river itself. What was needed was some way to distinguish between nitrate in the river originating in artificial fertilizer and nitrate originating from the breakdown of humus or other organic materials.

Here I recalled an observation made in my laboratory some twenty years earlier when we were using a heavy (nonradioactive) isotope of nitrogen to trace the synthesis of viruses in plants. In nature, the nitrogen atom exists in two forms which are chemically identical and differ only in their atomic weights. One of them, nitrogen 14 (weight: 14 atomic units), makes up about 99.6 per cent of all natural nitrogen; the other form, nitrogen 15 (weight: 15 atomic units), makes up the remaining approximately 0.4 per cent. The ratio between the prevalence of the two forms of nitrogen can be determined with remarkable precision in an electronic instrument, the mass spectrometer.

From mass-spectrometer measurements we soon learned that whereas the artificial fertilizers used in Illinois all had nitrogen isotope ratios approximately the same as that found in the air (a natural consequence of the fact that they were made, chemically, from air nitrogen), nitrogen in soil, manure, and sewage was considerably enriched in nitrogen 15. This meant that measurements of the isotope ratio in nitrate taken from the Sangamon River, or from soil drainage water, might show whether the nitrate was derived from artificial fertilizer or from organic matter in soil, manure, or sewage.

We decided to make such measurements. Fortunately, a University Center associate, Dr. John Goers, had been raised in Illinois and knew the Decatur area and some of its people well. He obtained the cooperation of a group of farmers near the town of Cerro Gordo whose land lay in the Sangamon River watershed. All the land in the area is artificially drained by a system of tile pipes which lie about three or four feet beneath the surface. Tramping about the fields with his farmer friends, Dr. Goers located the outlet points of various drainage tiles and made arrangements to collect from time to time the water that flowed from them. These samples were brought back to the laboratory, measured for nitrate content, and the nitrogen analyzed with respect to nitrogen 15/nitrogen 14 ratio. It was found that those drains yielding high nitrate levels were low in nitrogen 15 content and vice versa. This meant that whatever source was responsible for high nitrate levels in soil drainage water must have itself been relatively low in nitrogen 15 content. The only possible nitrogen source with that characteristic is artificial fertilizer nitrogen. Other, more detailed, studies confirmed this conclusion and showed as well that a minimum of 60 per cent of the nitrate in Lake Decatur is derived from fertilizer used on the adjacent farms. There is now little doubt that the nitrate problem in Lake Decatur arises from the intensive use of artificial fertilizer nitrogen on the neighboring farms.

It should be noted that our university is not an agricultural institution and indeed, like many of the nation's independent universities, has been guided by the precept that its main mission is the propagation of "pure" knowledge. This has been particularly true in the science departments, where the goal is the pursuit of "basic" science—study of the fundamental properties of nature. Especially in biology, this has meant in recent years that research has largely been concerned with the finer details of chemical and physical processes in living things. Usually such events cannot be studied in whole living systems, where they are so numerous and elaborately interconnected that the nature of any single process is obscured by the effects of others. Instead, research tends to be concentrated on test tube systems of reactive molecules isolated from living things. This kind of research, "molecular" biology, has become almost synonymous with "pure" biology.

However, some of us have been concerned that such an approach is inapplicable to the actual biological processes that occur in nature—for example, in Illinois soil—where the system's intrinsic complexity must be understood rather than avoided by artificially isolating its parts in the laboratory. Indeed, a general controversy has now arisen in the United States scientific community, which reflects to some degree the demand by many of our students for studies which are "relevant" to the real problems of the world. The controversy centers around the question of whether basic science ought to be pursued for its own sake, or whether equally basic research can be done in the complex arena of nature as it exists outside the laboratory. More will be said about this later on, but an incident relevant to our nitrogen studies is worth recording here.

One of my university colleagues, Dr. Daniel H. Kohl, is an expert and gifted researcher on the electronic processes that couple the driving force of solar energy to the chemical changes that are the ultimate consequences of photosynthesis in plants. Dr. Kohl is concerned with more than electrons, however, and has an equally strong interest in the environmental crisis and its consequences for human welfare. Given this motivation, it is not surprising that he expressed an interest in joining our study on the isotope analysis of the fate of fertilizer nitrogen in Illinois. Indeed, he is responsible for much of the recent success of the study not only in the laboratory, but also in the equally important arena of ordinary human relations with the Illinois farmers who, with great understanding, given the potential impact of the work on their own livelihoods, aided us with valuable information and resources. It is disturbing, but illuminating, to record that Dr. Kohl's decision to undertake this work was made over the intense objection of most of his departmental colleagues, who were convinced that such work was an unacceptable diversion from the department's devotion to "pure" research.

Since then, much of the controversy has faded away, as it becomes increasingly evident not only to the Decatur health officials, but to farmers, agronomists, and "pure" biologists alike, that the fertilizer problem is serious and of far-ranging scientific and social significance. This was very apparent when we reported the results of our isotope studies at an unusual kind of scientific seminar in the fall of 1970 at the Cerro Gordo high school with the local farmers, health department officials, and agronomists from the University of Illinois. We presented our results, explained our interpretation of them, and reported our conclusion that the high nitrate levels in the Decatur water supply were largely due to the intensive use of fertilizer nitrogen on the surrounding farms.

The discussion went on far into the night. After a lively interchange with the agronomist, it was generally agreed that the data were meaningful. One agronomist reported that agricultural agents were already advising local farmers to start thinking about the possibility of using less fertilizer nitrogen. Some months later that same agronomist, one of the nation's leading agricultural experts, was appointed to the Illinois Pollution Control Board, where he introduced a measure unprecedented in United States agriculture: state regulations to govern the use of fertilizer.

Most rewarding was the response of the farmers. From their own remarkable scientific insights, they advanced useful suggestions for the further development of our research. Indeed, since then several farmers have offered the use of their own land for experimental studies to determine the effects of reduced fertilizer levels on the nitrogen output of drainage water. But perhaps the most significant feature of this discussion in the high school at Cerro Gordo was the warm evidence that the farmers, who had the most to lose from any reforms in nitrogen usage, were as deeply concerned as the health officials about the hazard to the Decatur water supply. They made it clear that they were prepared to consider any suggestions that might resolve the conflict between Decatur's need for healthful water and their own need to make a living.

Since then our work has continued at a much more rapid pace. We have assembled a team of biologists, chemists, geologists, soil scientists, biochemists, anthropologists, and economists to work out the broad range of problems that must be considered. On the one hand, we are studying the incidence of methemoglobinemia in the area in order to evaluate the potential cost in health of elevated nitrate levels. At the same time, detailed studies have been started to work out the

89

consequences for the farmer of any proposed reduction in fertilizer usage.

Similar studies are being carried out by other researchers. Very recently one of them, Dr. Abraham Gelperin of the University of Illinois, reported the result of a study of infant death rates in various Illinois counties. He reported that in five counties the death rate for baby girls (but not boys) born during the months when nitrate levels were high (April, May, and June) was 5.5 per 1000 as compared to 2.5 per 1000 for the months when nitrate levels were low (August, September, and October). Dr. Gelperin concluded: The evidence indicated that high levels of nitrate in the water, as found in these counties, may increase the infant mortality rate among female babies.

This may be the first evidence of the cost in human health of the intensive use of fertilizer nitrogen.

What we learn in the cornfields around Decatur will be applicable elsewhere. In central California, intensive use of fertilizer nitrogen is suspected of causing sharp increases in nitrate levels in the wells that yield the water supply for many areas. A similar problem has appeared in Israel and in Germany. All this reflects the unexpected result of an important technological advance, which was permitted to intrude significantly on the environment before we were aware that it would not only improve agriculture, but also harm human health.

6

LAKE
ERIE
WATER

The most blatant example of the environmental crisis in the United States is Lake Erie, a huge inland sea large enough to symbolize the permanence of nature. Lake Erie has been a major natural resource for a rich region comprising a half dozen large cities with a population of thirteen million, a huge and varied industry, lush farm lands, and profitable fisheries. But in the process of creating this wealth, the lake has been changed, so polluted that the original biological systems that maintained the social value of the lake have largely been killed off. The fate of Lake Erie is a measure of the damage we inflict on our natural resources in order to create the nation's wealth.

In the last decade, the people living near Lake Erie have had ample evidence of its deterioration. Nearly all the beaches they once enjoyed have been closed by pollution; each summer huge mounds of decaying fish and algae pile up on the shore; the once sparkling water is dense with muck; oil discharged into one of its tributary rivers has burst into flame. Lake Erie's living balance has been upset and if the lake is not yet "dead," it certainly appears to be in the grip of a fatal disease.

Lake Erie is about 12,000 years old. It was created by the great advancing ice sheet that gouged out the beds of the Great Lakes and later melted, filling the newly made depressions with clear water. Minerals from the surrounding rocks dissolved in the water of the newborn lake and streams carried into it material washed out of the soil of the adjacent lands. Now the biological life of the lake could begin. Microscopic plants—algae—grew and reproduced, creating their living substance from hydrogen taken from water, nitrogen and phosphorus provided by dissolved nitrate and phosphate salts, and carbon derived from the carbon dioxide of the air.

Once algae grow in it, a body of water can sustain a complex web of life: the small animals that eat the algae; the fish that feed on them; the bacteria of decay that return organic animal wastes to their inorganic forms—carbon dioxide, nitrate, and phosphate—which can then support the growth of fresh algae. This makes up the basic, fresh-water ecological cycle.

When the first observations of Lake Erie were recorded in the seventeenth century, it supported a large and varied population of fish. The waters of the lake were clear and sparsely populated with algae, for the nutrient salts leaching into the lake were only enough to produce a limited plant crop, which was also kept in check by the animals that fed on the algae. For two hundred years Lake Erie continued in this state of biological balance.

But beginning at the turn of this century, reports

from Lake Erie fisheries revealed sudden changes in the life of the lake. First, there was the near disappearance of the lake sturgeon, a delectable, valuable fish long common in the lake. Before 1900, Lake Erie yielded a million-pound annual crop of sturgeon, but ten years later the yield had fallen to 77,000 pounds, never to recover again; in 1964 only 4,000 pounds of sturgeon were taken. In 1920 northern pike, which had until then yielded million-pound catches, all but disappeared. In the 1930's the cisco, which once represented half the total fish crop of Lake Erie, dropped from a yield of 14,000,000 pounds to 764,000 pounds and never recovered; from 1960 to 1964 the annual cisco catch was 8,000 pounds. In 1940 the Sauger-pike crop suddenly became reduced, reaching a scant 1,000 pounds in the years 1960 to 1964. A few years later the whitefish abruptly disappeared from the lake, and in the 1960's the blue pike met the same fate. The total fish catch, in pounds, is now not much different from what it was in 1900, but the valuable fish have been replaced by "rough" fish—perch, sheepshead, catfish, and carp, and by the sudden invasion of smelt from the ocean in the 1950's. The money value of the catch has declined sharply.

The fish, then, gave the first warning that the biology of Lake Erie was changing and fixed the start of the change at roughly 1900. In 1928 the Buffalo Society of Natural Sciences studied the lake and reported no noticeable changes in the lake's chemical and living constituents which might account for the losses in fish. One suspected cause was pollution from sewage and industrial wastes emanating from the cities on the lake shore, but the report concluded that "it is possible to safely say that the lake as a whole is remarkably free from pollution. . . . The oft repeated statement that waste from the Detroit River and the cities at the western end of the lake is invading the eastern area and destroying fishing is without foundation. Nowhere in the open lake is objectionable pollution of any kind found in the water or silt deposits located on the bottom."

Another possible cause of the fish kills was insufficient oxygen in the lake water to support the more active species. The oxygen level of lake water is, in fact, a very sensitive index of pollution. When raw, untreated sewage enters a lake, it contributes a good deal of organic matter to the water. The more organic matter entering the lake, the greater the amount of oxygen needed to convert it to inorganic salts; this "biological oxygen demand," or BOD, is therefore a measure of the amount of organic pollution in the water.

Certain features of water movement in a lake seriously affect the oxygen problem. Oxygen enters the body of the lake water from its surface, where it makes contact with the air and where light needed for photosynthetic oxygen production is most intense. This means that oxygen can reach the deeper parts of the lake only if there is good top-to-bottom circulation. Where the lake is shallow—as it is in the western basin of Lake Erie—wave action churns the entire water mass and circulates oxygen-rich water throughout its volume. However, in deeper waters, as in Lake Erie's central basin, such vertical circulation is only intermittent.

In the summer months, particularly in calm weather, the central basin of Lake Erie becomes stratified in such a way as to prevent vertical circulation of oxygen. If the BOD of the lake water or the lake bottom is sufficiently great, the bottom waters may then lose most or all of their oxygen. Fish that seek the bottom water because they require its cool temperatures will then find insufficient oxygen there. In Lake Erie many fish spend their early life on the lake bottom where they may die if the oxygen content becomes too low.

This explains why pollution from untreated sewage wastes, which increases the biological oxygen demand of the lake waters, can lead to low oxygen levels near the lake bottom in the summer months. The biologists of the 1928 survey of Lake Erie were aware of this problem. However, they found only a small depletion of oxygen in the lake water and concluded that the amounts of sewage were not enough to affect the oxygen content of the lake.

Not until 1953 did biologists find the first real clue to the problem. In that summer the western basin of Lake Erie—in which the waters are usually well mixed throughout the year—experienced one of its occasional periods of stratification. Throughout the month of August wind velocities were unusually low, the skies were clear, and temperatures high. On September 1, Dr. N. W. Britt of the Ohio State University's Institute of Hydrobiology cruised among the islands of the western basin recording water temperatures, measuring oxygen content, and studying samples of the lake bottom. His records show that in the period from September 1 to September 4 thermal stratification developed in the western basin. As a result, the water at the bottom of the lake became depleted of oxygen; instead of the normal saturation level of about 5 parts of oxygen per million parts of water, the bottom waters contained only 1 ppm of oxygen or less.

As an ecologist, Dr. Britt was concerned not only with the physical environment in the lake, but also with its effect on the lake's living creatures. He had a particular interest in the May fly. For as long as anyone remembered, the May fly was a familiar feature of the Lake Erie area. Each summer lacy-winged adult May flies emerged from the lake in hordes as the nymphs that covered the lake bottom matured. Once on the wing, they congregated, in the summer nights, around every nearby light. May flies, adult and nymphs, are an important food for the lake's fish; the Gray Drake, a favorite dry fly among fishermen, is designed to imitate the adult May fly. The nymphs can live only in bottom areas that are well supplied with oxygen.

In the western basin of Lake Erie, a number of careful bottom surveys between 1929 and 1953 had shown that May fly nymphs were the most common lake-bottom animals. Counts of from 300 to 500 May fly nymphs per square meter of lake bottom were typical. On September 5, 1953, at a measuring station near South Bass Island, Dr. Britt dredged up the sediment from the lake bottom. The sediment was washed on a fine-meshed screen, and the animals remaining on the screen identified and counted. He found 93 May fly nymphs in a sample representing one fifth of a square meter of lake bottom—a normal count of 465 nymphs per square meter—but they were all dead. The nymphs were only partly decomposed, and since decomposition would be rapid at the warm summer temperatures of the lake, Dr. Britt concluded that the nymphs "had been dead only a few hours, or at most only a few days." They had died, he reasoned, because of the brief thermal stratification and the resulting low oxygen content of the water between September 1 and 4.

From September 14 to 26, a total of sixty-one bottom samples were taken in the area. Where, in previous years, biologists had found hundreds of May fly nymphs per square meter of lake bottom, there was now an average of forty-four. Dr. Britt had happened on, and recorded for science, a crucial turning point in the biology of the western basin of Lake Erie. Although the May fly nymphs made a brief recovery in 1954, thereafter they disappeared. Clouds of May flies are no longer seen in the summer nights near Lake Erie.

While the May fly nymphs require a good oxygen supply, other bottom-living animals do not—bloodworms and fingernail clams in particular. A comparison of the bottom-dwelling animals in western Lake Erie in 1930 and 1961 is revealing. In 1930 May fly nymphs everywhere dominated the bottom fauna; in the open areas of the lake there were hundreds per square meter, the population thinning out only close to the outflow of the polluted river waters at Detroit, Toledo, and Monroe. Heavy bloodworm populations were found only near the polluted river waters. In 1961 bloodworms were found in high populations out into the body of the lake, and nowhere were there more than a few May fly nymphs per square meter.

Again, these animal counts show that, beginning in 1953, the pollution level in western Lake Erie had become sufficiently high to use up the oxygen in the bottom waters. Although this situation prevailed for only a few summer days, it was enough to cause a permanent change in the lake's population of bottom-dwelling animals.

The early records for bottom animals of the lake's central basin are not so complete, but the recent evidence is clear. Although the 1928 survey of the oxygen content of the central basin recorded no bottom areas with little or no oxygen, investigations between 1955 and 1964 reported serious oxygen deficits. A 1964 survey revealed that one fourth of the total lake bottom fell to from 0 to 2 ppm of oxygen during the summer thermal stratification.

Thus by the 1960's the western and central portions of the lake had switched from a well-oxygenated biological system to an oxygen-poor one. Important fish food had disappeared and fish that sought the cool bottom waters in the summer could not survive there for lack of oxygen. Only in the eastern basin, which is so deep that the water mass contains sufficient oxygen near its bottom even in the summer period of thermal stratification, were fish able to find cool waters well saturated with oxygen throughout the year. For the first time in its 12,000-year history, Lake Erie has begun to suffer serious oxygen deficits—with consequences fatal to its animal life. What are the possible causes of such oxygen deficits?

For a long time biologists have known about the oxygen demand created by the bacterial decay of organic wastes. A practical expression of this knowledge is the modern sewage treatment plant, which is, in effect, a way of domesticating the microbial activities that degrade wastes in natural streams and lakes. Sewage treatment involves a primary step in which indigestible solids are removed. This is followed by secondary treatment in a tank or pond rich in microbial decay organisms and usually artificially supplied with oxygen. Here, the organic materials that make up the bulk of sewage wastes are converted by microbial oxidation to inorganic substances. If the system works well, the resulting water is a clear dilute solution of the inorganic products of sewage treatment, of which nitrate and phosphate are most important. The waste's demand for oxygen is held within the secondary treatment pond where it can be met by an artificial air supply. The inorganic products of sewage treatment, which are free of BOD, can then be released to rivers and lakes without causing an immediate drain on the oxygen available in the natural waters. Industrial wastes—for example, from packing plants and canneries—may also represent a considerable BOD and can also be treated to convert the oxygen-demanding organic materials to inorganic ones.

The total mass of organic waste that reaches Lake Erie each year requires, for its conversion to inorganic salts, the consumption of about 180 million pounds of oxygen. A possible explanation of the recent oxygen deficits in the lake is the withdrawal of oxygen from lake water by the action of bacteria on this organic material. This possibility can be readily checked, for detailed measurements of the 1964 summer oxygen deficit permit us to calculate the minimum amount of oxygen that would have had to be withdrawn from the waters of the lake to bring about this deficit. It was found that the oxygen deficit in the bottom waters of the central basin alone was 270 million pounds of oxygen. This deficit developed over a period of only several weeks in only a part of the total mass of lake water, and must have been partially mitigated by oxygen entering the lake water. This means that Lake Erie, as a whole, must receive annually sufficient oxygen-demanding material to require the consumption of very considerably more than 270 million pounds of oxygen. If the organic wastes reaching the lake in a year can account for the consumption of only 180 million pounds of oxygen, somewhere in the lake there must be a very much larger oxygen demand, which is the main cause of the dangerously low levels of oxygen in lake water in recent summers. The key to the Lake Erie problem lies in discovering the nature and location of this huge, hidden source of oxygen demand.

In seeking for it, we need to recall that an effective primary and secondary sewage treatment plant will convert nearly all (about 90 per cent) of the organic matter originally present in the raw sewage into inorganic products. In this way, nearly all of the oxygen-consuming organic wastes in sewage are converted to nitrate and phosphate and discharged to surface waters which carry them out to sea.

It is now clear that this aim is being frustrated in Lake Erie, as it is in a growing number of the nation's water systems. Most of the inorganic products released into the lake as a result of waste treatment do *not* flow out of Lake Erie into the sea, but are reconverted into organic matter, much of which remains in the lake, where it makes the huge demand for oxygen that has been so disastrous for the lake's biology.

Algae are crucial in this process. One of the symptoms of the sickness of Lake Erie has been the appearance each summer of huge algal "blooms"—vast areas of the lake where, under the impact of excessive nutrients, algal growths give the lake the literal appearance and consistency of pea soup. In recent years such massive algal growths have discolored wide reaches of the lake waters, and great mounds of algae have washed up on beaches. Algal blooms grow quickly; they die off equally fast and, sinking into the lake, foul it with algal organic matter. This process, called *eutrophication,* or overfertilization, is largely responsible for Lake Erie's growing oxygen deficit.

Some recent calculations provide a startling picture

of the seriousness of the eutrophication problem. The current phosphate "budget" for Lake Erie has been worked out; the amount of phosphate reaching the lake from treated wastes and other sources has been estimated at 174,000 pounds per day; the amount that leaves the lake via the Niagara River has been measured at 24,000 pounds per day; the difference, 150,000 pounds of phosphate per day, or 55 million pounds per year, remains in the lake. This phosphate stays in the lake because it is built into the overgrowths of algae stimulated by the excess nutrients.

A vital question remains: if much more phosphorus enters the lake than leaves it each year, where are the huge amounts that must have accumulated over the years?

One possibility is that the lake's total algal population has increased each year by the amount of new growth resulting from the annual increment of nutrients. But this explanation is unworkable, if only because nearly all of the algae grown in the productive summer months die off in October and November. Indeed, this is the clue to the puzzle of the missing material: the nitrogen and phosphorus salts added to the lake accumulate in it in the form of dead algae, which, as they die, sink to the bottom—where their substance remains. In effect, a good deal of the waste poured into Lake Erie has accumulated in the lake bottom as the residue of algae and other living organisms. Thus, instead of Lake Erie forming a waterway for sending wastes to the sea, it has become a trap that is gradually collecting in its bottom much of the waste material dumped into it over the years—a kind of huge underwater cesspool!

Unfortunately, there has not yet been a study of the chemistry and biology of the Lake Erie bottom sufficiently detailed to explain its effects on the biology of the lake as a whole. However, such studies have been made on several small lakes in the English Lake District, and these reveal new facts of ominous importance for the future of Lake Erie. The English work, reported by C. H. Mortimer in 1941, which compared the chemical behavior of two forms of iron, iron II and iron III, in the bottom mud of several lakes, at least offers an explanation for the Lake Erie problem. Iron III forms insoluble complexes with the materials of the bottom mud; thus protected, a lake can accumulate an enormous mass of oxygen-demanding material in its muddy bottom without depleting the oxygen content of the overlying water. However, in the absence of oxygen, iron III is converted to iron II, which cannot bind the bottom materials and permit them to enter the overlying water. When serious oxygen depletion occurs in the summer months, there is a risk that the protective layer of iron III will break down—exposing the biology of the lake to the heavy impact of the accumulated algal nutrients for so long stored in the mud.

All this means that in using Lake Erie as a dumping ground for municipal and industrial organic wastes and for agricultural fertilizer drainage, there has accumulated—in the bottom mud—a huge and growing oxygen debt. For many years the special chemistry of iron made it possible to avoid payment of this debt, which has piled up for 100 years or more. But now the lake has begun to exceed the limit of the iron III–Iron II system that has protected it from biological disaster. As a result, in some future especially hot and windless summer, Lake Erie may be faced with a sudden demand to repay a century's accumulated oxygen debt. This would be a biological cataclysm that could possibly exhaust, for a time, most of the oxygen in the greater part of the lake waters. Such a catastrophe would make the lake's present plight seem slight by comparison.

The above is only a bald, scientific account of the destruction of the life of Lake Erie. It begs the insistent question: by whose hand was this deed done? When explanations are demanded, the response is often a plea of innocence or ignorance, evasion or a recourse to the influence of uncontrollable forces.

Consider, for example, one of the most common "explanations" for the plight of Lake Erie—that it is suffering from the premature onset of a natural "aging" process. This idea has the comforting effect of reducing the onus for the death of the lake's self-purifying biological system by entering the claim that death was, in any case, inevitable. The basic notion here is that all lakes very slowly change from a relatively unfertile oxygen-rich state to a eutrophic one, as nutrient salts over the course of many centuries gradually leach into the lake from the surrounding land. According to this view, Lake Erie is suffering from a kind of premature old age—a condition of high fertility, rich algal growth, and oxygen depletion that all lakes reach only after thousands of years, but which has developed in Lake Erie much faster.

In this connection, it is useful to take a look at the speed with which the eutrophic changes in Lake Erie have taken place. For at least some aspects of the lake's biological condition, there are good records available that go back almost one hundred years. These records show that a number of substances that are present in wastes—salts of sodium, potassium, and calcium—have been increasing in amount in Lake Erie water only since 1900. The increases were gradual at first, but since

103

1940 have risen more sharply. The significance of these changes can be seen by comparing them with corresponding records for Lake Superior, a lake which is larger than Lake Erie and in a relatively unpopulated area so that it receives, relative to its size, much less pollution than Lake Erie. None of the changes in salt concentrations observed in Lake Erie since 1900 are evident in the Lake Superior records; the salt concentrations have been essentially constant from the beginning of the record about one hundred years ago to today. Unfortunately, there are no comparable long-range records for phosphate and nitrate, but the available data show that these values have also increased in Lake Erie but not in Lake Superior.

Even more striking is the historical record of the algal population of Lake Erie. This is available in the tabulations of the Cleveland Waterworks, which since 1919 has made a daily count of the number of algal cells found in one millimeter of Lake Erie water taken at the point of the city's water supply intake in the lake. In 1927 the annual average count was about 100 algae per milliliter; in 1945 the count had increased to about 800; in 1964 it reached 2,500. The 1927 count is typical of a "young" nonaging lake; there is no evidence here that Lake Erie was aging before 1927.

These observations offer no evidence at all that Lake Erie was aging—even slowly—before 1900. In fact, the whole concept that lakes gradually, over geological time, become transformed into the eutrophic condition may be questionable. There have been recent studies based on estimates of metallic elements in lake bottom sediments, which are indicative of oxygen conditions during the history of a lake. They show, for instance, that very soon after its formation, the eutrophic lake,

Esthwaite Water in England, very rapidly (over the course of some hundreds of years) developed a low-oxygen condition, and that except for periodic short-term fluctuations, this condition has been maintained steadily for the last 9,000 years. Similar measurements made on sediment samples of a nearby lake, Windermere, which is at present not eutrophic, indicate that it has also maintained its condition steadily for the last 9,000 years.

Thus neither in the case of a presently eutrophic lake (Esthwaite Water) nor of a presently noneutrophic lake (Windermere) is there any evidence of gradual changes in the degree of eutrophication. Similar results have been obtained from a study of Linsley Pond in Connecticut, which is often cited as an example of a naturally "aged" lake. Here, too, as in Esthwaite Water, the metal content of the bottom sediment shows that the lake developed a eutrophic condition very rapidly soon after it was formed (by glacial action about 10,000 years ago)—which has remained unchanged ever since.

Human intervention—not enhancement of supposedly natural eutrophication—is wholly responsible for the present deterioration of Lake Erie and for its grimly uncertain future. The guilt is all ours.

Another source of confusion—and conveniently, of evasion—is the moderate complexity of the processes that lead to algal overgrowth, or eutrophication, which is the acknowledged source of most of the Lake Erie problem. Algal growth requires three chief nutrients: carbon dioxide, nitrate, and phosphate. *All* must be present in sufficient amounts if the algae are to grow. If any one of the three is missing, then algal growth can be triggered by supplying it. Thus, depending on the local condition of the water, any one of the three nutrients may be "responsible" for the algal overgrowth This tripartite complicity leaves a good deal of room for evasive tactics, for the notion that every effect must have a singular "cause" is conveniently embedded in public awareness of science. Thus, when the detergent manufacturers were confronted with evidence that detergents have greatly increased the phosphate content of surface waters and might induce eutrophication, they blamed the algal overgrowths on nitrate. On the other hand, in response to evidence that nitrate leaching from heavily fertilized farmland causes eutrophication, the agriculturalists are likely to call attention to phosphate. Most recently, much has been made of the "discovery" that carbon dioxide may trigger an algal bloom—as indeed it will, if both phosphate and nitrate are so plentiful in the water that carbon dioxide entering from the air is insufficient to support the algal growth that might otherwise be possible.

The total answer is that any one of the three algal nutrients may set off an algal bloom, providing that the other two are in adequate supply. When any of the three nutrients is present in excessive amounts, the water system becomes vulnerable to the influence of the other two. None of the three is safely present in water at high concentration if pollution due to algal overgrowths is to be avoided.

Perhaps the most common evasion is, in human terms, the most understandable—the role played by modern sewage treatment in inducing algal overgrowths. It is self-evident from the Lake Erie story that apart from phosphate due to detergents in municipal sewage and nitrate leaching from heavily fertilized farmland, most of the algae-feeding nutrients enter Lake Erie from the secondary effluent of sewage treatment plants. The design of these plants is, from the ecological point of view, faulty. This is a simple fact, but extraordinarily difficult to admit, given the huge and continuing investment in the construction of these plants. Following five years of study and numerous conferences and consultations, the Federal Water Pollution Control Administration issued a summary report in 1968 on the Lake Erie problem. While the report emphasizes the importance of eutrophication and the need for installing more "modern sewage treatment" plants, it fails to mention the fact that such plants, operating successfully, will worsen eutrophication.

Lake Erie dramatizes the massive destruction of natural resources by environmental pollution. It is not unique; ecological changes similar to those that have occurred in Lake Erie are under way in Lake Michigan, Lake Ontario, and Lake Constance; early stages of man-made eutrophication have been detected in the Baltic Sea, and even in Lake Baikal, which is the least eutrophic lake in the world. Massive as it is, the pollution of Lake Erie warns of even greater ecological destruction to come.

Perhaps one of the most meaningful ways to sense the impact of the environmental crisis is to confront the question which is always asked about Lake Erie: how can we restore it? I believe that the only valid answer is that no one knows. For it should be clear that even if overnight all of the pollutants now pouring into Lake Erie were stopped, there would still remain the problem of the accumulated mass of pollutants in the lake bottom. To my knowledge, no one has proposed a means of solving that problem which is even remotely feasible. It is entirely likely, I believe, that practically speaking Lake Erie will *never* be returned to anything approximating the condition it was in, say, twenty-five to fifty years ago.

This, then, is the outcome of our assault on Lake Erie: we have grossly, irreversibly changed the biological character of the lake and have greatly reduced, now and for the foreseeable future, its value to man. Clearly we cannot continue on this course much longer.

7

MAN
IN THE
ECOSPHERE

The environmental crisis is a sign that the ecosphere is now so heavily strained that its continued stability is threatened. It is a warning that we must discover the source of this suicidal drive and master it before it destroys the environment—and ourselves.

Environmental deterioration is caused by human action and exerts painful effects on the human condition. The environmental crisis is therefore not only an ecological problem, but also a social one. This adds to the intrinsic complexity of the ecosphere the further complications of human activities: the number of people supported by the earth's natural system; the sciences that tell us what we know about nature; the technology that converts this knowledge to practical action; the resultant industrial and agricultural production that extracts new wealth from the earth's skin; the economic systems that govern the distribution and uses of wealth; the social, cultural, and political processes that shape all the rest. Where, in this welter of events, can we find an explanation of the environmental crisis?

Again, as in the case of the ecosphere, we are confronted with a task for which modern science is poorly prepared: the analysis of an intrinsically complex system. The earlier discussion of the ecosphere suggests that here too it might be useful to adopt the expedient of seeking out a train of relationships which link one factor to the next. It should be remembered that this is an expedient which is not designed to yield an exclusive, unique description of the over-all system of relationships, but only a partial one that can serve some intended purpose. The purpose most relevant to environmental problems would be to discover how human activities depend on the environment and, in turn, how these activities influence it.

The key to understanding such a network is to find the ways in which each part depends on the rest. For example, in the case of the aquatic ecosystem we know that fish depend on algae for food, the production of organic waste depends on fish, the production of inorganic nutrients depends on the organic wastes, and algae depend for their growth on inorganic nutrients. Such a cycle of dependencies is a useful way to think about the relationship between any part of the system and the behavior of the whole. In the same way, we can seek relationships which link a series of human activities to the ecosystem on which they depend and which they in turn affect.

Suppose we begin with the ecosphere. This, together with the earth's mineral resources, is the source of all the goods produced by human labor or wealth. Thus, wealth depends on the ecosphere. In turn, people depend on wealth. For development, an adult human being requires a certain supply of goods—for food, clothing, shelter, transportation, communication, and the general care and amenities of life.

And it is a truism that without people, there would be neither science nor technology, industry nor agriculture, nor the economic, social, cultural and political processes that govern the whole. Those who are so concerned with "overpopulation" often regale us with figures that describe the galloping progression of human beings that inhabited the earth: 5 million in prehistoric times; 250 million at the birth of Christ; 500 million at 1650; 1,000 million at 1850; 3,500 million at present; and some 6,000 million projected for 2000. It is worth remembering that a similarly rapid growth can be seen in the number, variety, and usefulness of machines, buildings, conveyances, and cooking utensils; in the number, variety, and intellectual richness of literary works, paintings, musical compositions, and scientific articles. The earth has experienced not only a "population explosion," but also, and more meaningfully, a "civilization explosion." People, and indeed their growth in number, are the source of the vastly elaborated network of events that comprises the civilization of man: the new knowledge of nature generated by science, the power of technology to guide natural forces, the huge increase in material wealth, the rich elaboration of economic, cultural, social, and political processes.

To elucidate the interaction of man and his habitat, we must seek out, then, among all these human activities, those which form a sequence that enables us to return to our starting point, the ecosphere. Such a singular choice is, of course, arbitrary. For nearly everything that people imagine or do *can* influence their attitude toward the world in which they live, and their action on it.

For example, painting, music, or sculpture all reflect human experience in the world, including nature, or the ecosphere. And who would wish to deny that a great painting, or a song, can in turn influence human action on the environment? My intention is not to slight these human activities or to deny their power in the world, but to provide a sharper focus on the material base of human life on the earth.

Accordingly, to continue this demonstration of the web of interactions between man and nature, I shall choose from among the activities which are dependent on people only one—science. Science is, after all, the means by which human beings learn the nature of the world in which they live, knowledge that is the essential guide to what human beings do in that world. Particularly in relation to the ecosphere, much of what we do is now guided, consciously, by what science tell us (or what we think it tells us) about nature.

Immediately dependent on science—the accumulated knowledge of how nature operates—is technology, which generates a practical means of using scientific knowledge for useful ends. Although in the past technology was often developed by trial and error, rather than directly from organized scientific knowledge, in modern times nearly all technological advances are consciously guided by science.

In turn, and again especially in modern conditions, industrial and agricultural production are dependent on technology. The dominance of technology in the development of United States productivity has been thoroughly documented, for example by John Kenneth Galbraith. And in all modern societies, production depends on the operation of the processes that govern the distribution and exchange of wealth—the economic system.

Finally, it is the operation of the economic system that governs the extraction of new wealth from the ecosphere. For a wealth-production activity is operable only insofar as it is expected to yield some desired value; and value is, in turn, defined by the economic system. Here we return, in this cyclical course, to the ecosystem, since all wealth-producing enterprises depend on the ecosphere for the biological capital that is essential to every productive enterprise.

Thus, wealth, which is essential to produce people and to maintain all their activities, is itself produced by human actions which are guided by science, mediated by technology, governed by an economic system, and exerted through the ecosphere. Of course, this simple sequence is not intended to describe the operation of the whole of human society, which is not a simple circular process, but rather a complex, multiply branched network. Thus, wealth extracted from the earth's natural resources is not only used to satisfy immediate human needs, to produce people; it is also used to produce new devices, tools, factories, transportation, communication systems, hospitals, museums, works of art—or weapons of war.

It is also important to remember that the connection between science and technology and the economic system is a two-way affair. While economic activity depends on productive processes generated by science and technology, the reverse is also true. The economic system, and the political ideology it expresses, imposes important constraints on the development of science and technology. One of these is simply money, which is provided by government agencies, private foundations, and business enterprises to support research and development. Those who provide this support can, and do, influence the course of science and technology simply by choosing the areas they favor. Environmental research provides an illuminating example. Before the recent public concern over environmental problems, such research received only scant support in the United States. In recent years, support for basic research on problems selected by scientists themselves has become much more scarce, while funds available for research directed toward the understanding of environmental problems have increased. As a result, many more scientists have now elected to study problems of environmental significance. Thus, science and technology are not independent sources of information to be used or ignored by the social system, but rather are subject to considerable social direction. Nevertheless it remains true that whatever action is taken by productive enterprises or government agencies relevant to the ecosystem must depend on science for the necessary knowledge and on technology for the necessary means.

What has been described thus far is, of course, only a static picture of what is, in reality, a dynamic, changing process—the course of civilization. Again, it is useful to select from this vast domain the highly simplified sequence described earlier in order to gain some sense of how it operates in time.

Let us begin with the extraction of wealth from the ecosystem. As wealth is produced and in part converted into people, the number of people increases. For there is considerable evidence that increased wealth reduces mortality, which—if the birth rate does not also decline —leads to an increase in population. Since human beings, like all living things, are self-propagated, there is a built-in tendency for the population to grow in size, so long as sufficient wealth is available to support the newly added people. In turn, the increasing number of people tends to intensify activities that depend on people —science, technology, production, and wealth.

It is sometimes supposed that this self-accelerating interaction between the increase in wealth and technological competence and population growth is bound to set off an explosive "population bomb" unless deliberate steps are taken to control birth rate. In fact, there is strong evidence that the process itself sets up a counterforce that slows population growth considerably. This process, known to demographers as the "demographic transition," has occurred in most of the industrialized nations of the world. At first, in the early stages of the eighteenth-century agricultural and industrial revolution, increasing wealth reduced mortality so that—with the birth rate unchanged—populations grew rapidly. Later, with further improvement in living standards, in the nineteenth century, birth rates declined and population growth slowed down. The reasons for this change are not biological, but social. Especially important is the changing role of children. When living standards were relatively low—for example, in the early stages of the industrial revolution—their labor was essential to the family's survival; child labor was common. Later, with improved living standards, adult labor alone became sufficient to maintain family income; compulsory schools were established and the children, no longer necessary economic assets, became economic liabilities. At the same time, since social services improved, parents were less likely to depend on children as a form of old-age insurance. The natural result was a reduced birth rate, which occurred even without the benefit of modern methods of contraception. Thus, although population growth is an inherent feature of the progressive development of productive activities, it tends to be limited by the same force that stimulates it—the accumulation of social wealth and resources. In nations that are now in their developing stages, where populations are in rapid growth, the demographic transition has been grossly affected by certain new developments; these are considered later on.

A kind of self-propagating tendency can also be recognized within the areas of science and technology. These are parts of human culture, and represent an accumulating, evolving assemblage of facts, ideas, and attitudes—which are recorded and thus perpetuated. The body of scientific literature and the practical, lasting evidence of technological achievements become starting points for further advances. In this sense, science and technology, like the population, are self-generating, and, at least for the present, grow at an ever-increasing rate. The science "information explosion" is exemplified in the growth curve of scientific papers; the number doubles, at present, every fifteen years. Technology, as exemplified by the proliferation of new instruments and techniques generated by a germinal invention—for example, the transistor—also grows at an accelerating rate. Thus science and technology tend to take off, radially so to speak, and generate their own growth, so long as the social factors on which they depend permit.

Self-generated growth is also characteristic of the sectors represented by the wealth extracted from the earth by industrial and agricultural production. Particularly in modern industrial systems, production leads to the accumulation of capital goods and financial resources and therefore to the further expansion of production and of its wealth-creating capacity. All modern economic systems are designed to grow by means of such self-generated expansion. Clearly, these sectors of the system constitute another self-driven force that tends to expand the size of the over-all cycle of production and human activity on the earth. The continued capability of economic systems to sustain such growth is open to serious question, a matter that is taken up in a later chapter.

We return now to the one remaining, profoundly basic, sector of the man–nature system—the ecosphere and the earth's mineral resources. Here matters are very different. First, this is the only part of the over-all system that is not created by human effort. It pre-existed human beings on the earth; its fundamental properties were established long before the appearance of man. And, in contrast to the human sectors of the system, this natural segment is intrinsically *incapable of continued growth or expansion*.

The earth and the ecosphere are fixed in mass. The solar radiation that drives the dynamic events in the ecosphere is, on the time-scale of human life, fixed in amount (but gradually declining with the extinction of the sun over a period of many billion years). Moreover, because the ecosphere is governed by cyclical processes, the earth and ecosphere must operate in a state of balance. It is a fundamental fact of nature, then, that the base of human existence represented by the ecosphere and mineral resources is limited in its size and rate of activity. One can argue whether the ecosphere, in its pre-human, natural condition or in its present one, operates near its intrinsic limit; but that there is some limit, and that the system's operation does not permit indefinitely continued growth, is undeniable.

Kept in proper balance, the earth's ecological cycle is self-renewable, at least over the time-scale involved in human history. In this time-scale, it can operate and support some number of human beings as one of its constituents more or less indefinitely. However, mineral resources, if used, can only move in one direction —downward in amount. Unlike the constituents of the ecosphere, mineral resources are *nonrenewable*. Fossil fuels, such as coal, oil, and natural gas, were deposited in the earth during a special period of its evolution that has not since been repeated—with the exception of the slow accumulation of very slight modern fuel deposits such as peat. Once fossil fuels are used, solar energy trapped within them millions of years ago is dissipated irrevocably.

The earth's store of metals, laid down by not-to-be-repeated geological events, is also nonrenewable. Of course, since matter is never destroyed, metals taken from the earth's ores remain on the earth after use and in theory could be used again. However, when iron, for example, is taken from the earth as a concentrated ore, converted into useful products that later are scattered, as rust, across the face of the globe, what is lost, irrevocably, is energy. Whenever any material is scattered from a concentrated origin and mingles with other substances, a property known as "entropy" is increased. And an increase in entropy always involves a loss in available energy. This is perhaps more easily seen in reverse: that the gathering together of scattered material into an ordered arrangement requires the addition of energy. (Anyone who has tried to reassemble a jigsaw puzzle from its scattered parts has experienced this law of nature.) Since any use of a metallic resource inevitably involves some scattering of the material, if only from the effects of friction, the *availablility* of the resource tends constantly downward and can be reversed only at the expense of added energy—which is itself a limited resource.

There is nothing inevitable about the high rate at which most metallic resources are now scattered after use and so lost to reuse. If we wished, nearly all the copper, for example, produced from ore and built into a product could be recovered and used again when the product outlives its usefulness. All that is required is to place sufficiently high value on the metal. This is of course exactly what has been done with precious metals such as gold and platinum. As a result, only a small proportion of all of the precious metals ever mined has been lost to reuse. If all metals were valued as much as gold, the problem of mineral depletion would be solved for a very long time. Depletion of metal is not so much governed by the amount of metal used as by the value placed on it and therefore its degree of reuse.

We come, then, to a fundamental paradox of man's life on the earth: that human civilization involves a series of cyclically interdependent processes, most of which have a built-in tendency to grow, except one— the natural, irreplaceable, absolutely essential resources represented by the earth's minerals and the ecosphere. A clash between the propensity of the man-dependent sectors of the cycle to grow and the intractable limits of the natural sector of the cycle is inevitable. Clearly, if human activity on the earth—civilization—is to remain in harmony with the whole global system, and survive, it *must* accommodate to the demands of the natural sector, the ecosphere. Environmental deterioration is a signal that we have failed, thus far, to achieve this essential accommodation.

This much is self-evident from what we now know about environmental pollution. The fouling of surface waters is the result of the overloading of the natural, limited cycle of the aquatic ecosystem either by direct dumping of organic matter, in the form of sewage and industrial wastes, or indirectly by the release of algal nutrients produced by waste treatment or leached from overfertilized soil. Water pollution is a signal that the limited, natural, self-purifying cycle has broken down under stress. Similarly, air pollution is a signal that human activities have overloaded the self-cleansing capacity of the weather system so that the natural winds, rain, and snow are no longer capable of cleaning the air. The deterioration of the soil is a sign that the soil system has been overdriven, that organic matter, in the form of food, is being extracted from the cycle at a rate that exceeds the rate of rebuilding of the soil's humus. The technical expedient of attempting to evade this problem by loading the soil with inorganic fertilizer is capable of restoring the crop yield—but at the expense of increasing pollution of the surface waters. Pollution by man-made synthetics, such as pesticides, detergents, and plastics, and by the dissemination of materials not naturally part of the environmental system, such as lead and artificial radioactive substances, is a sign that these materials cannot be accommodated by the self-purifying capabilities of the natural system and therefore accumulate in places harmful to the ecosystem and to man. In the same way, environmental pollution by a metal such as mercury—and the depletion of this mineral resource—is a consequence only of our willingness to "lose" it, because it is insufficiently valuable, according to present economic criteria, to be reclaimed.

Clearly, something is gravely wrong.

121

8

POPULATION
AND
"AFFLUENCE"

The environmental crisis tells us that there is something seriously wrong with the way in which human beings have occupied their habitat, the earth. The fault must lie not with nature, but with man. For no one has argued, to my knowledge, that the recent advent of pollutants on the earth is the result of some natural change independent of man. Indeed, the few remaining areas of the world that are relatively untouched by the powerful hand of man are, to that degree, free of smog, foul water, and deteriorating soil. Environmental deterioration must be due to some fault in the human activities on the earth.

One explanation that is sometimes offered is that man is a "dirty" animal—that unlike other animals man is likely to "foul his own nest." Somehow, according to this view, people lack other animals' tidy nature and increasingly foul the world as their numbers increase. This explanation is basically faulty, for the "neatness" of animals in nature is not the result of their own sanitary activities. What removes these wastes is the activity of *other* living things, which use them as nutrients. In an ecological cycle no waste can accumulate because nothing is wasted. Thus, a living thing that is a natural part of an ecosystem cannot, by its own biological activities, degrade that ecosystem; an ecosystem is always stressed from without. Human beings, as animals, are no less tidy than other living organisms. They pollute the environment only because they have broken out of the closed, cyclical network in which all other living things are held.

So long as human beings held their place in the terrestrial ecosystem—consuming food produced by the soil and oxygen released by plants, returning organic wastes to the soil and carbon dioxide to the plants—they could do no serious ecological harm. However, once removed from this cycle, for example to a city, so that bodily wastes are not returned to the soil but to surface water, the human population is separated from the ecosystem of which it was originally a part. Now the wastes become external to the aquatic system on which they intrude, overwhelm the system's self-adjustment, and pollute it.

Certain human activities—agriculture, forestry, and fishing—directly exploit the productivity of a particular ecosystem. In these cases, a constituent of the ecosystem that has economic value—an agricultural crop, timber, or fish—is withdrawn from the ecosystem. This represents an external drain on the system that must be carefully adjusted to natural and man-made inputs to the ecosystem if collapse is to be avoided. A heavy drain may drive the system out of balance toward collapse. Examples include destructive erosion of agricultural or forest lands following overly intense exploitation or the incipient destruction of the whaling industry due to the extinction of whales.

Environmental stress may also arise if the amount of a particular ecosystem component is deliberately augmented from without, either to dispose of human waste or in an effort to accelerate the system's rate of turnover and thereby increase the yield of an extractable good. An example of the first sort is the dumping of sewage into surface waters. An example of the second sort is the use of nitrogen fertilizer in agriculture.

Finally, since human beings are uniquely capable of producing materials not found in nature, environmental degradation may be due to the resultant intrusion into an ecosystem of a substance wholly foreign to it. Perhaps the simplest example is a synthetic plastic, which unlike natural materials, is not degraded by biological decay. It therefore persists as rubbish or is burned— in both cases causing pollution. In the same way, a toxic substance such as DDT or lead, which plays no role in the chemistry of life and interferes with the actions of substances that do, is bound to cause ecological damage if sufficiently concentrated. In general, any productive activity which introduces substances foreign to the natural environment runs a considerable risk of polluting it.

Our task, then, is to discover how human activities generate *environmental impacts*—that is, external intrusions into the ecosystem which tend to degrade its natural capacity for self-adjustment.

As a first step we might look at the history of the pollution problem in an highly industrialized country such as the United States. Unfortunately, despite the national proclivity to collect and store in the memories of the ubiquitous computer all sorts of statistics—from an individual's tax records to his attendance at political rallies—historical data on pollution levels are very spotty. However, a rather striking picture does emerge from the data that are available: *most pollution problems made their first appearance, or became very much worse, in the years following World War II.*

A good example of this trend is provided by phosphate, an important pollutant of surface waters. In the thirty-year period from 1910 to 1940 annual phosphate output from municipal sewage somewhat more than doubled, from about 17 million pounds (calculated as phosphorus) to about 40 million pounds. Thereafter the rate of phosphate output rose rapidly, so that in the next thirty-year period, 1940 to 1970, it increased more than sevenfold to about 300 million pounds per year. Some other examples of increases in annual pollutant output since 1946: nitrogen oxides from automobiles (which trigger the formation of smog), 630 per cent; tetraethyl lead from gasoline, 415 per cent; mercury from chloralkali plants, 2,100 per cent; synthetic pesticides (between 1950 and 1967 only), 270 per cent; inorganic nitrogen fertilizer (some of which leaches into surface water and pollutes it), 789 per cent; nonreturnable beer bottles, 595 per cent. Many pollutants were totally absent before World War II, having made their environmental debut in the war years: smog (first noticed in Los Angeles in 1943), manmade radioactive elements (first produced in the wartime atomic bomb project), DDT (widely used for the first time in 1944), detergents (which began to displace soap in 1946), synthetic plastics (which became a contributor to the rubbish problem only after the war).

These striking changes in the postwar pace of environmental deterioration provide an important clue to the origin of the pollution problem. The last fifty years have seen a sweeping revolution in science, which has generated powerful changes in technology and in its application to industry, agriculture, transportation, and communication. World War II is a decisive turning point in this historical transition. The twenty-five years preceding the war is the main period of the sweeping modern revolution in basic science, especially in physics and chemistry, upon which so much of the new productive technology is based. In the approximate period of the war itself, under the pressure of military demands, much of the new scientific knowledge was rapidly converted into new technologies and productive enterprises. Since the war, the technologies have rapidly transformed the nature of industrial and agricultural production. The period of World War II is, therefore, a great divide between the scientific evolution that preceded it and the technological revolution that followed it.

We can find important clues to the development of postwar technology in the nature of the prewar scientific revolution. Beginning in the 1920's, physics broke away from the ideas that had dominated the field since Newton's time. Spurred by discoveries about the properties of atoms, a wholly new conception of the nature of matter was developed. Experiment and theory advanced until physicists gained a remarkably effective understanding of the properties of subatomic particles and of the ways in which they interact to generate the properties of the atom as a whole. This new knowledge produced new, more powerful techniques for smashing the hitherto indestructible atom, driving out of its nucleus extremely energetic particles. Natural and artificial radioactivity was discovered. By the late 1930's it became clear, on theoretical grounds, that vast quantities of energy could be released from the atomic nucleus. During World War II, this theory was converted into practice, giving rise to nuclear weapons and reactors—and to the hazards of artificial radioactivity and the potential for catastrophic war.

The new physical theories also helped to explain the behavior of electrons, especially in solids—knowledge that in the postwar years led to the invention of the transistor and to the proliferating solid-state electronic components. This provided the technological base for the modern computer, not to speak of the transistor radio.

Chemistry, too, made remarkable progress in the prewar period. Particularly significant for later environmental effects were advances in the chemistry of organic compounds. These substances were first discovered by eighteenth-century chemists in the juices of living things. Gradually chemists learned the molecular composition of some of the simpler varieties of natural organic substances. Chemists developed a powerful desire to imitate nature—to synthesize in the laboratory the organic substances uniquely produced by life.

The first man-made organic substance, urea, was synthesized in 1828. From this simple beginning (urea contains only one carbon atom), chemists learned how to make laboratory replicas of increasingly complex natural products. Once techniques for putting together organic molecules were worked out, an enormous variety of different products could be made. This is the natural consequence of the escalating mathematics of the possible atomic combinations in organic compounds. For example, although molecules that are classed as sugars contain only three types of atoms—carbon, oxygen, and hydrogen—which can be related to each other in only a few different ways, there are sixteen different molecular arrangements for sugars that contain six carbons (one of these is the familiar glucose, or grape sugar). The number of different kinds of organic molecules that can, in theory, exist is so large as to have no meaningful limit.

Around the turn of the century chemists learned a number of practical ways of creating many of the theoretically possible molecular arrangements. This knowledge—that the variety of possible organic compounds is essentially limitless and that ways of achieving at least some of the possible combinations were at hand—proved irresistible. It was as though language had suddenly been invented, followed inevitably by a vast outburst of creative writing. Instead of new poems, the chemists created new molecules. Like some poems, some of the new molecules were simply the concrete end-product of the joyful process of creation —testimony to what the chemist had learned. Other molecules, again like certain poems, were created for the sake of what they taught the creator—newly defined steps toward more difficult creations. Finally, there were new molecules created with a particular purpose in mind—let us say to color a fabric—the analogy, perhaps, of an advertising jingle.

The net result represents, in terms of the number of new man-made objects, probably the most rapid burst of creativity in human history. Acceleration was built into the process, for each newly created molecule became, itself, the starting point for building many new ones.

As a result, there accumulated on the chemists'

shelves a huge array of new substances, similar to the natural materials of life in that they were based on the chemistry of carbon, but most of them absent from the realm of living things. As new useful materials were sought, some of the chemicals were taken off the shelf—either because of a resemblance to some natural substance or at random—and tried out in practice. This is how sulfanilamide—which a dyestuff chemist had synthesized in 1908—was found in 1935 to kill bacteria, and DDT—which had sat on a Swiss chemical laboratory shelf since 1874—was found in 1939 to kill insects.

Meanwhile a good deal was learned about the chemical basis of important molecular properties—the kind of molecular structure that governed a substance's color, elasticity, fibrous strength, or its ability to kill bacteria, insects, or weeds. It then became possible to *design* new molecules for a particular purpose, rather than search the chemical storeroom for likely candidates. Although many such advances had occurred by the time of World War II, very few had as yet been converted to industrial practice on a significant scale. That came later.

Thus, the prewar scientific revolution produced, in modern physics and chemistry, sciences capable of manipulating nature—of creating, for the first time on earth, wholly new forms of matter. But until World War II the practical consequences were slight compared to the size and richness of the accumulated store of knowledge. What the physicists had learned about atomic structure appeared outside the laboratory only in a few kinds of electrical equipment, such as certain lamps and x-ray apparatus. In industry, physical phenomena still appeared largely in the form of mechanical motion, electricity, heat, and light. In the same way the chemical industry was largely based on the older substances—minerals and other inorganic chemicals. But the new tools, unprecedented in their power and sweeping in their novelty, were there, waiting only on the urgency of the war and the stimulus of postwar reconstruction to be set to work. Only later was the potentially fatal flaw in the scientific foundation of the new technology discovered. It was like a two-legged stool: well founded in physics and chemistry, but flawed by a missing third leg—the biology of the environment.

All this is a useful guide in our search for the causes of the environmental crisis. Is it only a coincidence that in the years following World War II there was not only a great outburst of technological innovation, but also an equally large upsurge in environmental pollution? Is it possible that the new technology is the major cause of the environmental crisis?

This is part of the background of the sharp rise in pollution levels in the United States since 1946. But there have been other changes as well, and these too might be related to the pollution problem. Pollution is often blamed, for example, on a rising population and level of affluence. It is easy to demonstrate that the changes in pollution level in the United States since World War II cannot be accounted for simply by the increased population, which in that period rose by only 42 per cent. Of course, this is but a simplistic response to a simplistic proposal. It is conceivable that even a 40 to 50 per cent increase in population size *might* be the real cause of a much larger increase in pollution intensity. For example, in order to provide the food, clothing, and shelter necessary for that many more people, it might be necessary to intensify production—and therefore the resulting pollution—by a much greater proportion because the increased production of goods might require the use of inefficient activities (for example, obsolete factories might need to be pressed into use). In this case, production activities would need to expand much more than 40 to 50 per cent to meet the needs of so large an increase in population. In effect, this would imply a reduction in productivity (that is, the value produced per unit labor used in the process). In actual fact, matters are just the other way around; there have been sharp *increases* in productivity since 1946. Moreover, the chemical industries, which are particularly heavy polluters, have shown especially large increases in productivity; between 1958 and 1968 productivity in chemical industries increased by 73 per cent as compared with a 39 per cent increase for all manufacturing. So changes in productive efficiency can hardly account for the discrepancy between recent increases in pollution levels and the growth of the population.

Another popular idea is that increased population has led to the rapid growth of cities, where internal crowding and deteriorated social conditions lead to a worsening of the pollution problem. This notion, too, fails to account for the actual intensity of the environmental crisis. For one thing, a number of serious pollution problems, such as those due to radioactive fallout, fertilizer, pesticides, mercury, and many other industrial pollutants are not of urban origin. It is true, however, that the size and population density of a city will have a disproportionately large effect on the amount of pollution produced per person, because of the "edge" effect. (That is, as a city becomes larger, the ratio between its circumference and its area declines; since wastes must be removed at the city's boundaries, one might expect waste levels to rise for the same effort to remove them per unit area.) This effect may explain differences in the incidence of diseases related to air pollution among cities of different sizes. Thus the per capita incidence of lung cancer in the largest cities (1 million or more population) is about 37 per cent higher than it is in cities from 250,000 to 1 million population. However, here too, the effect is too small to explain the observed increases in the intensity of pollution.

The distribution of population does have a serious effect on environmental pollution due to automotive transport. Consider, for example, the consequences of the population shifts that are so typical of United States cities: rising populations of blacks and other minority groups in urban ghettos; migration of more affluent social groups to the suburbs. These processes separate the homes and places of work of both ghetto dwellers and suburbanites. Those suburbanites who work in the city, but are unwilling to live there, need to commute; ghetto dwellers who seek work in outlying industries, but are unable to live in the suburbs, must also commute, in reverse. This helps to explain why automobile vehicle-miles traveled within metropolitan areas, per capita, have increased from 1,050 in 1946 to 1,790 in 1966. Thus, the intensification of environmental problems associated with urbanization is not so much due to the increasing size of the population as it is to the maldistribution of the living and working places in metropolitan areas.

In sum, there appears to be no way to account for the rapid growth in pollution levels in the United States since 1946 by the concurrent growth in the over-all size of the population. Neither simple increase in numbers, the multiplicative effects of urban crowding, nor a supposed decrease in productive efficiency can explain the sharp increases in pollution which are the mark of the environmental crisis. The explanation must lie elsewhere.

The upshot of these considerations is that the ratio between the amount of pollution generated in the United States and the size of the population has increased sharply since 1946. The country produces more pollution, for the size of its population, than it used to. This relationship can be converted to a mathematically equivalent but—as we shall see—highly misleading statement: that there has been a sharp increase in the amount of pollution produced *per person*. For example, if pollution has increased tenfold while population has increased by 43 per cent, then pollution per person has increased about sevenfold $(1.43 \times 7 = 10$ approximately). Since biological wastes produced per person have certainly not increased by this much, this observation usually leads to the further conclusion that each of us has become more affluent, responsible for the use of more goods and therefore for the production of more wastes. A favorite statistic introduced at this point is that the United States contains about 6 per cent of the world's population, but uses from 40 to 50 per cent of the world's goods and that this kind of affluent society is, in the nature of things, also an "effluent society."

Again, it is useful to look at the facts about "affluence" in the United States. We can think of affluence in terms of the average amount of goods devoted, per person, to individual welfare. As a very rough measure —which, as we shall see, is vastly inflated—we might use the Gross National Product available per person. In 1946 GNP per capita was $2,222; in 1966 it was $3,354 (expressed in 1958 dollars to correct for inflation). This represents an increase of about 50 per cent, which by itself is clearly insufficient to account for the observed increases in pollution per capita.

Since the GNP is a crude over-all average of the goods and services produced in the country, it is more informative to break it down into specific items, especially as between those essential to life, such as food, clothing, and shelter, and amenities, such as personal automobiles, television sets, and electric corn-poppers.

With respect to food, the over-all picture for the 1946–68 period is quite clear: no significant changes have taken place in per capita availability of the major food categories, such as total calories and protein, in the United States. Total calories actually declined somewhat, from about 3,380 per person per day in 1946 to about 3,250 per person per day in 1968. Protein available dropped slightly in the first few years after World War II, remained constant at about 95 grams per person per day until 1963, when it began to rise slightly, reaching the value of 99 grams per person per day in 1968; this represents a slight decrease from 1946 to 1968.

These figures are reflected in over-all agricultural production data for the United States. In the postwar period, total grain production per capita has not varied from year to year by more than a few per cent. In the same period, per capita consumption of certain important diet accessories—calcium, vitamins A and C, and thiamin—actually declined about 11 to 20 per cent. This situation may reflect the temporary improvement in nutritional balance due to wartime food programs, and the unfortunate decline in the quality of the United States diet when these programs were abandoned.

In general, then, in total quantity per capita, food consumption in the United States during the 1946–68 period has remained essentially unchanged, although there has been some decline in certain aspects of diet quality. Clearly, there is no sign of increasing affluence with respect to food consumption.

The situation with respect to clothing is quite similar: essentially no change in per capita production. For example, annual production of shoes per capita in the United States remained constant at about three pairs between 1946 and 1966. In that period, per capita domestic production of all types of hosiery was more variable, but there was no significant over-all change between 1946 and 1966. While rapidly changing styles in that period caused large variations in the relative proportion of different types of outer clothing used per capita (for example, men's and women's suits declined considerably, while the production of separate skirts, blouses, trousers, and sport shirts increased), the over-all per capita production of clothing remained essentially unchanged. Total use of fiber was forty-five pounds per capita in 1950 and forty-nine pounds per capita in 1968—an increase of only 9 per cent. Again, we must conclude that, at least in the crude terms of the amounts of clothing produced per capita, there is no sign of increasing affluence in the United States in the period following 1946.

With respect to shelter, the following figures are relevant: housing units occupied in 1946 were 0.272 per capita, in 1966 they were 0.295 per capita. These

135

figures do not take into account the quality of housing. In any case, they do not indicate any marked increase in affluence with respect to housing. This situation is also reflected in the production figures for housing materials, which show little change per capita in the period following 1946.

We can sum up the possible contribution of increased affluence to the United States pollution problem as follows: per capita production of goods to meet major human needs—food, clothing, and shelter—have not increased significantly between 1946 and 1968 and have even declined in some respects. There has been an increase in the per capita utilization of electric power, fuels, and paper products, but these changes cannot fully account for the striking rise in pollution levels. If affluence is measured in terms of certain household amenities, such as television sets, radios, and electric can-openers and corn-poppers, and in leisure items such as snowmobiles and boats, then there have been certain striking increases. But again, these items are simply too small a part of the nation's over-all production to account for the observed increase in pollution level.

What these figures tell us is that, in the most general terms—apart from certain items mentioned above—United States production has about kept pace with the growth of the United States population in the period from 1946 to 1968. This means that over-all production of basic items, such as food, steel, and fabrics has increased in proportion to the rise in population, let us say from 40 to 50 per cent. This over-all increase in total United States production falls far short of the concurrent rise in pollution levels, which is in the range of 200 to 2,000 per cent, to suffice as an explanation of the latter. It seems clear, then, that despite the frequent assertions that blame the environmental crisis on "overpopulation," "affluence," or both, we must seek elsewhere for an explanation.

9

THE
TECHNOLOGICAL
FLAW

We have now arrived at the following position in the search for the causes of the environmental crisis in the United States. We know that *something* went wrong in the country after World War II, for most of our serious pollution problems either began in the postwar years or have greatly worsened since then. While two factors frequently blamed for the environmental crisis, population and affluence, have intensified in that time, these increases are much too small to account for the 200 to 2,000 per cent rise in pollution levels since 1946. The product of these two factors, which represents the total output of goods (total production equals population times production per capita), is also insufficient to account for the intensification of pollution. Total production—as measured by GNP—has increased by 126 per cent since 1946, while most pollution levels have risen by at least several times that rate. Something else besides growth in population and affluence must be deeply involved in the environmental crisis.

138

"Economic growth" is a popular whipping boy in certain ecological circles. As indicated earlier, there are good theoretical grounds why economic growth *can* lead to pollution. The rate of exploitation of the ecosystem, which generates economic growth, cannot increase indefinitely without overdriving the system and pushing it to the point of collapse. However, this theoretical relationship does not mean that any increase in economic activity automatically means more pollution. What happens to the environment depends on *how* the growth is achieved. During the nineteenth century the nation's economic growth was in part sustained by rapacious lumbering, which denuded whole hillsides and eroded the soil. On the other hand, the economic growth that in the 1930's began to lift the United States out of the Depression was enhanced by an ecologically sound measure, the soil conservation program. This program helped to restore the fertility of the depleted soil and thereby contributed to economic growth. Such ecologically sound economic growth not only avoids environmental deterioration, but can even reverse it. For example, improved conservation of pasture lands, which has been economically beneficial in the western part of the Missouri River drainage basin, seems to have reduced the level of nitrate pollution in that stretch of the river. In contrast, further downstream, in Nebraska, agricultural growth has been achieved counterecologically by intensifying the use of fertilizer, which leads to serious nitrate pollution problems.

In other words, the fact that the economy has grown —that GNP has increased—tells us very little about the possible environmental consequences. For that, we need to know *how* the economy has grown.

The growth of the United States economy is recorded

in elaborate detail in a variety of government statistics
—huge volumes tabulating the amounts of various
goods produced annually, the expenditures involved, the
value of the goods sold, and so forth. Although these
endless columns of figures are rather intimidating, there
are some useful ways to extract meaningful facts from
them. In particular, it is helpful to compute the rate
of growth of each productive activity, a procedure that
nowadays can be accomplished by committing the
tables of numbers to an appropriately programmed
computer. In order to compare one kind of economic
activity with another, it is useful to arrange the computer to yield a figure for the percentage increase, or
decrease, in production or consumption.

Not long ago, two of my colleagues and I went
through the statistical tables and selected from them the
data for several hundred items, which together represent
a major and representative part of over-all United
States agricultural and industrial production. For each
item, the average annual percentage change in production or consumption was computed for the years since
1946, or since the earliest date for which the statistics
were available. Then we computed the over-all change
for the entire twenty-five-year period—a twenty-five-
year growth rate. When this list is rearranged in decreasing order of growth rate, a picture of *how* the
United States economy has grown since World War II
begins to emerge.

The winner of this economic sweepstakes, with the
highest postwar growth rate, is the production of nonreturnable soda bottles, which has increased about 53,000
per cent in that time. The loser, ironically, is the horse;
work animal horsepower has declined by 87 per cent
of its original postwar value. The runners-up are an

interesting but seemingly mixed bag. In second place is production of synthetic fibers, up 5,980 per cent; third is mercury used for chlorine production, up 3,930 per cent; succeeding places are held as follows: mercury used in mildew-resistant paint, up 3,120 per cent; air conditioner compressor units, up 2,850 per cent; plastics, up 1,960 per cent; fertilizer nitrogen, up 1,050 per cent; electric housewares (such as can-openers and corn-poppers), up 1,040 per cent; synthetic organic chemicals, up 950 per cent; aluminum, up 680 per cent; chlorine gas, up 600 per cent; electric power, up 530 per cent; pesticides, up 390 per cent; wood pulp, up 313 per cent; truck freight, up 222 per cent; consumer electronics (TV sets, tape recorders), up 217 per cent; motor fuel consumption, up 190 per cent; cement, up 150 per cent.

Then there is a group of productive activities that, as indicated earlier, have grown at about the pace of the population (i.e., up about 42 per cent): food production and consumption, total production of textiles and clothes, household utilities, and steel, copper, and other basic metals.

Finally there are the losers, which increase more slowly than the population or actually shrink in total production: railroad freight, up 17 per cent; lumber, down 1 per cent; cotton fiber, down 7 per cent; returnable beer bottles, down 36 per cent; wool, down 42 per cent; soap, down 76 per cent; and, at the end of the line, work animal horsepower, down 87 per cent.

What emerges from all these data is striking evidence that while production for most basic needs—food, clothing, housing—has just about kept up with the 40 to 50 per cent or so increase in population (that is, production *per capita* has been essentially constant), the *kinds* of goods produced to meet these needs have changed drastically. New production technologies have displaced old ones. Soap powder has been displaced by synthetic detergents; natural fibers (cotton and wool) have been displaced by synthetic ones; steel and lumber have been displaced by aluminum, plastics, and concrete; railroad freight has been displaced by truck freight; returnable bottles have been displaced by nonreturnable ones. On the road, the low-powered automobile engines of the 1920's and 1930's have been displaced by high-powered ones. On the farm, while per capita production has remained about constant, the amount of harvested acreage has decreased; in effect, fertilizer has displaced land. Older methods of insect control have been displaced by synthetic insecticides, such as DDT, and for controlling weeds the cultivator has been displaced by the herbicide spray. Range-feeding of livestock has been displaced by feedlots.

In each of these cases, what has changed drastically is the technology of production rather than over-all output of the economic good. Of course, part of the economic growth in the United States since 1946 has been based on some newly introduced goods: air conditioners, television sets, tape recorders, and snowmobiles, all of which have increased absolutely without displacing an older product.

Distilled in this way, the mass of production statistics begins to form a meaningful pattern. In general, the growth of the United States economy since 1946 has had a surprisingly small effect on the degree to which individual needs for basic economic goods have been met. That statistical fiction, the "average American," now consumes, each year, about as many calories, protein, and other foods (although somewhat less of vitamins); uses about the same amount of clothes and cleaners; occupies about the same amount of newly constructed housing; requires about as much freight; and drinks about the same amount of beer (twenty-six gallons per capita!) as he did in 1946. However, his food is now grown on less land with much more fertilizer and pesticides than before; his clothes are more likely to be made of synthetic fibers than of cotton or wool; he launders with synthetic detergents rather than soap; he lives and works in buildings that depend more heavily on aluminum, concrete, and plastic than on steel and lumber; the goods he uses are increasingly shipped by truck rather than rail; he drinks beer out of nonreturnable bottles or cans rather than out of returnable bottles or at the tavern bar. He is more likely to live and work in air-conditioned surroundings than before. He also drives about twice as far as he did in 1946, in a heavier car, on synthetic rather than natural rubber tires, using more gasoline per mile, containing more tetraethyl lead, fed into an engine of increased horsepower and compression ratio.

These primary changes have led to others. To provide the raw materials needed for the new synthetic fibers, pesticides, detergents, plastics, and rubber, the production of synthetic organic chemicals has also grown very rapidly. The synthesis of organic chemicals uses a good deal of chlorine. Result: chlorine production has increased sharply. To make chlorine, an electric current is passed through a salt solution by way of a mercury electrode. Consequently, mercury consumption for this purpose has increased—by 3,930 per cent in the twenty-five-year postwar period. Chemical products, along with cement for concrete and aluminum (also winners in the growth race), use rather large amounts of electric power. Not surprisingly, then, that item, too, has increased considerably since 1946.

All this reminds us of what we have already been told by advertising—which incidentally has *also* grown; for example, the use of newsprint for advertising has grown faster than its use for news—that we are blessed with an economy based on very modern technologies. What the advertisements do not tell us—as we are urged to buy synthetic shirts and detergents, aluminum furniture, beer in no-return bottles, and Detroit's latest creation—is that *all this "progress" has greatly increased the impact on the environment.*

This pattern of economic growth is the major reason for the environmental crisis. A good deal of the mystery and confusion about the sudden emergence of the environmental crisis can be removed by pinpointing, pollutant by pollutant, how the postwar technological transformation of the United States economy has produced not only the much-heralded 126 per cent rise in GNP, but also, at a rate about ten times faster than the growth of GNP, the rising levels of environmental pollution.

Agriculture is a good place to start. To most people, the "new technology" connotes computers, elaborate automation, nuclear power, and space exploration; these are the technologies that are often blamed for the discordant problems of our technological age. In comparison, the farm seems rather innocent. Yet, some of the most serious environmental failures can be traced to the technological transformation of the United States farm.

Among the many organized human activities, farming lies particularly close to nature. Before it was transformed by modern technology, the farm was no more than a place where, to serve the convenience of man, several quite natural biological activities were localized: the growth of plants in the soil and the nurture of animals on the crops. Plants and animals were nourished, grew, and reproduced by means long established in nature. Their interrelationships were equally natural; the crops withdrew nutrients, such as inorganic nitrogen from the soil; the nutrients were derived by gradual bacterial action from the store of soil's organic matter; the organic store was maintained by the return of plant debris and animal wastes to the soil and by the fixation of nitrogen from the air into useful, organic form.

Here, the ecological cycles are nearly in balance, and with a little care, the natural fertility of soil can be maintained—as it has been, for example, in European countries and in many parts of the Orient—for centuries. Particularly important is the retention of animal manure in the soil and the similar utilization of every available scrap of vegetable matter—including the return to the soil of the garbage generated in the cities by the food produced on the farm.

Almost every knowledgeable European observer who has visited the United States has been shocked by our carefree attitude toward soil husbandry. Not surprisingly, the American farmer has been in a constant struggle to survive economically. In the great Depression of the 1930's, some of the severest hardships were endured by farmers, as the soil was first degraded by poor husbandry and later literally lost to the winds and the rivers because of the resultant erosion. In the postwar period, new agricultural technology came to the rescue. This new technology has been so successful— as measured in the hard currency of the farmer's economic return—that it has become enshrined in a new kind of farm management so far removed from the ancient plan of farming as to merit a wholly new name —"agribusiness."

Agribusiness is founded on several technological developments, chiefly farm machinery, genetically controlled plant varieties, feedlots, inorganic fertilizers (especially nitrogen), and synthetic pesticides. But much of the new technology has been an ecological disaster; agribusiness is a main contributor to the environmental crisis.

Consider, for example, feedlots. Here cattle, removed from pasture, spend a considerable period of time being fattened in preparation for market. Since the animals are confined, their wastes become heavily deposited in a local area. The natural rate of conversion of organic waste to humus is limited, so that in a feedlot most of the nitrogenous waste is converted to soluble forms (ammonia and nitrate). This material is rapidly evaporated or leached into ground water beneath the soil or may run directly into surface waters during rainstorms. This is responsible, in part, for the appearance of high nitrate levels in some rural wells supplied by ground water, and for serious pollution problems due to algal overgrowths in a number of streams in the Midwest. Where untreated feedlot manure is allowed to reach surface water, it imposes a heavy oxygen demand on streams that may be already overloaded by municipal wastes.

A livestock animal produces much more waste than a human being. Much of this waste is now confined to feedlots. For example, in 1966 more than ten million cattle were maintained in feedlots before slaughter, an increase of 66 per cent over the preceding eight

146

years. This represents about one half of the total United States cattle population. Feedlots now produce more organic waste than the total sewage from all U.S. municipalities. Our sewage disposal problem is, in effect, more than twice its usually estimated size.

The physical separation of livestock from the soil is related to an even more complex chain of events, which again leads to severe ecological problems. Animals confined in feedlots are supplied with grain rather than pasturage. When, as it has been in much of the Midwest, the soil is used for intensive grain production rather than pasturage, the humus content is depleted; farmers then resort to increasingly heavy applications of inorganic fertilizer, especially of nitrogen, setting off the ecologically disruptive sequence that has already been described.

At this point, a fertilizer salesman—and some agronomists—might counter with the argument that feedlots and intensive use of fertilizer have been essential to increase food production enough to keep up with the rising population of the United States and the world. The actual statistics on this matter are worth some attention, for they shed a new light not only on the role of new technologies in agricultural production, but also on the pollution problem.

Between 1949 and 1968 total United States agricultural production increased by about 45 per cent. Since the United States population grew by 34 per cent in that time, the over-all increase in production was just about enough to keep up with population; crop production *per capita* increased 6 per cent. In that period, the annual use of fertilizer nitrogen increased by 648 per cent, surprisingly larger than the increase in crop production. One reason for this disparity also turns up

147

in the agricultural statistics: between 1949 and 1968 harvested acreage *declined* by 16 per cent. Clearly, more crop was being produced on less land (the yield per acre increased by 77 per cent). Intensive use of fertilizer nitrogen is the most important means of achieving this improvement in yield per acre. Thus, the intensive use of fertilizer nitrogen allowed "agribusiness" to just about meet the population's need for food—and at the same time to reduce the acreage used for that purpose.

These same statistics also explain the resulting water pollution problem. In 1949, an average of about 11,000 tons of fertilizer nitrogen were used *per USDA unit of crop production,* while in 1968 about 57,000 tons of nitrogen were used for the *same* crop yield. This means that the efficiency with which nitrogen contributes to the growth of the crop declined fivefold. Obviously, a good deal of the fertilizer nitrogen did not enter the crop and must have ended up elsewhere in the ecosystem.

For an explanation of this phenomenon we can go back to the Illinois farms described earlier in Chapter 5. In that state, on the average, in 1949 about 20,000 tons of fertilizer nitrogen were used to produce a corn yield of about 50 bushels per acre. In 1968 the area used about 600,000 tons of nitrogen to produce an average of about 93 bushels of corn per acre. The reason for the disparity between the increase in fertilizer and yield is a biological one: the corn plant, after all, does have a limited capacity for growth, so that more and more fertilizer must be used to force the plant to produce the last few bushels of increased yield. Therefore, in order to achieve such high yields the farmer *must* use more nitrogen than the plant can take up. Much of the leftover nitrogen leaches from the soil and pollutes the rivers; it is literally impossible to obtain such high fertilizer-induced yields without polluting the environment. And given the farmer's present economic situation, he cannot survive *unless* he pollutes. The economic break-even point in the area is in the range of 80 bushels of corn per acre; to get the last 20 bushels of corn that mean the difference between profit and loss, as described earlier, the farmer must nearly double his use of fertilizer nitrogen. But only part of the added nitrogen goes into the crop; the difference goes into the river and pollutes water supplies—for example, at Decatur, Illinois, as we have seen.

What the new fertilizer technology has accomplished for the farmer is clear: more crop can be produced on less acreage than before. Since the cost of fertilizer, relative to the resultant gain in crop sales, is lower than that of any other economic input, and since the Land Bank pays the farmer for acreage not in crops, the new technology pays him well. The cost—in environmental degradation—is borne by his neighbors in town who find their water polluted. The new technology is an economic success—but only because it is an ecological failure.

The pesticide story is quite similar: increased annual use, at reduced efficiency, leading to an excessive environmental impact. Thus, following the introduction of the new synthetic insecticides such as DDT, the amount of pesticides used in the United States *per unit agricultural production* increased between 1950 and 1967 by 168 per cent. By killing off natural insect predators of the target pest, while the latter tends to become resistant, the new insecticides become increasingly inefficient. As a result, increasing amounts must be used simply to maintain crop yield. For example, in Arizona insecticide use on cotton tripled between 1965 and 1967 with an appreciable *drop* in yield—an agricultural treadmill, which forces us to move ever faster to keep in place. And again, the decreasing efficiency means an increasing release of pesticides into the environment—where they become a threat to wildlife and man.

In a way, this ecological view of modern agricultural technology only increases one's admiration for the business acumen of those who purvey it. In this light, the nitrogen fertilizer industry must surely take its place as one of the cleverest business operations of all time. Before the advent of inorganic nitrogen fertilizer, the farmer had to rely heavily on nitrogen-fixing bacteria to maintain the soil's fertility. These bacteria naturally inhabit the soil either in or around the roots of plants and can make up for the inevitable loss of nitrogen in food shipped off the farm for sale or otherwise lost by natural processes. The bacteria are a free economic good, available at no cost other than the effort involved in crop rotation and other necessary husbandry of the soil. Now comes the fertilizer salesman with impressive —and quite valid—evidence that crop yields can be increased sharply by supplying inorganic nitrogen in amounts that much more than make up the soil deficit. And not only does the new, saleable product replace what nature freely provided, it also helps to kill off the competition. For there is considerable laboratory evidence that in the presence of inorganic nitrogen, bacterial nitrogen fixation stops. Under the impact of heavy use of inorganic nitrogen fertilizer, the nitrogen-fixing bacteria originally living in the soil may not survive, or if they do, they may mutate into nonfixing forms.

It is probable, I believe, that wherever inorganic nitrogen fertilizers have been in continuous and intensive use, the natural population of nitrogen-fixing bacteria has been sharply reduced. As a result, it will become increasingly difficult to give up the intensive use of fertilizer nitrogen, as this main source of natural nitrogen fertility is lost. To the salesman, nitrogen fertilizer is the "perfect" product—it wipes out the competition as it is used.

The new insecticides are equally good business propositions, for killing off the beneficial insects that previously kept insect pests in check, they deprive us of the natural, freely available competitor to the new technological product. When farmers attempt to give up their reliance on synthetic insecticides, they often find it necessary to import new insect predators to replace the ones that originally kept the pests under control.

Like an addictive drug, fertilizer nitrogen and synthetic pesticides literally create increased demand as they are used; the buyer becomes hooked on the product.

In marketing terms, detergents are probably one of the most successful of modern technological innovations. In a scant twenty-five years this new invention has captured more than two thirds of the laundry market from one of man's oldest, best-established, and most useful inventions—soap. This technological displacement is typical of many that have occurred since World War II: the replacement of a natural organic product by an unnatural synthetic one. In each case the

151

new technology has worsened the environmental impact of the economic good.

Soap is produced by reacting a natural product, fat, with alkali. A typical fat used in soap-making is palm oil. This is produced by the palm tree, using water and carbon dioxide as raw materials, and sunlight to provide the necessary energy. These are all freely available, renewable resources. No environmental impact results from the synthesis of the palm oil molecule. Of course, with inadequate husbandry a palm plantation can deplete the soil, and when the oil is extracted from the coconut, fuel is used and the resultant burning contributes to air pollution. The manufacture of soap from oil and alkali also consumes fuel and produces wastes.

Once used and sent down the drain, soap is broken down by the bacteria of decay—for the natural fat is readily attacked by the bacterial enzymes. In most places, this bacterial action takes place within the confines of a sewage treatment plant. What is then emitted to surface waters is only carbon dioxide and water, since fat contains only carbon, hydrogen, and oxygen atoms. Hence there is little or no impact on the aquatic esosystem due to the biological oxygen demand (which accompanies bacterial degradation of organic wastes) arising from soap wastes. Nor is the product of soap degradation, carbon dioxide, usually an important ecological intrusion since it is already in plentiful supply from other environmental sources. In its production and use, soap has a relatively light impact on the environment.

In comparison with soap, the production of detergents is likely to exert a more intense environmental impact. Detergents are synthesized from organic raw materials originally present in petroleum along with a number of other substances. To obtain the raw materials, the petroleum is subjected to distillation and other energy-consuming processes—and the burned fuel pollutes the air. Then the purified raw materials are used in a series of chemical reactions, involving chlorine and high temperatures, finally yielding the active cleaning agent. This is then mixed with a variety of additives, designed to soften hard water, bleach stains, "brighten" wash (this additive strongly reflects light and dazzles the eye to achieve a simulated whiteness), and otherwise gladden the heart of the advertising copy writer. Suitably boxed, this is the detergent. The total energy used to produce the active agent alone—and therefore the resultant air pollution—is probably three times that needed to produce oil for soap manufacture. And to produce the needed chlorine, mercury is used—and released to the environment as a pollutant. In substituting man-made chemical processes for natural ones, detergent manufacture inevitably produces a greater environmental stress than does the manufacture of soap.

Once used, detergents become serious sources of additional pollution. Here the contrast with soap is striking. Soap has been used for thousands of years, everywhere in the world, in a wide variety of ecological, economic, and cultural settings—without any record, to my knowledge, of pollution problems. In contrast, in only twenty-five years, detergents have established a notoriously bad environmental record wherever they have been used.

The first detergents marketed were synthesized from petroleum derivatives composed of branched molecules. Since the enzymes of the decay bacteria cannot attack such molecules, they passed through sewage treatment plants unchanged. The industry only became aware of the problem when mounds of detergent foam appeared in streams and in some places water drawn from taps foamed like beer. In 1965, under the threat of legislation, "biodegradeable" detergents were introduced in the United States; these had unbranched molecules that decay bacteria could attack. However, at one end of the molecule the new detergents also had a benzene unit; in aquatic systems benzene can be converted to phenol (carbolic acid), a toxic material. In fact, the new degradable detergents are more likely to kill fish than the old ones, although they do not produce the nuisance of foam.

Another pollution problem arises from the phosphate content of detergents, whether degradable or not, for phosphate can stimulate algal overgrowths, which on their death overburden the aquatic ecosystem with organic matter. Phosphate is added to detergents for two purposes: to combat hard water (because it helps to tie up materials, such as calcium, which cause water hardness) and to help suspend dirt particles so that they can be readily rinsed away. Soap itself accomplishes the second of these functions, but not the first. In hard water, soap is rather ineffective, but can be improved by adding a water-softening agent such as phosphate. Thus, phosphate is needed only to solve the hard-water problem. But where water is hard, it can be treated by a household water-softener, a device which could also be built into washing machines. In other words, successful washing can be accomplished without resorting to phosphate, which when added to detergents, worsens their already serious environmental effects. Thus the actual need to replace soap is slight. As a recent chemical engineering textbook states: "There is absolutely no reason why old-fashioned soap cannot be used for most household and commercial cleaning."

In recent years detergent manufacturers have been beleaguered by environmental complaints: first against nondegradable detergents, then against phosphates, and most recently when, at considerable expense, they attempted to replace phosphates with NTA (nitrilotriacetic acid)—only to have that step criticized by the United States Public Health Service because NTA was found to cause birth defects in laboratory animals. The question arises: is the economic good to be derived from detergents worth all this trouble? The economic good to be derived from detergents is the ability to clean. On these grounds, a detergent is no better an economic good than soap—but it is, far more than soap, an ecological "bad."

It will be argued, of course, that the mere fact that detergents have driven soap from the market must mean that users find them more desirable than soap and therefore a better economic good. This argument loses most of its force when advertising is taken into account. A study in England shows that the sales of different brands of detergents are directly proportional to their relative advertising expenditures. Nor is this a matter of merely acquainting the buyer with the virtues of the product with the expectation that these virtues will then sustain further purchases. For, when advertising is cut back, sales fall off. In 1949 Unilever spent 60 per cent of the total costs for advertising detergents in England and enjoyed 60 per cent of the total sales; by 1951 its advertising budget had been reduced to 20 per cent of the total and sales had fallen off to 10 per cent. The lesson was learned, however; by 1955 advertising expenditures—and sales—had tripled from the 1951 low. It would appear that advertising, rather than the detergent's virtues, is the most important determinant of sales.

If, on these grounds, we regard the economic good to be derived from soap and detergents as about equal, we can then look into the ratio between environmental cost, as measured by phosphate content, and economic good. Thus, in 1946 every ton of cleaner (counting the *active* cleaning agent in detergent as equivalent to an equal weight of soap) sold in the United States contained about 7 pounds of phosphate phosphorus—which after use entered waterways where it contributed to the problem of algal overgrowths. In 1968 some 137 pounds of phosphate phosphorus were emitted into environmental systems per ton of cleaners used. The technological displacement of soap by detergents has caused a twentyfold intensification of the impact of phosphate from cleaners on the environment—at no basic gain to the consumer. The displacement of soap by detergents has made us no cleaner than we were; but it has made the environment more foul.

Textile production reflects another important displacement of natural organic materials by unnatural synthetic ones. Some relevant statistics: in 1950 in the United States about 45 pounds of fiber were used per capita by fabric mills. Of this total, cotton and wool accounted for about 35 pounds per capita, modified cellulose fibers (such as rayon) for about 9 pounds per capita, and wholly man-made synthetic fibers (such as nylon) for about 1 pound per capita. In 1968 total fiber consumption was 49 pounds per capita. However, now, cotton and wool accounted for 22 pounds per capita, modified cellulose fibers for 9 pounds per capita, and synthetic fibers for 18 pounds per capita. "Affluence"—per capita use of fiber—was essentially unchanged, but natural materials had been considerably displaced by synthetic ones. This technological displacement has intensified the stress on the environment.

To produce fiber, whether natural or synthetic, both raw materials and a source of energy are required. The molecules that make up a fiber are themselves threadlike polymers—chains of repeated smaller units. In cotton the polymer is cellulose, long molecules composed of hundreds of glucose units linked end to end. Energy is needed to assemble such an elaborate structure—both to form the necessary glucose units and to join them into the molecular thread. The energy required to form the cotton fiber is, of course, taken up by the cotton plant from a free, *renewable* resource —sunlight. The energy needed to form wool, which is made up of the protein polymer keratin, is obtained from the sheep's food, which is, in turn, derived from sunlight.

The crucial link between an energetic process and the environment is the temperature at which the process operates. Living things do their energetic business without heating up the air or polluting it with noxious combustion products. Whether in the cotton plant or the sheep, the chemical reactions that put the natural polymers together operate at rather low temperatures, and the energy is transferred efficiently. Nothing is burned, nothing wasted. This is, after all, the hallmark of life— that it can function well in the earth's environment, at the temperatures common on the planet. The chemical composition of a complex system such as the earth's surface is determined by its general temperature, for as the temperature of a system is raised, otherwise inactive constituents can react, thereby changing its chemical composition. For example, at the range of temperatures on the earth, chemical reaction between oxygen and nitrogen is negligible, so that the existence of these gases in the air, and the absence of their reaction products, such as nitrogen oxides, reflects the earth's temperature range. Thus, nitrogen oxides are rare at the earth's general temperature, even though the ingredients—oxygen and nitrogen gas—are intimately mixed in large amounts in the air—because these two gases do not react appreciably except at much higher temperatures. Living things, having evolved in the absence of nitrogen oxides, have developed a number of chemical processes that would be damaged if nitrogen oxides were present. As a result, living things are susceptible to toxic effects from nitrogen oxides and are therefore at risk wherever abnormally high temperatures occur and nitrogen oxides are produced.

The energy required for the synthesis of a synthetic fiber like nylon comes from two sources. Part of it is contained in the raw materials; since these are usually derived from petroleum or natural gas, their energy represents solar energy previously trapped by fossil plants. This is, of course, a nonrenewable source of energy and therefore, in the ecological sense, wasteful.

Another part of the energy used in nylon synthesis is needed to separate the various raw materials from petroleum or natural gas and to drive the various chemical reactions. Nylon, for example, is produced by a series of from six to ten chemical reactions, operating at temperatures ranging from 200°F. (near the boiling point of water) to 700°F. (about the melting point of lead). This means a considerable high-temperature combustion of fuel—and, for the reasons given, the resulting air pollution. Such reactions may release waste chemicals into the air or water, producing an environmental impact not incurred in the production of a natural fiber.

Of course the production of cotton or wool can also violate ecological principles, and does as presently practiced. In the United States cotton is now grown with intensive application of nitrogen fertilizer, insecticides, and pesticides, all of which produce serious environmental impacts that are avoided in the manufacture of synthetic fibers. In addition, the gasoline burned by tractors engaged in cotton production leads to air pollution. Some of these effects could be minimized; for example, more reliance could be placed on natural control of insect pests. Similarly, nylon production could be improved, ecologically, by reducing waste chemical emissions. However, what is at issue here is the fundamental point that even if all possible ecological improvements were made in the two processes, the natural one would still be more advantageous ecologically. Cotton involves a freely available, nonpolluting, renewable source of energy—sunlight—for the basic chemical synthesis, whereas in the chemical synthesis of a fiber, energy must be derived from a nonrenewable resource, and through high-temperature operations that emit ecologically harmful wastes. Even with the best possible controls such operations pollute the environment with waste heat.

Once produced, a synthetic fiber inevitably generates a greater impact on the environment than a natural fiber. Because it is man-made and unnatural, the synthetic fiber is not disposable without stressing the environment. On the other hand, the natural polymers in cotton and wool—cellulose and keratin—are important constituents of the soil ecosystem and therefore cannot accumulate as wastes if returned to the soil.

The ecological fate of cellulose, whether in a leaf, a cotton shirt, or a bit of paper, is well known. If it falls on the ground and becomes covered with soil, such cellulosic material enters into a series of complex biological processes. The cellulose structure is first invaded by molds; their cellulose-digesting enzymes release the constituent sugars into the soil. These stimulate the growth of bacteria. At the same time, the degradation of cellulose allows enzymatic attack on other polymeric components of the leaf, releasing soluble nitrogenous constituents to the soil. These too stimulate bacterial growth. The net result is the development of fresh microbial organic matter, which becomes converted to humus—a substance essential to the natural fertility of the soil. Because cellulose is an essential cog in the soil's ecological machinery, it simply cannot accumulate as a "waste." Keratin behaves similarly in the soil ecosystem. All this results from the crucial fact that for every polymer produced in nature by living things, there exist enzymes that have the specific capability of degrading that polymer. In the absence of such enzymes, the natural polymers are quite resistant to degradation, as is evident from the durability of fabrics protected from biological attack.

The contrast with synthetic fibers is striking. The structure of nylon and similar synthetic polymers is a human invention and does not occur in natural living things. Hence, unlike natural polymers, synthetic ones find no counterpart in the armamentarium of degradative enzymes in nature. Ecologically, synthetic polymers are literally indestructible. And, as in the case of natural polymers, there are no other natural agencies capable of degrading polymers at a significant rate. Hence, every bit of synthetic fiber or polymer that has been produced on the earth is either destroyed by burning—and thereby pollutes the air—or accumulates as rubbish.

This fact is apparent to anyone who has wandered along a beach in recent years and marveled at the array of plastic objects cast ashore. A close look at such objects—bits of nylon cordage, discarded beer-can packs, and plastic bottles—is even more revealing. Like other objects on the beach, bits of glass for example, the plastic objects are worn by wave action. Ecologically, it is always useful to ask about any given material in the environment, "Where does it go?" Where, then, does the material abraded from plastic objects go in the marine environment? The answer has just become apparent in a recent report. Nets which are used to collect microscopic organisms from the sea, now accumulate a new material: tiny fragments of plastic fibers, often red, blue, or orange. For technological displacement has been at work here; in recent years natural fibers such as hemp and jute have been nearly totally replaced by synthetic fibers in fishing lines and nets. While the natural fibers are subject to microbial decay, the synthetic ones are not and therefore accumulate.

It is illuminating, in this connection, to ask why synthetic cordage has replaced natural materials in fishing operations. A chief reason is that the synthetic fibers have the advantage of resisting degradation by molds, which, as already indicated, readily attack cellulosic materials such as hemp or jute. Thus, the property that enhances the economic value of the synthetic fiber over the natural one—its resistance to biological degradation —is precisely the property that increases the environmental impact of the synthetic material.

All modern plastics, like synthetic fibers, are composed of man-made, unnatural polymers. They are, therefore, ecologically nondegradable. It is sobering to contemplate the fate of the billions of pounds of plastic already produced. Some of it has of course been burned —thereby adding to the air not only the ordinary products of combustion, but in some cases particular toxic substances such as hydrochloric acid as well. The rest remains, in some form, somewhere on the earth.

Having been designed for their plasticity, the synthetic polymers are easily formed into almost any wanted shape or configuration. Huge numbers of chaotically varied plastic objects have been produced. Apart from the aesthetic consequences, there are serious ecological ones. As the ecosphere is increasingly cluttered with plastic objects nearly infinite in their shape and size, they will—through the workings of nature and the laws of probability—find their way into increasingly narrow nooks and crannies in the natural world. This situation has been poignantly symbolized by a recent photograph of a wild duck, its neck garlanded with a plastic beer-can pack. Consider the awesome improbability of this event. A particular plastic pack is formed in a factory, shipped to a brewer, fitted around six cans of beer, further transported until it reaches human hands that separate plastic from beer can. Then, tossed aside, it nevertheless persists until it comes to float on some woodland lake where a wild duck, too trustingly innocent of modern technology, plunges its head into the plastic noose. Such events—which bring into improbable, wildly incongruous, but fatal conjunction some plastic object and some unwitting creature of the earth —can only become increasingly frequent as plastic factories continue to emit their endless stream of indestructible objects, each predestined by its triumphant escape from the limited life of natural materials, to become waste.

The vast development of modern synthetic organic materials has also triggered other, equally unexpected, stresses on the environment. Some of these products, unlike plastics, are not inert, but biochemically active. In some cases, the effect is intentional—to kill insects or weeds, or to defoliate forests and crops in Vietnam. However, living things share a number of similar biochemical systems, so that an unnatural substance that affects an intended organism is likely to affect others, in different ways, as well. DDT, which attacks biochemical processes in the insect nervous system, also influences the behavior of enzymes in the livers of birds —inhibiting the formation of eggshells, which readily break after they are laid. The weed-killer 2,4,5-T, sprayed in huge amounts on the forests and croplands of Vietnam, distorts the plants' biochemistry and denudes them of leaves; now this same substance has been found to induce birth defects in laboratory animals and may be the cause of increased birth defects among recently newborn Vietnamese babies. Such substances are in effect drugs and ought to be dispersed with appropriate foresight and control. Such control is impossible when tons of these ecological drugs are sprayed across the countryside from the air.

To provide raw materials for the synthesis of the new materials—synthetic fibers, plastics, detergents, pesticides, and drugs—there has been a huge, concurrent increase in the production of organic chemicals generally (up 746 per cent since 1946). This change has carried in its wake several other consequences, which have increased the stress on the environment. Such a chain of consequences links the production of synthetic detergents to mercury-poisoned fish. One step in the synthesis of the degradable detergents now in common use, linear alkyl sulfonates, is the conversion of a paraffin compound to a chlorinated form. Chlorine is a common reagent in organic reactions; chlorine atoms, attached to an organic molecule, are often effective in promoting the formation of chemical links to other molecules. As a result, chlorine production in the United States has increased with the rapid rise in the production of synthetic organic chemicals—an increase of 600 percent between 1947 and 1969. Chlorine is usually produced by passing an electric current through a solution of common salt (sodium chloride). Mercury is a valuable adjunct to this process, for it serves not only to conduct electricity, but also traps another product of the reaction, sodium, as an amalgam. As a result, the use of mercury for chlorine production in the United States has increased several thousand per cent since 1946. Following the electrolytic process, the sodium-laden mercury is reacted with water; this converts the sodium to the alkali sodium hydroxide, regenerating pure mercury for further use. In this process, large amounts of mercury and water are mixed and circulated; inevitably some of the mercury is lost, ending up eventually in the waste drainage system. The mercury is carried to the bottom of rivers and lakes; there bacteria convert the metallic mercury to a soluble form, methyl mercury—which poisons the fish. It is suspected that two chlorine plants on the shores of Lake St. Clair are responsible for bringing the mercury content of most of the lake's fish above acceptable limits.

Thus, mercury poisoning is a feature of the "plastic age."

When the automobile and the internal combustion engine were invented, no one knew that some seventy years later they would become the greatest single source of urban environmental pollution. It is often assumed that automotive pollution—from carbon monoxide, lead, and smog—is the inescapable result of the huge numbers of vehicles that choke the highways. This is, of course, part of the problem; in the years from 1947 to 1968 the total number of vehicles on United States roads increased 166 per cent; the total vehicle-miles traveled have gone up by 174 per cent. However, at least two major automotive pollutants, lead and photochemical smog, have increased much faster than even the proliferating roads and cars. For example, studies of the amounts of lead deposited yearly in glaciers show that the annual entry of lead into the environment, almost entirely from gasoline, has increased by about 300 per cent in the last 25 years—considerably faster than the increase in the total consumption of gasoline in that time (up 159 per cent). The smog situation is even more puzzling. As indicated in Chapter 4, photochemical smog made its debut in Los Angeles in 1943. Since then it has appeared in most of the nation's large cities and has become vastly more intense in Los Angeles itself. A reasonable estimate of the over-all increase in smog levels in United States cities since World War II would be tenfold or so, or in the range of 1,000 per cent. Again, this increase is much greater than the concurrent rise in automobile travel. Clearly something else besides the number of cars and the mileage traveled has changed.

What has changed is the automobile. Cynics are sometimes prone to dismiss the annual changes in Detroit car models as superficial ones, designed not so much by engineers as by advertising excutives. Unfortunately, the engineers have been at work too, and beneath the annual transformation of the automobile's gaudy and increasingly fragile skin, technological changes, especially in the engine, have transformed it—into a highly efficient smog generator.

The industry's statistics, together with a few additional ones available from government reports, provide a detailed record of this technological mischief. In the internal combustion engine, gasoline is mixed with air in the cylinders, and the mixture is then ignited at a suitable moment, by means of an electric spark. Just before it is ignited the fuel-air mixture is compressed by the cylinder piston. The cylinder pressure has a great deal to do with the amount of power that the engine can deliver; generally, the greater the pressure the higher the power output. For reasons which are yet fully to be explained, the automobile industry long ago became committed to increasing the engine's power. In 1925, when the first records became available, the average passenger car engine delivered 55 horsepower; by 1946 the average was 100 horsepower. Between 1946 and 1958 average horsepower was driven upward by the engineers to reach 240 in 1958. In that year, in response to foreign competition, United States manufacturers introduced the "compact" car, with a smaller engine. As a result, between 1958 and 1961, average horsepower dropped from 240 to 175. Then, a curious nearly biological phenomenon occurred—the "compact" cars gradually grew in size and in engine power, so that between 1961 and 1968, average horsepower climbed again, to 250.

To achieve increased horsepower, it was necessary to increase engine compression; the relevant measure, "compression ratio," rose from 5.9 in 1946 to 9.3 in 1961. It then dipped briefly, along with horsepower, but, recovering from that aberration, climbed upward again, reaching an average of 9.5 in 1968. Thus, the low-powered, low-compression engine was displaced between 1946 and 1968. This technological displacement, like many others in that period, has strongly intensified the impact of automobile travel on the environment.

First, because high-powered engines are less efficient in their use of fuel—especially when run at low speeds, as they are in the car-choked city streets—the amount of gasoline burned per mile traveled increased. In 1946 passenger cars averaged about fifteen miles per gallon; by 1968 the average was about fourteen miles per gallon. This meant more fuel combustion—and therefore more air pollution from gasoline combustion products—*per vehicle-mile traveled*.

A second, more acute, pollution problem arises from the special engineering needs of the high-compression engine. At high cylinder pressures, the explosive combustion is uneven, causing a jarring "knock" which decreases engine power. To suppress engine knock, it became necessary to add tetraethyl lead to the gasoline. All of this lead—which is a toxic material—is emitted into the air from the engine exhaust. As the average compression ratio rose, so did the lead content of the gasoline. In 1946 gasoline used in the United States contained—and emitted into the environment—about 50,000 tons of lead; by 1968 the lead emitted had increased to 260,000 tons. In that period the amount of lead used *per vehicle-mile traveled* increased from 280 to 500 pounds per million vehicle-miles. In other words, because of the increase in engine power and compression ratio, for the same amount of actual *use*, cars now pollute the environment with nearly twice as much lead as they did in the immediate postwar period.

Finally there is the matter of photochemical smog, which is probably the most unexpected environmental outcome of recent automotive "progress." As already pointed out in Chapter 4, photochemical smog is triggered by the emission of nitrogen oxides—in urban areas, largely from automotive vehicles—into the air. The natural levels of nitrogen oxides in the air are ordinarily very low, and as already indicated, living things do not tolerate this substance very well. However, when air is heated, for example, during fuel combustion in the cylinder, the nitrogen and oxygen react and nitrogen oxides are emitted from the engine exhaust. As compression ratio increased, so did the engine's operating temperature; this has sharply increased the amount of nitrogen oxides emitted per unit of engine use. Nitrogen oxide emission is also affected by a series of other engine characteristics; when these are taken into account, it can be estimated that whereas the average 1946 passenger car emitted about 500 parts per million of nitrogen oxides in its exhaust, in the average 1968 automobile this figure rose to 1200 ppm. Thus, the emission of nitrogen oxides per vehicle-mile use more than doubled over this period of time. Taking into account increased mileage and gasoline consumption from 1946 to 1968, and the increase in nitrogen oxide emission per vehicle-mile, it is found that total emissions of nitrogen oxides have increased about sevenfold—a rise that begins to account for the sharp increase in smog levels. Here, again, is a counter-ecological change in technology.

In a sense, the increase in automobile travel during

the last twenty-five years is also a counterecological consequence of a technological change—in the distribution of residences and places of work. That the increase in per capita travel is at least in part related to the increased work-residence travel incident upon the changes in population distribution is suggested by traffic studies. These show that about 90 per cent of all automobile trips are ten miles or less in length; this class of trips represents about 30 per cent of total automobile mileage traveled. The mean work-residence travel distance in United States metropolitan areas is about five miles for central city dwellers and about six miles for those living in suburban areas. This is statistical evidence of what millions of people know from their own daily frustration: that twice a day, in most urban areas, the roads are clogged with people driving to and from work—a consequence of the separation between place of work and residence and the absence of adequate means of mass transportation.

A related technological displacement that turns up in the United States growth pattern since 1946 is the displacement of railroad freight haulage by trucks. The ecological cost of this displacement is evident in the following figures. The energy required to move one ton of freight one mile by rail now averages about 624 btu (British thermal units), while trucks require about 3,460 btu per ton-mile. This means that, *for the same freight haulage,* trucks burn nearly six times as much fuel as railroads—and emit about six times as much environmental pollution. At the same time, the amount of power required to produce the cement and steel needed to lay down a mile of four-lane highway (essential for truck traffic) is 3.6 times the power needed to produce the steel track for comparable rail traffic. Finally, the highway takes up a 400-foot right of way, while the railroad takes only 100 feet. In all these ways, the displacement of railroad traffic by automotive vehicles not only for freight but also for passenger travel has intensified the environmental impact incurred per unit of economic good (i.e., ton-miles of freight).

Electric power is one of the fast-growing features of the postwar United States economy. This industry is also the source of major pollution problems: sulfur dioxide, nitrogen oxides, and dust emitted by fossil-fuel burning plants; radioactive emissions and the small but enormously catastrophic potential of an accident from the operation of nuclear power plants; and the emission of waste heat to the air and nearby surface waters by both types of plants. This growth in the use of electric power is, justifiably, associated with the modernity of our economy and—with much less cause—to our supposed "affluence." The statistics appear to be straightforward enough. In the United States, annual power consumption is about 20,540 kilowatt hours per capita (the United States consumes 34 per cent of the world's electric power output), as opposed to about 2,900 kw-h per capita for Chile, 260 kw-h per capita for India, and 230 kw-h per capita for Thailand. However, electric power, unconverted, is not in itself capable of satisfying any known human need, and its contribution to human welfare needs to be measured in terms of the economic goods that power can produce. Here we discover another serious failing—when measured in terms of human welfare—of postwar technology: the new productive technologies are more costly than the technologies they have displaced, in consumption of electric power and other forms of fuel-generated energy *per unit economic good*. For example, aluminum, which has increasingly displaced steel and lumber as a construction material, requires for its production about 15 times more fuel energy than steel and about 150 times more fuel energy than lumber. Even taking into account that less aluminum, by weight, is needed for a given purpose than steel, the power discrepancy remains. For example, the energy required to produce metal for an aluminum beer can is 6.3 times that needed for a steel beer can.

The displacement of natural products by synthetic organic chemicals and of lumber and steel by concrete has a similar effect, for both chemical manufacturing and the production of cement for concrete are intense consumers of electric power. Aluminum and chemical production alone account for about 28 per cent of total industrial use of electric power in the United States. Thus the expansion of power production in the United States is not an accurate measure of increased economic good, being badly inflated by the growing tendency to displace power-thrifty goods with power-consumptive ones. The cost of this inefficiency is heavily borne by the environment.

Another technological displacement is readily visible to the modern householder in the daily acquisition of rubbish, most of it from packaging. It is a useful exercise to examine the statistics relevant to some economic good—beer, let us say—and determine from them the origin of the resultant impact on the environment. We can begin the exercise by recalling that the relevant economic good is chiefly the beer, not the bottle or can in which it is delivered. The relevant pollutant is the nonreturnable bottle or can, for these, when "disposed of" in rubbish, cannot be assimilated in any natural ecological cycle. Therefore, they either accumulate or must be reprocessed at some expenditure of energy and cost in power-produced pollutants. The exercise consists in determining the relative effects of the

171

three factors that might lead to an increased output of pollution, in this case, in the period from 1950 to 1967. In that time, the total consumption of nonreturnable beer bottles increased by 595 per cent and the consumption of beer increased by 37 per cent. Since the population increased by 30 per cent, the "affluence" factor, or the amount of beer consumed per capita, remained essentially constant (actually a 5 per cent increase). The remainder of the increased output of pollutant—beer bottles—is due to the technological factor —that is, the number of nonreturnable bottles produced per gallon of beer, which increased by 408 per cent. The realtive importance of the three factors is evident.

It will be argued, of course, that the use of a nonreturnable beer bottle is more desirable than a returnable one to the individual beer drinker. After all, some human effort must be expended to return the bottle to the point of purchase. We can modify the earlier evaluation, then, by asserting that for the sake of whatever improvement in well-being is involved in avoiding the effort of returning the bottle, the production of beer in nonreturnable bottles incurs a 408 per cent intensification of environmental impact. No such subtlety is involved in comparing the environmental impacts of two alternative nonreturnable beer containers: steel beer cans and aluminum ones. The energy involved in producing the aluminum can—and therefore the amount of combustion and the resultant output of pollutants —is 6.3 times that required for a steel can.

Similar computations can be made for the added environmental impact incurred when extra layers of packaging are added to foods and other goods or when plastic wrappers (nondegradable) are substituted for degradable cellulosic ones. In general, modern industrial technology has encased economic goods of no significantly increased human value in increasingly larger amounts of environmentally harmful wrappings. Result: the mounting heaps of rubbish that symbolize the advent of the technological age.

It should be recognized that such computations of environmental impact are still in a primitive, only partially developed stage. What is needed, and what—it is to be hoped—will be worked out before long, is an ecological analysis of every major aspect of the production, use, and disposition of goods. What is needed is a kind of "ecological impact inventory" for each productive activity, which will enable us to attach a sort of pollution price tag to each product. We would then know, for example, for each pound of detergent: how much air pollution is generated by the electric power and fuel burned to manufacture its chemical ingredients; how much water pollution is due to the mercury "loss" by the factory in the course of manufacturing the chlorine needed to produce it; the water pollution due to the detergent and phosphate entering sewage systems; the ecological effect of fluoride and arsenic (which may contaminate the phosphate), and of mercury, which might contaminate any alkali used to compound the detergent. Such pollution price tags are needed for all major products if we are to judge their relative *social* value. The foregoing account shows how far we are from this goal, and once again reminds us how blind we are about the environmental effects of modern technology.

It is useful, at this point, to return to a question asked earlier: what are the relative effects of the three factors that might be expected to influence the intensity of environmental pollution—population size, degree of affluence, and the tendency of the productive technology to pollute? A rather simple mathematical relationship connects the amount of pollutant emitted into the environment to these factors: pollutant emitted is equal to the product of the three factors—population times the amount of a given economic good per capita times output of pollutant per unit of the economic good produced. In the United States all three factors have changed since 1946. By comparing these changes with the concurrent increase in total pollutant output, it is possible to assign to each of the three factors the fraction of the over-all increase in pollutant output for which it is responsible. Since the increase of population, affluence and technology are multiplied together, and not added, to make the total increment in pollution, there is no convenient yet mathematically correct way of directly comparing each factor's relative importance to the whole. However, by expressing the ratios of the impacts for two different years in logarithmic terms, it is possible to evaluate the contribution of the change in any one factor; for example, population (as given by the ratio of the populations in the two years) in terms of the fraction which the *logarithm* of that ratio represented of the *logarithm* of the corresponding ratio of the total impacts. Since in multiplication logarithms are *added,* it becomes possible by this means to compute a relative measure of the contribution of each of the three factors to the total impact. When this computation is carried out for the economic goods considered above— agricultural production (pollutant outputs: nitrogen fertilizer, pesticides), cleaners (pollutant output: phosphate), passenger car travel (pollutant outputs: lead and nitrogen oxides), and beer consumption (pollutant output: beer bottles)—a rather clear picture emerges.

The logarithm of the increase in population accounts (as expressed by the ratios of the values for the two years) for from 12 to 20 per cent of the logarithm of the various increases in total pollutant output since 1946. The logarithm of the affluence factor (i.e., amount of economic good per capita), accounts for from 1 to 5 per cent of the logarithm of the total increase in pollutant output, except in the case of passenger travel, where the contribution rises to about 40 per cent of the total. This reflects a considerable increase in vehicle miles traveled per capita. However, as already pointed out, a good deal of this increase does not reflect improved welfare, but rather the unfortunate need for increased travel incident upon the decay of the inner cities and the growth of suburbs. The technology factor —that is, the logarithms of the increased output of pollutants per unit production resulting from the introduction of new productive technologies since 1946— accounts for 80 to 85 per cent of the logarithm of the total output of pollutants, except in the case of passenger travel, where it accounts for about 40 per cent of the total.

However, from the qualitative evidence on other pollution problems discussed earlier, it is already apparent that they follow a similar pattern: most of the sharp increase in pollution levels is due not so much to population or affluence as to changes in productive technology.

The over-all evidence seems clear. The chief reason for the environmental crisis that has engulfed the United States in recent years is the sweeping transformation of productive technology since World War II. The economy has grown enough to give the United States population about the same amount of basic goods, per capita, as it did in 1946. However, productive technologies with intense impacts on the environment have displaced less destructive ones. The environmental crisis is the inevitable result of this counterecological pattern of growth.

175

10

THE
SOCIAL
ISSUES

The preceding sections of this book were concerned with the origins of the environmental crisis. The analysis makes it plain, I believe, that the crisis is not the outcome of a natural catastrophe or of the misdirected force of human biological activities. The earth is polluted neither because man is some kind of especially dirty animal nor because there are too many of us. The fault lies with human society—with the ways in which society has elected to win, distribute, and use the wealth that has been extracted by human labor from the planet's resources. Once the social origins of the crisis become clear, we can begin to design appropriate social actions to resolve it. These are the concerns of the present chapter.

In modern industrial societies the most important link between society and the ecosystem on which it depends is technology. There is considerable evidence that many of the new technologies which now dominate production in an advanced country such as the United

States are in conflict with the ecosystem. They therefore degrade the environment. How can we account for this fault in modern technology?

At this point, it is important to take notice of the special status of science and technology in modern society. Technology often seems to act like an autonomous force, relatively independent of and more competent than the mere human beings who practice it. For example, confident prediction of future events is usually regarded as beyond the capability of ordinary people. Not so for technology. According to a leading technophile, Simon Ramo:

> Gather any group of competent technologists, put them to the job of trying to anticipate developments in their fields of expertise, and there is a very good chance that they will list a substantial fraction of the important things that will indeed happen in the period that they indicate.

Technology, it seems, has a crystal ball—that works.

One reason that technologists tend to be so certain about the technological future is suggested by one of the most astute observers of the social role of technology, John Kenneth Galbraith, who states:

> It is a commonplace of modern technology that problems have solutions before there is knowledge of how they are to be solved.

In this brief statement, Galbraith has brilliantly characterized technology: it is built on faith—in itself. Indeed, the power of technology is so evident and overwhelming as seemingly to intimidate even its critics. Thus Jacques

177

Ellul, one of the severest critics of effects of technology on human values, writes:

> Technique has become autonomous; it has fashioned an omnivorous world which obeys its own laws and which has renounced all tradition. . . . Technique has progressively mastered *all* the elements of civilization . . . man himself is overpowered by technique and becomes its object.

Thus both the proponents of technology and those who favor the "counterculture" seem to look on technology as a kind of self-sufficient, autonomous juggernaut, relatively immune to human fallibility and somehow ungovernable by human will. Those who admire the competence of technology suggest that human beings need to accommodate to it. Thus, according to Ramo:

> We must now plan on sharing the earth with machines. . . . We become partners. The machines require, for their optimum performance, certain patterns of society. We too have preferred arrangements. But we want what the machines can furnish, and so we must compromise. We must alter the rules of society, so that we and they can be compatible.

Here, Ramo assumes that machines have some autonomous "optimum performance," whereas human beings can only claim "preferred arrangements." Given this imbalance, the resultant "compromise" is inevitable; he calls for change in the rules of society, not machines.

The resulting frustrations of those who believe in the priority of human values has been admirably expressed by Archibald MacLeish:

After Hiroshima it was obvious that the loyalty of science was not to humanity but to truth—its own truth—and that the law of science was not the law of the good—what humanity thinks of as good, meaning moral, decent, humane—but the law of the possible. What it is possible for science to know science must know. What it is possible for technology to do technology will have done. . . . The frustration—and it is a real and debasing frustration—in which we are mired today will not leave us until we believe in ourselves again, assume again the mastery of our lives, the management of our means.

Against this background, it is significant that the *fallibility* of technology has become an important issue in the environmental crisis. Thus, when President Nixon surprised the people who had elected him on a platform that emphasized "crime in the streets" by devoting most of his first State of the Union message to the environmental crisis, he proposed to solve it by mobilizing the energy "of the same reservoir of inventive genius that created those problems in the first place."

While President Nixon's statement is a welcome confirmation of the ecological failure of modern technology which has been documented in previous chapters, it would seem prudent to examine his proposed solution rather closely. For, if technology is indeed to blame for the environmental crisis, it might be wise to discover wherein its "inventive genius" has failed us—and to correct that flaw—before entrusting our future survival to technology's faith in itself. It would be prudent, then, to examine the past record of technological efforts and to discover why they have failed so often in the environment.

The technology of sewage treatment is a good example. The basic problem has already been described earlier. When sewage, which contains considerable organic matter, is dumped into a river or lake, it generates an inordinate demand for oxygen, which is consumed as the bacteria of decay convert organic matter to inorganic breakdown products. As a result, this practice has commonly depleted the oxygen supply of surface waters, killing off the bacteria of decay and thereby halting the aquatic cycle of self-purification. Enter the sanitation technologist. First the technological problem is defined: how can the oxygen demand of sewage be reduced before it enters surface waters? Then the means are designed: the bacteria of decay are domesticated by establishing them in a treatment plant, artificially supplied with sufficient oxygen to accommodate the entering organic matter. What is released from the treatment plant is largely the inorganic residues of bacterial action. Since these have no oxygen demand, the problem, as stated, has been solved; modern sewage treatment technology has been created.

This, briefly, is the technological scenario—a story which, in confirmation of the technological faith, seems to end happily. Unfortunately, off stage, in nature's rivers and streams, the scenario does not work out so well. The treated sewage affluents are now rich in the inorganic residues of decay—carbon dioxide, nitrate, and phosphate—which in the natural cycle support the growth of algae. Now heavily fertilized, the algae bloom furiously, soon die, releasing organic matter, which regenerates the oxygen demand that sewage technology had removed. The technologist's success is undone. The reason for this failure is clear: the technologist defined his problem too narrowly, taking into his field of vision only one segment of what in nature is an endless cycle that will collapse if stressed *anywhere*. This same fault lies behind every ecological failure of modern technology: attention to a single facet of what in nature is a complex whole.

Consider another example—detergents. Here the technological aim was solely to develop a synthetic cleaning agent to replace soap. Research on the original synthetic detergents was designed to answer only the questions relevant to this single aim: is the detergent a good washing agent? Is it soft on milady's hands? Will it turn linen whiter than white? Will it sell? No one asked about the fate of the detergent when it goes down the drain and emerges into the ecosystem. Many "consumer acceptability" tests were performed on detergents. But the ultimate consumers of the detergents, the bacteria in surface waters and sewage disposal systems, were ignored. The result was a technological failure, for the original nondegradable detergents had to be withdrawn from the market.

Even with this unhappy experience in public view, detergent technologists persisted in their narrow-visioned ways. I recall an experience several years ago following a discussion of the eutrophication problem before a group of chemical engineers. After I had pointed out how nitrate and phosphate entering surface waters stimulate algal overgrowths and the importance of removing phosphates from detergents, an employee of a large detergent manufacturer spoke up. His firm, he said, was working hard to find a substitute for detergent phosphate. When I asked whether their research had uncovered any good leads, he replied eagerly: "Yes, a polynitrate."

Later, the industry actually began to build plants to manufacture a nitrate-based substitute for phosphate,

NTA, only to suspend the project when NTA was found to cause birth defects in laboratory animals. Similarly, when manufacturers were required to replace nondegradable detergents, which because of their branched molecules resist bacterial degradation, they concentrated on this single difficulty and produced unbranched "degradable" detergent molecules. They ignored the benzene group attached to the new molecule—which in surface water may be converted to phenol, a toxic substance.

Technology's tubular vision is also responsible for the fertilizer problem. Here the single aim was to increase agricultural yields; no attention was given to the fate of the excess nitrate in the ecosystem, until the resulting pollution of surface waters was upon us.

Pesticide technology was aimed solely at the insect pest, ignoring its inevitable effects on the insects' predators—which in nature control the pests—on wildlife and on man.

The modern high-powered automobile is a monument to a single-minded technology which called for little else but power, ignoring the inevitable effect on the environment of the resultant, noxious combustion products produced by the heat of high-compression engines.

Synthetic plastics are the end products of a vast amount of elaborate research and development, all focused exclusively on a particular use for which the plastic is intended: as a fiber, bottle, or packaging material. No one troubled over the fate of the material when it has outlived its usefulness and is intruded into the environment.

The Aswan Dam, like many other large engineering projects, was designed to produce power and to store water for a permanent irrigation system; the effect of the irrigation ditches on the spread of a serious disease, schistosomiasis, was neglected.

Mercury was introduced into chemical manufacturing to take advantage of its special electrical and chemical properties; that waste mercury would move through the aquatic ecosystem and accumulate in fish came as a sudden, unpleasant surprise.

Nuclear bombs were designed as explosives; for a long time—until forced by outside pressure—the responsible government agencies tried to evade the fact that they had designed not merely a new explosive, but an instrument of global ecological catastrophe.

These pollution problems arise not out of some minor inadequacies in the new technologies, but because of their very success in accomplishing their designed aims. A modern sewage treatment plant causes algal over-growths and resultant pollution *because* it produces, as it is designed to do, so much plant nutrient in its effluent. Modern, highly concentrated, nitrogen fertilizers result in the drainage of nitrate pollutants into streams and lakes just *because* they succeed in the aim of raising the nutrient level of the soil. The modern high-compression gasoline engine contributes to smog and nitrate pollution *because* it successfully meets its design criterion—the development of a high level of power. Modern synthetic insecticides kill birds, fish, and useful insects just *because* they are successfully absorbed by insects and kill them, as they are intended to do. Plastics clutter the landscape *because* they are unnatural, synthetic substances designed to resist degradation—precisely the properties that are the basis of their technological value.

Here we can begin to sense an explanation of the contradiction between the supposed infallibility of technology and its evident failures in the environment. The new technologies were, in fact, *not* failures—when tested against their stated aims. Thus, the stated aim of nuclear weapons technology—to explode bombs—has been brilliantly achieved; thousands of Japanese graves and the radioactivity of our bones, after all, testify to that. In the same sense, a sewage treatment plant is a success, for it does, after all, achieve its goal of reducing the biological oxygen demand of sewage. Similarly, nitrogen fertilizer does accomplish what the agronomist set out to achieve—an increased crop yield. Synthetic pesticides do kill insects, detergents do wash clothes, and plastics do effectively contain beer cans.

It becomes clear, then, that we are concerned not with some fault in technology which is only coincident to its value, but with a failure that derives from its basic *success* in industrial and agricultural production. If the ecological failure of modern technology is due to its success in accomplishing what it sets out to do, then the fault lies in its *aims*.

Why, then, should modern technology be guided by aims that are so consistently off the ecological mark? Again we can turn to Galbraith for help. Here is Galbraith's definition of technology, especially as it relates to production:

> Technology means the systematic application of scientific or other organized knowledge to practical tasks. *Its most important consequence, at least for the purpose of economics, is in forcing the division and subdivision of any such task into its component parts. Thus, and only thus, can organized knowledge be brought to bear on performance.* Specifically, there is no way that organized knowledge can be brought to bear on the production of an automobile as a

whole or even on the manufacture of a body or chassis. It can only be applied if the task is so subdivided that it begins to be coterminous with some established area of scientific or engineering knowledge. Though metallurgical knowledge cannot be applied to the manufacture of the whole vehicle, it can be used in the design of the cooling system or the engine block. While knowledge of mechanical engineering cannot be brought to bear on the manufacture of the vehicle, it can be applied to the machining of the crankshaft. While chemistry cannot be applied to the composition of the car as a whole, it can be used to decide on the composition of the finish or trim. . . . Nearly all of the consequences of technology, and much of the shape of modern industry, derive from this need to divide and subdivide tasks.

Now the reason for the ecological failure of technology becomes clear: unlike the automobile, the ecosystem cannot be subdivided into manageable parts, for its properties reside in the whole, in the connections between the parts. A process that insists on dealing only with the separated parts is bound to fail. Galbraith's description of how technology is applied to the production of an automobile—fragment by fragment— is precisely how it has been used in the series of blunders that have generated the environmental crisis. It explains why technology can design a useful fertilizer, a powerful automobile, or an efficient nuclear bomb. But since technology, as presently construed, cannot cope with the *whole* system on which the fertilizer, the automobile, or the nuclear bomb intrudes, disastrous ecological surprises—water pollution, smog, and global radioactive fallout—are inevitable. Ecological failure is apparently a necessary consequence of the nature of modern technology, as Galbraith defines it.

Add to this the faith "that problems have solutions before there is knowledge of how they are to be solved" and it becomes clear why in the age of technology we have acted blindly, massively, on nature *before* we were aware of the consequences. In popular imagery the technologist is often seen as a modern wizard, a kind of scientific sorcerer. It now appears that he is less sorcerer than sorcerer's apprentice.

It might be useful, at this point, to show that technology properly guided by appropriate scientific knowledge *can* be successful in the ecosystem, if its aims are directed toward the system as a whole rather than at some apparently accessible part. Consider, once more, the problem of sewage disposal. An ecologically sound technology would begin with a definition of the natural process that "disposes" of organic waste such as sewage. This is, of course, the soil ecosystem, which reincorporates organic matter into the natural nutritive cycle. Given that many people no longer live in close proximity to the soil but are collected in cities, clearly the ecologically appropriate technological means of removing sewage from the city is to return it to the soil.

Suppose, then, that the sewage, instead of being introduced into surface waters as it is now, whether directly or following treatment, is instead transported from urban collection systems by pipeline to agricultural areas, where—after appropriate sterilization procedures—it is incorporated into the soil. Such a pipeline would literally reincorporate the urban population into the soil's ecological cycle. This would restore the integrity of that cycle and incidentally end the need for inorganic nitrogen fertilizer, which also puts a stress on the aquatic cycle. The urban population is then no longer external to the soil cycle and is therefore incapable either of generating a negative biological stress upon it or of exerting a positive biological stress on the aquatic ecosystem. But note that this state of zero environmental impact is not achieved by a return to primitive conditions; it is not the people who are returned to the land, but the sewage. This requires a new technological advance: the construction of a sewage pipeline system.

Ecological survival does not mean the abandonment of technology. Rather, it requires that technology be derived from a scientific analysis that is appropriate to the natural world on which technology intrudes.

This suggests that behind the ecological failure of modern technology lies a corresponding failure in its scientific base. For, to cite Galbraith once more, the fragmented nature of technology is dictated by the need to make the technological task "coterminous with some established areas of scientific or engineering knowledge." The fault in technology, then, appears to derive from the fragmented nature of its scientific base.

There is, indeed, a specific fault in our system of science, and in the resultant understanding of the natural world, which, I believe, helps to explain the ecological failure of technology. This fault is reductionism, the view that effective understanding of a complex system can be achieved by investigating the properties of its isolated parts. The reductionist methodology, which is so characteristic of much of modern research, is not an effective means of analyzing the vast natural systems that are threatened by degradation. For example, water pollutants stress a total ecological web and its numerous organisms; the effects on the whole natural system are not adequately described by laboratory studies of pure cultures of separate organisms. The leading exponent of the opposite approach, *holism*, is René Dubos of Rockefeller University, who has done such excellent work in analyzing the interdependence between man and nature.

The reductionist approach has had a particularly adverse effect on what we know about the biological systems that are at risk in the environment. Biology has become a flourishing and well-supported science in the United States; it is producing a wealth of new knowledge and is training many scientists skilled in its new methodology. But modern biological research is now dominated by the conviction that the most fruitful way to understand life is to discover a specific molecular event that can be identified as "the mechanism" of a particular biological process. The complexities of soil biology or the delicate balance of the nitrogen cycle in a river, which are not reducible to simple molecular mechanisms, are now often regarded as uninteresting relics of some ancient craft. In the pure glow of molecular biology, studying the biology of sewage is a dull and distasteful exercise hardly worth the attention of a "modern" biologist.

This helps to explain a curious paradox in the status of environmental science in the United States. Since World War II there has been an unprecedented growth of biological research; yet we remain astonishingly ignorant of the profound changes that, during that same period, have occurred in our own biological surroundings. For example, we lack historical data regarding the levels of lead, mercury, cadmium, and other metallic pollutants in the soil, water, and air; national measurements of smog and other urban air pollutants began only recently and are still inadequate. In the absence of such baseline data it is difficult to interpret the present pollution levels. I once asked a government research official to explain this deficiency. The answer was forthright: proposals for research to measure the levels of environmental pollutants were nearly always rejected under the rubric "pedestrian research." After all, what could such data contribute to "fundamental" biological knowledge, which was always construed in terms of molecular theories exclusively derived from test-tube data? Fortunately, in the last few years, in direct response to the environmental crisis, the National Science Foundation has taken the leadership to institute a wholly new kind of program of research support: Research Applied to National Needs. That we must now develop a major new research program on "national needs," is tragic evidence that previous programs have failed to meet them.

Nor is reductionism limited to biology; it is, rather, the dominant viewpoint of modern science as a whole. It often leads sociologists to become psychologists, psychologists to become physiologists, physiologists to become cellular biologists, and turns cellular biologists into chemists, chemists into physicists, and physicists into mathematicians. Reductionism tends to isolate scientific disciplines from each other, and all of them from the real world. In each case, the discipline appears to be moving away from observation of the natural, real object: biologists tend to study not the natural living organism, but cells and ultimately molecules isolated from them. One result of this approach is that communication among the disciplines becomes difficult unless the subject is reduced to the simplest common denominator; the biologist is unable to communicate with the chemist unless he reduces his analytical biological problem to a molecular one. But the problem is then likely to become irrelevant to the real world. The failure of communication among such specialized basic sciences is an important source of difficulty in understanding environmental problems. For example, the chemists who developed the processes for synthesizing branched-chain detergents might have been forewarned about the ultimate failure of their products if they had been in close contact with biochemists—who already knew that such branched molecules tend to resist enzymatic attack and would therefore persist in disposal systems.

Reductionism has also tended to isolate scientific disciplines from the problems that affect the human condition. Such problems, environmental degradation for example, involve inherently complex systems. Life, as we live it, is not encompassed by a single academic discipline. Real problems that touch our lives and impinge on what we value rarely fit into the neat categories of the college catalog, such as physical chemistry, nuclear physics, or molecular biology.

For example, to encompass in our minds the terrifying deterioration of our cities, we need to know not only the principles of economics, architecture, and social planning, but also the physics and chemistry of the air, the biology of water systems, and the ecology of the domestic rat and the cockroach. In a word, we need to understand science and technology that is *relevant* to the human condition.

However, we in the scientific community have been brought up in a different tradition. We have a justified pride in our intellectual independence and know—for we often have to battle to maintain it—how essential this independence is to the search for truth. But scientists may sometimes tend to translate intellectual independence ino a kind of mandatory avoidance of all problems that do not arise in their own minds—an approach that may cut them off from the real and urgent needs of society, and often from their students as well. As a result, science has become too isolated from the real problems of the world and a poor instrument for understanding the threats to its survival.

In sum, we can trace the origin of the environmental crisis through the following sequence. Environmental degradation largely results from the introduction of new industrial and agricultural production technologies. These technologies are ecologically faulty because they are designed to solve singular, separate problems and fail to take into account the inevitable "side-effects" that arise because, in nature, no part is isolated from the whole ecological fabric. In turn, the fragmented design of technology reflects its scientific foundation, for science is divided into disciplines that are largely governed by the notion that complex systems can be understood only if they are first broken into their separate component parts. This reductionist bias has also tended to shield basic science from a concern for real-life problems, such as environmental degradation.

The isolation of science from such practical problems has another unfortunate consequence. Most people are less interested in the discipline of science than they are in its practical effects on their daily lives. And the separation between science and the problems that concern people has tended to limit what most people know about the scientific background of environmental issues. Yet such *public* knowledge is essential to the solution of every environmental problem. For these depend not only on scientific data, but ultimately on a public judgment which balances the benefits to be gained from a particular technology against the associated environmental hazards.

In effect, the citizen faces an important question about modern technology: does it pay? Whether we ask this in the direct language of profit and loss or in the more abstract language of social welfare, the question is crucial. Sooner or later, every human endeavor—if it is to continue—must pass this simple test: is it worth what it costs?

It might appear that for most environmental issues this question has already been answered. After all, power companies seem eager to build plants for nuclear fuels rather than fossil ones and farmers rapidly adopt new insecticides and fertilizers. Apparently their cost accounting tells them that the new technologies yield the best available margin between income and costs. The environmental crisis tells us, however, that these calculations are not complete—that certain costs have not yet been taken into account.

For example, what are the true costs of operating a coal-fired power plant in an urban area? The obvious costs—capital outlay, maintenance, operating costs, taxes—are of course well known. But we have recently discovered that there are other costs and have even begun to put a dollar value upon them.

We now know that a coal-burning power plant produces not only electricity, but also a number of less desirable things: smoke and soot, oxides of sulfur and nitrogen, carbon dioxide, a variety of organic compounds, and heat. Each of these is a *non*good and costs someone something. Smoke and soot increase the householder's laundry and cleaning bills; oxides of sulfur increase the cost of building maintenance; for organic pollutants we pay the price—not only in dollars, but in human anguish—of some number of cases of lung cancer.

Some of these costs can be converted to dollar values. The United States Public Health Service estimates the over-all cost of air pollution at about $60 per person per year. About one third of urban air pollution is due to power production from fossil fuels, representing about $20 per person per year. This means that we must add to the cost of power production, for each urban family of four, about $80 per year—an appreciable sum relative to the annual bill for electricity.

The point of this calculation is obvious. The *hidden* costs of power production, such as air pollution, are *social* costs; they are met, not by a single producer, but by the *public*. To discover the true cost of the many benefits of modern technology, we need to look for, and evaluate, all the hidden social costs represented by environmental pollution.

Every environmental decision therefore involves a balance between benefits and hazards. This is expressed in the official United States policy regarding allowable public exposure to radiation from atomic operations which states:

> The establishment of radiation protection standards involves a balancing of the benefits to be derived from the controlled use of radiation and atomic energy against the risk of radiation exposure. This principle is based on the position adopted by the Federal Radiation Council that any radiation exposure involves some risk, the magnitude of which increases with the exposure . . . the various benefits to be expected as a result of the exposure, as evalu-

193

ated by the appropriate responsible group, must outweigh the potential hazard or risk.

On this basis, the government has adopted as a guideline that a particular radiation exposure—for example, 10 rads to the thyroid gland—is "acceptable" for the general public. But since every increase in radiation exposure thereby increases the risk to health, there is a definite risk associated with a 10-rad dose to the thyroid. One calculation suggests that it might increase the national incidence of thyroid cancer about tenfold; another estimate suggests only a 50 per cent increase. In any case, if we accept as the price of nuclear power, for example, that citizens shall endure 10-rads of exposure to their thyroids, then some people, at some time, will pay that price with their health.

The same is true of other environmental issues. For any effort to reduce an environmental hazard will compete with the benefits available from the technological process that produces it. If radiation emission standards are made more rigorous, the health hazard from nuclear power operations could be reduced, but the added expense of achieving them would increase the cost of power and might render the nuclear industry incapable of competing with fossil-fuel power plants. This would severely curtail a major federally financed technological program and raise serious political issues. Similarly, it would be possible to reduce nitrate pollution from feedlots by returning the wastes to the land, where in nature they belong. But this would reduce the economy of the feedlot operation. Organic fertilizers could be reintroduced in place of inorganic nitrogen fertilizer in order to reduce the environmental hazard of excess nitrate in surface waters; but since inorganic fertilizers are cheaper to buy and to spread, crop production costs would rise. Urban pollution involves many cost/benefit decisions. For example, smog levels cannot be reduced without supplanting urban automotive traffic with electric-powered mass transit systems, or possibly by introducing new types of vehicles. The first of these actions would impose a massive economic burden on cities that are already unable to meet their social obligations; the second course would mean a serious disruption of one of the mainstays of our economy, the automobile industry. In the same way, the government's decision in 1970 to close the biological warfare arsenal at Pine Bluff, Arkansas, was protested by the local chamber of commerce, which expressed a readiness to accept the possible environmental hazard—and to enjoy the benefits of the 200 jobs associated with the arsenal —for the sake of "deterring" an enemy with the threat of bacterial attack.

We come then to a crucial question: who is to be the Solomon of modern technology and weigh in the balance all the good that comes of it against the ecological, social costs? Or, who will strike the balance between the concern of the prudent manager of a nuclear power plant for economy and the concern of a mother over the health of her child?

Confronted by decisions on nuclear power, radiation, nitrate levels, photochemical smog, bacterial warfare, and all the other technicalities of environmental problems, it is tempting to call in the scientific expert. Scientists can, of course, evaluate the relevant benefits: how many kilowatt-hours of electricity a nuclear power plant can deliver and at what price, or the yield of corn to be expected from nitrogen fertilizer. They can also evaluate the related risks: the radiation dose to people in the vicinity of the power plant and the hazard to infants from nitrate levels exacerbated by fertilizers. These evaluations can be derived from appropriate scientific theories, principles, and data.

However, no scientific principle can guide the choice between some number of kilowatt hours of electric power and some number of cases of thyroid cancer, or between some number of bushels of corn and some number of cases of infant methemoglobinemia. These are *value* judgments; they are determined not by scientific principle, but by the value that we place on economic advantage and on human life or by our belief in the wisdom of committing the nation to mass transportation or to biological warfare. These are matters of morality, of social and political judgment. In a democracy they belong not in the hands of "experts," but in the hands of the people and their elected representatives.

The environmental crisis is the legacy of our unwitting assault on the natural systems that support us. It represents hidden costs that are mounting toward catastrophe. If it is to be resolved, these costs must be made explicit and balanced against the benefits of technology in open, public debate. But this debate will not come easily. For the public has little access to the necessary scientific data. Much of the needed information has been, and remains, wrapped in government and industrial secrecy. Unearthing the needed information and disseminating it to the public is, I believe, the unique responsibility of the scientific community. For to exercise its right of conscience, the public must have the relevant scientific facts in understandable terms. As the custodians of this knowledge, we in the scientific community owe it to our fellow citizens to help inform them about the crisis in the environment.

This partnership between scientist and citizen is, I believe, the clue to the remarkable upsurge of public action on environmental issues that we have witnessed in the United States in recent years. Here are some examples:

1. The Limited Nuclear Test Ban Treaty of 1963, a major reversal of United States foreign policy, is perhaps the first of the great ecological victories achieved by the partnership between the American public and the scientific community. For nearly a decade after Hiroshima, while the United States, the USSR, and Great Britain rapidly developed and tested nuclear weapons, the American public was kept in ignorance of the crucial environmental facts. No one knew that every explosion produced massive amounts of strontium 90 and other radioisotopes; that strontium 90 would be carried through the food chain and lodge in the developing bones of children; that *any* increase in radioactive exposure increases the risk of cancer and other radiation hazards. Rigid secrecy kept these facts from the public; the American people were paying the biological price of nuclear tests not even knowing that it had been asked of them.

However, beginning in about 1953, the independent scientific community began to agitate for the release of government-held data on fallout. By 1956 sufficient information had been released to provide scientists with an effective understanding of what was happening. At this point, led by Linus Pauling, scientists, first in the United States and later throughout the world, appealed through a petition for action to halt nuclear tests and the spread of fallout. This appeal brought no immediate action, but for the first time broad sections of the public began to understand the nuclear peril.

There then developed in the United States the scientists' information movement—the effort (referred to in Chapter 3) of independent scientists organized in local committees under the aegis of the Scientists' Institute for Public Information to inform the public about the basic scientific facts on fallout. This campaign restored the missing element in the political process—the grist of data was supplied to the public conscience.

We have a fairly good historical record of the consequences. Previously unconcerned senators were moved to support the Nuclear Test Ban Treaty by a flood of passionate letters from parents who objected to raising their children on milk contaminated with strontium 90. The senators were not so much impressed that their constituents were irate (they are accustomed to that), but that they knew how to spell strontium 90! Presumably the prospect of facing not merely an irate voter but an informed one stirred them to action. Of course, there was also purely political pressure for the treaty; but that pressure succeeded, I am convinced, because it was armed—with the facts.

When the Test Ban Treaty was achieved, some observers expected scientists to lose interest in fallout. Instead, many of them saw that fallout was only part of a larger problem—the untoward environmental effects of modern technology—in which public education was also vital. It was at this point that the St. Louis Committee for Nuclear Information substituted "Environmental" for "Nuclear" in its name and converted its bulletin into the magazine now known as *Environment*.

2. A more recent example is the public victory over

the Pentagon on the matter of disposal of nerve gas. For years a huge deadly supply of nerve gas was stored in tanks lying directly in the path of planes using the Denver airport. This menace went unnoticed until scientists of the Colorado Committee for Environmental Information issued to the public a factual statement which pointed out that an unlucky plane crash might wipe out most of the Denver population. This, and other explanations by independent scientists in *Environment,* of how nerve gas had killed 6,000 sheep in Utah (a fact long denied by the Army) and the resultant public outcry, finally persuaded the government to remove the gas. On the advice of its experts, the Army began to haul the gas by rail across the country in order to dump it in the Atlantic. At once scientists of the St. Louis Committee for Environmental Information pointed out the enormous risk involved in this procedure and showed that the material could be inactivated on the spot. Once more, the Army's position was reversed. Curiously, the new decision to detoxify the material, like the earlier one to ship it, was also validated by the government's committees of experts. They corrected their initial mistake, and the government's policy was changed, but only after the relevant facts were unearthed by the scientific community—and brought to public attention.

3. For years the government spent billions of dollars and precious human resources on the development and production of biological weapons, only to abandon them not long ago when, despite the constraints of military secrecy, a few crucial facts about their uncontrollable dangers—if they were ever used—were brought home to the public by independent scientists: Matthew Meselson of Harvard, E. G. Pfeiffer of the University of

Montana, Arthur Galston of Yale, and Victor Sidel of the Einstein Medical College, among others.

4. And what led to the recent government decision to halt the spread of DDT in the environment? Surely not the advice of industrial experts, who, along with many government advisers, for many years spoke only of the advantages of this insecticide. No, it was Rachel Carson who calmly and courageously unearthed the ecological facts and brought them eloquently to the public attention. Following her lead, other scientists spoke up. Armed with the facts, citizens sued for action. Tragically late, action was taken. Nor is this task complete; as the U.S. markets for DDT are blocked, manufacturers increasingly ship the pesticide abroad.

5. The defeat of the SST over the massive, persistent opposition of the Nixon administration, the aircraft industry, and a number of labor unions is recognized as a crucial turning point in environmental politics. In 1969 Senator Gaylord Nelson of Wisconsin and his colleagues could muster only nineteen votes against the SST in the Senate; in 1970 they defeated it by fifty-two votes. What happened in the intervening year is clear enough: the public became acquainted with the facts about the SST—its sonic boom, its possible effects on the ozone blanket that shields the earth from solar ultraviolet radiation, and its economic futility—and voiced their opposition. Their representatives listened. As one senator put it when asked to explain why he switched from support to opposition to the SST: "I read my mail."

6. And let us also pay tribute to Mr. Norvald Fimreite, a graduate student of zoology at the University of Western Ontario, for he holds the world record, I believe, for the fastest, one-man, large-scale ecological

action. On March 19, 1970, he wrote to the Canadian Department of Fisheries and Forestry to report that he had found 7.09 ppm of mercury—a value fourteen times greater than the allowable limit—in pickerel from waters that feed Lake Erie. The Canadian government responded at once. Within a month chloralkali plants were pinpointed as a source of the mercury; they have been forced to change their operations. Meanwhile the Canadian government has banned the taking of fish in the area; sport and commercial fishing have been halted and the polluters are threatened with legal action.

There are many other examples: the nuclear reactor planned for Bodega Bay, California, and abandoned when a local citizens' committee, aided by the St. Louis Committee for Environmental Information, helped publicize a report that showed that, since it sat on the great San Andreas fault, the reactor might rupture in an earthquake; the Minnesota Committee for Environmental Information which made a study that led the state of Minnesota to adopt new reactor emission standards—much more stringent than AEC standards; the Northern California Committee for Environmental Information, which was instrumental in making Berkeley the first city to commit itself to natural, biological control of insects in its parks and streets; the scientists of the Rochester Committee for Environmental Information, who collected water samples that revealed the inadequacy of the city's sewage treatment—a new bond issue resulted; the New York Scientists' Committee for Public Information which unearthed an official report that showed that a new cross-town expressway, about to be adopted, would probably generate enough carbon monoxide to cause pedestrians to stagger in the streets—despite well-advanced plans, the project was dropped.

Add to all this the valiant efforts of Ralph Nader and the devoted students who have worked with him to uncover and make public the facts about air and water pollution and the inadequacies of protective regulations. And add, also, the legal actions taken by conservation organizations, by community groups, or simply by single, determined citizens to halt environmental hazards. All these efforts have been based not only on public morality, but on facts—unearthed by scientists and brought into public view through the newspapers, radio, television.

There is one grim reason for all these successes: the country has been vastly ignorant of the extent and depth of the environmental crisis because crucial facts remained buried in inaccessible reports or shielded by official and industrial secrecy. When the facts were revealed, citizens were ready to weigh the benefits against the risks and make the moral judgment which is the spark to political action.

All this has taken some people by surprise. For there is a myth in some political circles that public policy is determined more by narrow self-interest than by concerns for values as nebulous as the integrity of the environment. They would argue as well that there is no way to establish the general public attitude toward the moral acceptability of a given balance between benefit and risk and that, realistically, this judgement can only be made by some appropriate governmental agency. The answer to this argument is that public opinion has, in fact, already established rather well-defined limits to the risks that are acceptable for the benefits to be derived from a wide range of activities.

The benefit/risk issue is associated with many aspects of personal life: driving a car, traveling in a train or an aircraft, skiing, working in an industrial plant or living near it, the use of x-rays for medical diagnosis, watching a color television set, using a microwave oven or a synthetic insecticide. These are personal, voluntary acts. Other benefit/risk issues relate to large-scale social enterprises in which the risks are taken involuntarily. These include the widespread use of pesticides and fertilizers in agriculture, all forms of power production, air pollution due to urban traffic, and indeed all of the massive sources of environmental pollution.

Recently efforts have been made to evaluate, from the available statistics, the quantitative balance between the benefits and risks associated with such activities that has been acepted by the general public. For a number of such activities, Chauncey Starr has evaluated the risk (which he defines as "the statistical probability of fatalities per hour of exposure of the individual to the activity considered") and the benefit, calculated from the dollar equivalent value derived by the individual from the activity. The ratio of benefit to risk that is acceptable to the public can be seen from a plot of the risk against the benefit, calculated in these terms.

The results of such a plot are quite striking. When the value of the benefit is small, the acceptable risk is also relatively low; as the value increases, the acceptable risk also rises—but at a rate that is very large relative to the increase in value (the acceptable risk rises, approximately, in proportion to the cube of the benefit). Also, as the beneficial value of various activities increases, the acceptable risk reaches an upper limit. Since a wide variety of activities fit this general formula, we must conclude that there has been, deeply inherent in our society, some general standard of public judgment regarding the acceptable balance between benefit and risk. Moreover, the influence of a purely moral factor such as the distinction between an involuntary and voluntary activity is measurable in the results. Involuntary and voluntary activities fall on *separate* curves of the same general shape, but for the same benefit the acceptable level for involuntary risks is 10,000 times less than that acceptable for voluntary ones. These calculations show that the acceptable benefit/risk ratio is determined by a general public consensus; where regulatory agencies are involved, their actions appear to reflect rather than create the common public view. In effect, they place a numerical value on a matter of public morality—that, in Starr's words, "we are loath to let others do unto us what we happily do to ourselves."

Now, however, it has become apparent that we are in the midst of a revolution in public attitude toward the acceptability of levels of environmental deterioration which have for a long time been tolerated without general complaint. The explanation for this change is suggested by the clear 10,000-fold difference between the acceptable benefit/risk ratios of voluntary and involuntary activities. This reflects a more stringent public morality when actions of some members of society impose risks on others who are given no choice in the matter. The new assaults on the environment considerably intensify this moral factor. The public has now become aware, I believe, that the new environmental pollutants represent an assault by the present generation not merely on involuntary *living* victims—who have some recourse, however difficult—but on generations not yet born and therefore utterly defenseless. In response, the public is in the process of establishing a new set of acceptable benefit/risk ratios. For a given benefit, the new ratio will accept only a risk that is far below even that acceptable for involuntary risks imposed on the present population. This, then, is the moral response to the assaults on the integrity of the environment which threaten the well-being and even the survival of succeeding generations.

In politics, environmental protection is sometimes regarded as a "motherhood" issue; no one can really oppose it. In fact, it is often suggested that environmental issues are so innocuous that they serve to divert people from more serious, controversial issues—a kind of ecological "cop-out" from the problems of poverty, racial discrimination, and war. In practice, it hasn't quite turned out that way; as a political issue, environmental protection is neither innocuous nor unrelated to basic questions of social justice.

For example, in the ghetto, environmental protection is sometimes regarded as an irrelevant diversion from the plight of the blacks. Some approaches to environmental action give substance to this view. This was dramatized during Earth Week 1970 at San Jose State College in California, where a student environmental program was climaxed by the burial of a brand new car, as a symbol of environmental rebellion. The event was picketed by black students who believed that the $2,500 paid for the car could have been better spent in the ghetto. The San Jose burial reflects a kind of personalized approach to the environmental crisis which is sometimes adopted by ecological crusaders. They reason—erroneously, as we have seen—that pollution is caused by the excessive consumption of goods and resources by the United States population. Since the wastes generated by this intense consumption pollute our environment, the eco-activist is advised to "consume less." In the absence of the added statistic that in the United States the per capita consumption by blacks is much less than that of the white population, such observations are not likely to make much sense to blacks or to anyone who is concerned with social justice.

Disaffiliation of blacks from the environmental movement would be particularly unfortunate, because in many ways blacks are the special victims of pollution. A white suburbanite can escape from the city's dirt, smog, carbon monoxide, lead, and noise when he goes home; the ghetto dweller not only works in a polluted environment, he lives in it. And in the ghetto he confronts his own, added environmental problems: rats and other vermin, the danger of lead poisoning when children eat bits of ancient, peeling paint. And, through its history, the black community can be a powerful ally in the fight against environmental degradation. The environmental crisis is a crisis of survival, an issue that is not familiar to middle-class Americans. They have not yet learned how to face such a soul-shaking threat; witness our continued failure to appreciate that the existence of ready-armed nuclear weapons means that doomsday may be tomorrow. For blacks, the issue of survival is several hundred years old. If they too have not yet mastered it, they have at least had a good deal of experience that may be enormously valuable to a society that, now as a whole, must face the threat of extinction. Blacks need the environmental movement, and the movement needs the blacks.

There is also a close relationship between environmental issues and poverty. A classic illustration is provided by the recent events at Hilton Head, South Carolina. There, on a beautiful shoreline site, adjacent to large, well-kept estates, a chemical company proposed to build a large plant which, in the absence of unprecedented, expensive environmental controls, would certainly degrade the local environment. Opposed to the plant were the estate owners, conservationists, and shrimp fishermen who feared the aesthetic and ecological effects of the plant's effluents. In support of the plant were the chemical company and many of the poor people in the area, who saw the opportunity to relieve their long-standing unemployment. Where lies justice in this matter? It might be possible to compute the economic benefits of the plant and compare them with the economic costs of the effects of pollutants on shrimp fishing and on the local natural ambiance. Would it then be sufficient to compare the benefits with the costs and decide in favor of the more economical action? Clearly the matter cannot end there, for the environmental problem, even if "solved" in this way, raises other, more fundamental issues which are not solved by environmental action. For example, if the plant is blocked (which is in fact what happened), this action, in effect, says to the unemployed that their right to a job is less important than the integrity of the environment. The appropriate response may well be that a society that can find the means to save a marsh ought to be equally capable of finding the means to employ its citizens.

A similar situation arose in connection with the SST; unions strongly supported the project because its abandonment would throw some thousands of workers out of jobs. To a person thus unemployed, the immediate response may well be anger directed against the "eco-freaks" who opposed the SST. On further reflection, such a person might wonder about the rationality of an economic system that forces a person to fight for a job with the knowledge that the product would wake babies in the night and increase the incidence of ultraviolet-induced skin cancers.

There is an equally close link between environmental problems and the issues of war and peace. Like detergents and DDT, nuclear armament is a huge technological blunder. When in the 1950's the Pentagon generals and their scientific advisers decided to rely on nuclear weapons for the nation's defense, they were apparently unaware of what the scientific community, its voice strongly amplified by public response, has since told them: that it will not work, that no nation would survive a nuclear war.

In the same way, the Pentagon replied to an inquiry from the AAAS that it would not use herbicides in Vietnam if it believed that these agents would have "long-term ecological effects" on that tortured land. Now we know from the efforts of the AAAS and other independent scientists that the United States has indeed conducted ecological warfare in Vietnam. In response, the government has, at last, greatly restricted the military use of herbicides in Vietnam. There is equal force in the fact that the United States government has now abandoned the manufacture of biological warfare agents, after long defending them—against opposition from the scientific community—as effective and necessary for the nation's "defense."

It seems to me that these ecological insights raise very profound questions about the competence of our military to defend the nation, as they are charged to do. It adds force to the mounting evidence of purely military blunders in the United States war in Southeast Asia. It raises the momentous issue of at last freeing mankind from the threat of annihilation, from the intolerable burden of living, every day, within minutes of castatrophe.

The environmental crisis is hardly a "motherhood" issue. Nor is it a diversion from other social questions. For as we begin to act on the environmental crisis, deeper issues emerge which reach to the core of our system of social justice and challenge basic political goals.

The force of this challenge is revealed by the implications of two alternative routes of environmental action: action *of* the public and action *by* the public. Those who favor the first route, march under Pogo's banner: "We have met the enemy and he is us." They are committed to personal acts that lessen environmental impact: they walk or bicycle rather than drive a car; they use returnable bottles and phosphate-free detergents; they produce no more than two children. These are the rudiments of a new, ecology-minded personal life-style. It is designed to minimize the two factors that intensify pollution that are under personal control: consumption and population size.

In contrast, action directed toward the third source of environmental impact—the counterecological design of production technology—is necessarily social, rather than personal. As indicated earlier, this factor has a far more powerful effect on pollution levels than the other two. It will be recalled that, as measured by the ratios of the logarithms, in the United States, population rise accounts for 12 to 20 per cent of the increases in postwar environmental impact, while the technological factor accounts for 40 to 85 per cent of these increases. If, to take a conservative illustration, the technological factor had had five times the effect of rising population, then there would have been the following alternative means by which we could have *prevented* the rise in pollution level since World War II. If we chose to allow population to grow, as it did, by about 43 per cent, then *a 30 per cent reduction* in environmental impact would have been required of productive technology. If, on the other hand, we chose to allow the environmental impact of technology to increase, as it did, by about 600 per cent (in this example), then *an 86 per cent reduction* in population size would have been required. (See note for the relevant computation.) It seems rather clear that of the two factors, technology is by far the more effective one. On the other hand it is not subject to direct personal control.

Which route should we take? Should people be urged to consume less and produce fewer children in order to reduce pollution levels? Or should we, rather, concentrate on the ecological reform of technology? Or both?

Since powerful resistance is likely to delay technological reforms, and reduction in consumption is hardly sensible in the face of continued poverty and need, it is often proposed that the primary effort should be made to slow the growth of the United States population. Apart from the fact that a large *reduction* in population would be needed to achieve a noticeable effect on pollution levels, this is, of course, a perfectly logical argument. So long as we continue to use it, ecologically faulty production technology will certainly do less damage to the environment if fewer people demand its products. Clearly, there are logical grounds for supporting *both* ecological reform of production technology and the reduction of population growth as a basis of environmental improvement.

But there is more than logic and ecology at work here. For this same principle can be applied with equal logic to nearly every social problem. Indeed, under the impetus of recent environmental concern, it has been. Here are two examples:

> A Secretary of Labor spends his years in office trying futilely to fight unemployment by creating more jobs; and only later, freed of the inhibitions of office and politics' restraints, faces the truth that there are too few jobs because there are too many people.

> Considering the problems of air and water pollution, poverty, clogged highways, overcrowded schools, inadequate courts and jails, urban blight, and so on, it is clear that the United States has more people than it can adequately maintain.

This, it seems to me, sets the problem in its proper context: the nation's social system is grossly incapable of supporting the people who created it in their present and expected numbers; they are therefore suffering poverty, unemployment, environmental pollution, inadequate schooling, injustice, and the tyranny of war. Now, if the reason for this incompetence is that, even with maximum efficiency and complete social equity, the nation no longer has sufficient resources to support the expected population, we have no choice but to control its size. However, according to the United States Commission on Population Growth and the American Future:

211

There is little question that the United States has the resources, if it chooses to use them, to meet the demands of a population growing at the current rate as well as to correct various social and economic inequities.

This being the case, it seems to me that there is a clear dichotomy between the two routes toward social progress. We are engaged in a kind of political "zero-sum game": to the degree that population size is reduced, to that degree may we be able to tolerate some of the technological, economic, and social faults that plague us; to the degree that we repair these faults, to that degree can the nation successfully support a growing population.

How these considerations are to be balanced against one another depends on the collective sense of social justice inherent in the American people. Insofar as they are themselves willing to accept the personal burden of relieving the crisis in the environment, in unemployment, in education, in health, in urban decay, they will voluntarily reduce births. Insofar as the American people are unwilling to undertake this personal action, they will need to seek relief by altering the economic, social, and political priorities that govern the disposition of the nation's resources.

All this assumes voluntary public choice. However, some population-minded ecologists hold that "we must have population control at home, hopefully through a system of incentives and penalties, but by compulsion if voluntary methods fail." The outcome would be to constrain, by compulsion, the public choice between the two basic paths toward social progress. More simply stated, this is political repression.

212

Nor is it possible to disguise this ugly fact by notions such as "mutual coercion, mutually agreed upon." If a majority of the United States population voluntarily practiced birth control adequate to population stabilization, there would be no need for coercion. The corollary is that *coercion is necessary only if a majority of the population refuses voluntarily to practice adequate birth control.* This means that the majority would need to be coerced by the minority. This is, indeed, political repression.

In a way, it is fortunate that the environmental crisis has generated so much discussion of the population problem. The nation has for many years been tormented by the contrast between its unparalleled wealth and its inability to provide for its people an adequate environment, employment, schooling, health and social services, and a peaceful life. For a long time, this stark reality has been obscured by evasions, excuses, and a cloud of technical details. It seems to me that this screen has now, somehow, been penetrated by the environmental crisis. We can now see more clearly that the multiple national crisis of which it is a part, in MacLeish's words,

> will not leave us until we believe in ourselves again, assume again the mastery of our lives, the management of our means.

213

11

THE
QUESTION
OF SURVIVAL

In the last few years, the environmental crisis has entered forcefully into the political arena, not only in the United States, but in Sweden, England, Germany, Japan, Italy, and the Soviet Union. During the preparations for the 1972 United Nations Conference on the Human Environment it has also become a subject of international debate.

In the United States, the political impact of environmental issues is so strong as to generate, in some quarters, the suspicion that many of them are really politics dressed up as ecology. As a result, ecology suffers somewhat from the kind of "credibility gap" that has been observed in the neighborhood of the White House in recent years. And like some recent United States presidents, ecologists are sometimes suspected of escalating an admittedly bad situation into a catastrophic one—by claiming that environmental deterioration is not merely a threat to the quality of life, but to life itself, that the very survival of human beings on the earth is at stake.

Even a "numbers game" has evolved: "How long," people want to know, "do we have to live?" Environmentalists' answers range from about one hundred to rather few years. One has even asserted that if the crisis is not on its way to solution by 1972, he will give up the campaign, for it will then be too late.

How real is the environmental threat to human survival? How much time *do* we have? Or is the issue of survival only scare tactics, an exaggeration made in the presumably good cause of forcing public action on the declining quality of life?

The issue of survival can be put into the form of a fairly rigorous question: are present ecological stresses so strong that—if not relieved—they will sufficiently degrade the ecosystem to make the earth uninhabitable by man? If the answer is yes, then human survival is indeed at stake in the environmental crisis. Obviously no serious discussion of the environmental crisis can get very far without confronting this question.

It should be said at the outset that while this question is a fairly rigorous one, any answer is a matter of judgment, not of fact. Nevertheless, it is a judgment that can, and should, be related to actual data and scientific principles.

My own judgment, based on the evidence now at hand, is that the present course of environmental degradation, at least in industrialized countries, represents a challenge to essential ecological systems that is so serious that, if continued, it will destroy the capability of the environment to support a reasonably civilized human society. Some number of human beings might well survive such a catastrophe, for the collapse of civilization would reduce the pace of environmental degradation. What would then remain would be a kind of neobarbarism with a highly uncertain future. The reasoning behind this judgment is described in what follows.

To begin with, it is prudent to take note of the inherent limitations of any discussion that hopes to comment on the future course of ecological change. Extension from past data to future trends—the process of extrapolation—has many pitfalls. The most serious difficulty is that any such numerical extension necessarily assumes that the future process will be governed by the same mechanisms that have controlled past events. Mark Twain's observation on the Mississippi River is pertinent here:

> In the space of one hundred and seventy-six years the Lower Mississippi has shortened itself two hundred and forty-two miles. That is an average of a trifle over one mile and a third per year. Therefore, any calm person, who is not blind or idiotic, can see that in the Old Oölitic Silurian Period, just a million years ago next November, the Lower Mississippi River was upward of one million three hundred miles long, and stuck out over the Gulf of Mexico like a fishing-rod. And by the same token any person can see that seven hundred and forty-two years from now the Lower Mississippi will be only a mile and three-quarters long, and Cairo and New Orleans will have joined their streets together, and be plodding comfortably along under a single mayor and a mutual board of aldermen. There is something fascinating about science. One gets such wholesale returns of conjecture out of such a trifling investment of fact.

This is a useful warning. It is particularly relevant to ecological events, for as shown earlier, their inherent

216

complexity often leads to sudden, qualitative changes in response to gradual, quantitative ones. For this reason, estimates of the future condition of an ecosystem can easily be confounded by the emergence of such qualitative changes, as the predicted quantitative effects intensify.

Only few quantitative extrapolations of the changing state of the environment can be made with reasonable accuracy. Probably the firmest estimate is that regarding the depletion of oxygen in United States surface waters. From the yearly rate of increase in the amount of organic wastes intruded into surface waters, the total amount of oxygen required to degrade them can be estimated for future years. Then, this quantity can be compared to the total oxygen content of U.S. surface waters. The time at which the two values become equal signals a statistical crisis: that the total oxygen content of surface waters is then insufficient to support the ecological purification of the total influx of organic waste. According to a 1966 report of the U.S. National Academy of Sciences, on the basis of present trends this will occur at about the year 2000. Of course, this does not mean that the oxygen content of every U.S. river and lake will then go to zero. If the present trend is maintained, some bodies of water would reach that point much sooner. Others, perhaps a stream in the distant reaches of the Rockies, might not change in oxygen content at all. However, although it is rather crude and purely statistical, this computation is a useful—and ominous—prediction. It tells us that within the next thirty years we can expect many of our rivers and lakes to meet the fate of Lake Erie and to become incapable of supporting the ecological cycle that accomplishes the self-purification of surface waters.

One possible response to this prediction is "So what?" If most of our rivers and lakes become foul with decaying organic matter, could we not get used to the odor, purify the water needed for domestic and industrial use by technological means (for example, by using the inexhaustible supply of power that the AEC promises in order to distill pure water from foul), and go about our business? The answer is that the predicted quantitative change in surface waters will probably generate qualitative changes in the ecosystem, which could gravely threaten human survival.

In natural aquatic systems, the organic matter content is rather low. In turn, this severely limits the number and variety of microorganisms (bacteria and molds), most of which require organic matter, that can live in these systems. In the soil ecosystem, matters are very different. Here high levels of organic matter are common and a great variety of bacteria and molds that live on it inhabit the soil. Now, it is commonly found that among these numerous soil microorganisms are many that cause disease in animals and man. This can be demonstrated by a simple laboratory experiment. A pinch of soil is added to a flask of sterile organic nutrient medium, and the microorganisms are allowed to grow for a time. Then the resulting microbial culture is injected into a mouse; the animal is almost certain to die of an infection. When such soil cultures are studied in detail, numerous species of bacteria and molds that are known to cause a variety of animal and human diseases, some of them fatal, can be identified.

Although the soil harbors this reservoir of pathogenic microorganisms, they actually cause disease only rarely. Typically this occurs when soil happens to penetrate an unprotected part of the body. For example, heavy inhalation of dusty soil can lead to lung disease. Ordinarily, such contact is limited because the soil is held in place by the roots of plants. If, as a result of ecological degradation, dust-bowl conditions develop, such lung diseases may occur more frequently. So long as the natural integrity of the ecosystem is maintained, animals and man are to a large degree isolated from soil-borne infections.

Now let us return to surface waters. These are, of course, in intimate contact with the soil and its burden of pathogenic microorganisms. Moreover, people come into equally intimate contact with water—by swimming in it, drinking it, or inhaling spray. There is, therefore, a ready physical path leading from the soil and its pathogens, through the water, to man. Nevertheless, soil-borne disease ordinarily remains rare in man. The reason is clear: in natural conditions, surface waters are a very effective *biological* barrier to the movement of pathogenic microorganisms from the soil to man because the water ordinarily contains insufficient organic matter to support the growth of the pathogens. Since the organisms do not reproduce in the nutrient-poor water, the few that may enter it from the soil become highly dilute and eventually die off; the statistical probability that they will invade the body of, let us say, a swimmer is negligible.

However, in the next thirty years or so, as many rivers and lakes become unnaturally burdened with organic matter, the natural biological barrier between soil and man will break down. Some of the pathogens might grow and reproduce in the water, reaching concentrations that make a human infection far more likely than before. For this reason, the projected ecological change in surface waters is much more serious than a smelly nuisance. It may expose human beings to a host of new and unaccustomed diseases for which immunity may be lacking. This is the real danger in the extensive pollution of surface waters with organic matter.

Unhappily, there is at least one hint that this process may have already begun. In 1965 a new disease, now known as meningioencephalitis, was reported from Florida. It occurred typically in teen-age children several days after prolonged swimming during warm summer months in a pond or river. A severe headache develops, leading to coma, and, with a high frequency, to death. The cause of this disease has now been established—it is an amoeba, a microscopic protozoan, that is very commonly found in soil. Apparently the amoeba enters the body from infected water through the nose and massively invades the victim's brain membranes. The ecological basis of the disease now seems clear. In the soil, this amoeba is usually found in an inactive form, a cyst. When a high concentration of bacteria develops in the neighborhood of the cyst, their secretions stimulate it and an active amoeba emerges which then lives on the bacteria. It seems likely then, that in organically polluted streams and ponds there may be enough bacteria to activate the amoebic cysts, as they enter the water from the soil where they are plentiful. Feeding on the bacteria, the amoebae then reproduce in the water, becoming sufficiently concentrated to invade successfully the brain of the unlucky swimmer.

A hint that other soil organisms may be growing in polluted water comes from New York harbor. There it has been observed that despite a considerable improvement in the numbers of bacteria released into the harbor from sewage outlets, the bacterial count has increased by several hundred per cent in recent years.

It is possible that this change is a result of the growth of soil bacteria in the polluted waters around New York.

Breakdown of the water barrier between man and the soil has other, equally serious implications. Among the common molds found in soil are certain species that are known to produce a very active carcinogen aflotoxin. These, too, grow on organic matter. Recent studies by an associate of the Center for the Biology of Natural Systems at Washington University show that many soil molds—including those that produce aflotoxin—can be isolated from streams heavily polluted with organic matter. Should these organisms become common, we will be faced with another serious hazard to health. Some of the molds normally found in soil, but which have now been detected in polluted water, can cause serious infections if they become established in the body (for example, in a wound). Unfortunately, some current medical practices increase the likelihood of such infections. For example, changes in body levels of steroid hormones, such as result from the use of cortisone or of contraceptive pills, may increase susceptibility to such mold infections.

The rapid spread of water pollution is exemplified by the results of a recent survey of European beaches. The survey showed that visitors to most of the beaches of France, Spain, Belgium, and Italy are twice as likely to acquire an infection if they go swimming than they are if they stay out of the water. From the Italian Riviera to the beaches of the Dutch coast, heavy organic pollution from sewage and industrial wastes and the accompanying high bacterial count has become prevalent. The rate of deterioration appears to be accelerating in recent years; this should be regarded, I believe, as a warning of possible catastrophic health problems in the coming years.

It is this kind of warning of things to come that leads me to conclude that *if* we permit most of our surface waters to become heavily polluted with organic matter, we may be faced with outbreaks of new, serious diseases that could go a long way toward rendering major parts of the land uninhabitable. The increasing pollution of surface waters with organic matter breaks down the natural ecological separation of man and animals from soil pathogens and may open up a veritable Pandora's box of disease and toxic hazards. If we do not check the present course of water pollution, I believe that the multiple effects of these hazards may in the future become an intolerable threat to human health. And in this case, the future is something like the next thirty years.

One important reason why new ecological dangers often arise in the course of gradual, quantitative changes is the phenomenon of *synergism*. A common example of this effect was mentioned earlier: if the levels of sulfur dioxide and a carcinogen in polluted air are both doubled, the resultant hazard is much more than doubled, because sulfur dioxide inhibits the lung's self-protective mechanism and makes it more susceptible to the carcinogen. In synergism, the over-all effect of a complex biological insult is always greater than the sum of the effects of its separate parts.

Such synergistic interactions can occur within the body and thereby intensify the effects of environmental hazards. An example is the interaction between NTA and metals such as mercury and cadmium. When laboratory animals are exposed to NTA in the presence of mercury and cadmium levels, a tenfold increase in fetal abnormalities occurs. This is the observation that has barred the use of NTA in detergents. The NTA/mercury-cadmium synergism is typical of the tendency of metals to form complexes with certain types of organic compounds that may sharply differ, in their chemical and biological properties, from either of the separate constituents.

Synergistic interactions can also occur within the ecosystem. An example is the impact of organic water pollutants on the hazard from mercury pollution. Very considerable amounts of metallic mercury have been dumped into rivers and lakes in the United States, Canada, and elsewhere by chloralkali plants. As it lies on the bottom of a lake or river, metallic mercury is relatively innocuous. But if the bottom mud is rich in bacteria and especially if the oxygen content is low, bacterial action converts the metal to an organic form, methyl mercury. This is very soluble in water, enters the bodies of fish, where it causes the widespread occurrence of unacceptable levels of mercury. This means that pollution of surface waters by organic matter seriously intensifies the hazard of mercury pollution. Recent studies also suggest that another element, arsenic—which has entered surface waters as a contaminant of phosphate (from detergents and other sources)—may follow a similar course. Bacteria seem to be able to methylate arsenic and convert it to a highly toxic organic form. As a result of such interactions, we must anticipate that new *kinds* of environmental hazards may suddenly emerge as the levels of organic matter in surface waters gradually increase. Mercury deposited on river and lake bottoms many years ago can remain there, harmlessly, for many years, then, quite suddenly, as organic pollution intensifies, the ecological status of the bottom mud is changed and mercury emerges as a serious environmental hazard.

Heavy industrialization pours increasing amounts of toxic metals into the air: mercury, lead, nickel, and cadmium, for example. From the air, these metals are carried down to the soil by rain and snow where they accumulate. The ecology of the soil is very vulnerable to the toxic effects of these metals, for they may inhibit the growth of necessary soil bacteria and of plants. In addition, new unnatural complexes of these metals with organic compounds in the soil may be formed. The NTA experience warns that some of these may become new environmental dangers. It is well within the bounds of reasonable extrapolation, I believe, that if we continue to accumulate such metals in the soil, its ability to support plant life—to produce food crops and timber— might eventually be reduced catastrophically. It is also possible that new metal-organic complexes that are harmless to crops will pass through them to man, in food, where they may not be so harmless.

Pollution of air with the oxides of sulfur is a similar hazard. The situation is best known in northern Europe, where Swedish data, for example, show a progressive increase in the acidity of rain and snow over recent years. This unnatural influx of acid into the soil is bound to have serious effects on plant growth and may already be reducing the rate of timber production. But again, the greater danger may be from qualitative changes in the growth of soil microorganisms and in the chemical interactions among soil constituents in these new, unnatural conditions. Pollutants which accumulate in the soil may drastically upset its vital ecological balance.

Those pollutants that do not end up in the soil are

eventually deposited in the oceans, which have begun to accumulate persistent pesticides (it has recently been computed that about 25 per cent of all the DDT produced is now in the ocean) and other synthetic organic pollutants. Relatively little is known, as yet, about the impact of these pollutants on the vital ecological systems in the ocean. These systems produce most of the oxygen in the atmosphere through photosynthesis. Although there is no evidence of changes of the oxygen content of the air, there are some indications that photosynthetic activity of marine organisms may be inhibited by DDT and other pollutants.

Another reason why we must expect the unexpected in environmental pollution is that new effects are so often set in motion long before we are aware that the problem exists. Consider the following sequence of events.

In the 1950's, the plastic industry developed new types of flexible, synthetic materials—polyvinyl plastics —with good wearing properties. They found a ready market in automobile upholstery, so that within a decade the interiors of nearly every American car contained yards of the new plastic. Since then nearly everyone has been in contact with the material. Many people have noticed on entering a plastic-upholstered car, which has had its windows closed for a day or so— especially in the summer heat—that the steering wheel is slippery and that the inner window surfaces are coated with a slippery, transparent film. Car drivers— myself included—have tolerated this effect for a number of years without complaint (which, for myself, I now painfully regret). But in a space capsule, matters are not so relaxed. Here NASA technicians noticed the same effects, but took them seriously because the film spoiled the efficiency of optical equipment. For this reason, NASA barred the use of polyvinyl plastics in space equipment about five years ago.

Now the scene shifts to hospital blood banks. There, important glass equipment used to store and transfuse blood and other fluids was replaced by polyvinyl equipment about ten years ago. This was an apparently advantageous step, for the new equipment, unlike the old, was unbreakable.

The scene shifts again, this time to military hospitals in Vietnam, where the new plastic transfusion equipment is in extensive use. Here in the last few years a new medical phenomenon "shock lung," a sometimes fatal disorder, is noticed in wounded after transfusions, especially of long-stored blood. The effect was reported in medical journals in 1959, but not related to the transfusion process.

Now it is 1970. At the Carnegie Institution's embryology laboratory in Baltimore, Dr. Robert De Haan is having a problem with an experiment. He finds that cultures of embryonic chick heart cells, which he has studied successfully for some time, are mysteriously dying. After some effort he discovers the cause: some toxic material is leaching out of polyvinyl containers into his culture medium, killing the cells. He soon informs a colleague, Dr. Robert J. Rubin of the Johns Hopkins Hospital, of this finding. Dr. Rubin is concerned, because this same material may be leaching from polyvinyl blood transfusion equipment. His studies confirm this expectation. Material incorporated into the polyvinyl plastic in the manufacturing process, which is designed to make it flexible, readily enters the stored blood. He finds the plasticizer and its metabolic breakdown products in the blood, urine, and tissues of patients receiving blood that has been stored in polyvinyl bags. He finds, too, that the plasticizer causes blood platelets to become sticky and clot—a condition that probably explains "shock lung."

All this is reported in a scientific journal in October 1970. In this paper the authors point out that their results may account for the earlier observation of plasticizers in some foods, which are often packaged in polyvinyl-coated containers. One of these reports attracts the attention of Mr. F. C. Gross, now at NASA, but formerly a chemist with the United States Food and Drug Administration. He had been working on the spaceship plasticizer problem. He telephones Dr. Rubin and points out that human exposure to plasticizers is not limited to blood transfusions or to plastic-packaged foods, but includes as well the air that many car passengers breathe.

Meanwhile, back in the scientific journals, now that the issue has been raised, one can find earlier studies which show that plastics contain not only plasticizers having toxic effects, but also other additives, known as "stabilizers," that are usually even more hazardous. In one 1968 scientific report, we read:

> One of the most successful stabilizers in the plastics industry for PVC (polyvinyl chloride) formulations are the organotin compounds [i.e., tin-containing organic compounds]. Unfortunately they are also among the most toxic. Even though this toxicity is widely known, organotin stabilizers are still used in certain plastics for medical use.

Now that the alarm has been sounded, researchers are busy studying the toxic effects of the numerous

227

varieties of stabilizers and plasticizers used in modern plastics. Eventually their results will show, it is to be hoped, what dangers we have endured in the last decade from automobile upholstery, food packages, medical and dental equipment, plastic toys and water hoses, and the new "wet-look" plastic garments. The present scientific results already show that the effects may be subtle and slow to appear. For example, some of the materials have significant effects on cell growth. And lurking in the background is the potentially ominous fact that the basic material used in many of these plastic additives— phthalic anhydride—is also a constituent part of the molecule of a now notorious substance—thalidomide.

Concerned with the chemical link between a substance known to cause serious fetal deformities and the phthalic acid derivatives used as plasticizers, several researchers at Baylor University in Texas have studied the effects of the latter on developing chick embryos. In their words,

> The purpose of this work was to determine whether certain esters of phthalic acid which are used in the formulation of polyvinyl chloride plastics, were capable of producing adverse effects in the developing chick embryo.

And here is their summary of the results:

> Dibutoxyethyl phthalate was capable of causing teratogenesis [embryonic defects] in these embryos. Congenital malformations such as crania bifida [cleft skull] and anophthalmia [malformed eye] were observed in newly hatched chicks receiving this phthalate ester into the yolk sac before the third day of embryonic life. Also marked exophthalmia, resulting

228

from the absence of bone tissue forming the orbit of the eye, and blindness due to failure of the cornea to develop were other malformations observable in chicks treated with the phthalate ester. The data suggested that dibutoxyethyl phthalate, di-2-methoxyethyl phthalate and octyl isodecyl phthalate are capable of causing damage to the central nervous system of the developing chick embryo. This was manifested after hatching by grossly abnormal behavior of chicks such as tremor, nonpurposeful bodily movement, and a total incapability of either standing or walking normally.

What is the point of this story? It is *not* reported here in order to suggest that we are all about to perish from exposure to plastic automobile upholstery. All that can be said at this time about the hazard to health is that there may be one. What our experience with the plasticizer problem reveals is something much more serious than the harm that it might engender. It reminds us of our ignorance—that we are hardly aware of the potential hazards from hundreds of similar substances that have so quickly become unbiquitous in our environment. It warns us that the blind, ecologically mindless progress of technology has massively altered our daily environment in ways that may, much later, emerge as a threat to health. Unwittingly, we have created for ourselves a new and dangerous world. We would be wise to move through it as though our lives were at stake.

There is a final threat to ecological survival that hardly needs to be documented here—nuclear war. A decade ago, the military and their supporters could still pretend that victory was possible in a nuclear war. In the face of repeated evidence by the independent scientific community, led by Linus Pauling and others, the pretense was maintained for a while. Now, although the nuclear threat to survival is acknowledged, the United States and presumably other nuclear powers are in a constant state of readiness to launch a suicidal war. However, no political leader appears to be willing any longer openly to claim that civilization could survive a nuclear war.

These are the kinds of considerations that lead to my judgment that the present course of environmental degradation, if unchecked, threatens the survival of civilized man. Although it might be convenient if the environmentalist, like some occult seer predicting the end of the world, could set a date for this catastrophe, the exercise would be futile and in any case unnecessary. It would be futile because the uncertainties are far too great to support anything more than guesses. One can try to guess at the point of no return—the time at which major ecological degradation might become irreparable. In my own judgment, a reasonable estimate for industrialized areas of the world, might be from twenty to fifty years, but it is only a guess.

In any case, this guesswork is unnecessary. For it seems to me that the world is now no longer willing to tolerate even the present level of environmental degradation, much less its intensification. It is now widely recognized, I believe, that we are already suffering too much from the effects of the environmental crisis, that with each passing year it becomes more difficult to reverse, and that the issue is not how far we can go to the brink of catastrophe, but how to act—now.

When survival is discussed, some ecologists predict that we are doomed to environmental catastrophe by the present rate of population growth. Catastrophic famine due to rapid population growth in developing nations has been predicted for as early as 1975. According to another prediction: "The battle to feed all humanity is over. . . . At this late date [i.e., 1971] nothing can prevent a substantial increase in the world death rate."

As a result of such highly publicized assertions, the notion that human survival is threatened merely by increase in numbers is now a fairly common one.

What is the evidence for such predictions? The issue of population growth is enormously complex and can be only considered in brief here. The role of population growth in the environmental crisis in an industrialized country such as the United States has already been analyzed extensively in Chapter 9. It seems clear from this analysis that population growth in the United States has only a minor influence on the intensification of environmental pollution. If United States agricultural and industrial operations were ecologically sound, the country could support many more people than it does now with far less environmental impact.

Although I am convinced that there are no *ecological* grounds to speak of the United States as "overpopulated," such a scientific evaluation is certainly no bar to reaching this conclusion on *other* grounds. For example, I know of one ecologist who regards the United States as overpopulated because he usually meets another person on his favorite mountain trail. Here are some other reasons that lead some people to conclude that the country is overpopulated; they are quoted from newspaper advertisements published by a group called the "Campaign to Check the Population Explosion":

A hungry over-crowded world will be a world of fear, chaos, poverty, riots, crime and war. No country will be safe, not even our own. . . . What can we do about it? A *crash* program is needed to control population growth both at home and abroad.

Our city slums are packed with youngsters—thousands of them idle, victims of discontent and drug addiction. And millions more will pour into the streets in the next few years at the present rate of procreation. You go out after dark at your own peril. Last year one out of every four hundred Americans was murdered, raped or robbed. *Birth Control is an answer.*

These advertisements express a strong opposition to robbery, rape, and murder; to discontent and drug addiction among slum youths; and to poverty, riots, and war. They propose to check these undesirable activities by reducing the number of people who engage in them, either directly or in the expectation that in a less-crowded society these activities will somehow become less prevalent. There are, of course, other methods—known to social science or through simple human experience—for ameliorating these social ills: economic security, adequate housing and social services, disarmament and effective education. But these alternatives are not mentioned in the advertisements; in my view, they put forward not a social or ecological analysis, but a political program. Crime, youthful discontent, and drugs are serious social problems in the United States. Population control is less a scientific response to these problems than a political one.

It should be emphasized at this point that there *are* what I regard to be very good reasons to disseminate, as widely as possible, both the knowledge and the means required effectively to practice contraception. This reflects my belief that every couple should have the right, and freely available means, to exercise whatever control they choose over the number of children they produce. What is being disputed here is not the usefulness of birth control, but what I regard to be immoral, misleading, and politically retrogressive reasons for urging it.

As noted earlier, there is room for argument about the proper role of efforts to control population growth in the strategy of resolving the environmental crisis. However, as already indicated, the choice between the relative emphasis placed on technological reform and on population control is a political one which reflects one's view of the relative importance of social control over personal acts and social processes.

Population-minded ecologists also point out that the *world-wide* growth of population, especially in the developing countries, is the real problem and that population control should be emphasized in the United States in order to "set an example" for the world. To evaluate this view we need to consider the potential ecological catastrophe that might result from continued population growth in developing countries.

The developing nations are poor; their rising populations press heavily on their scant resources; hunger is widespread and economic development difficult. In the poor nations, in contrast with a country like the United States, there does seem to be an immediate relation between the rate of population growth and the well-being of their peoples.

The world population problem is the subject of a vast and complex literature. The field is one which cuts across a broad range of disciplines: the physiology of reproduction, the biology of sex and race, the sociology

233

of families and larger groups, economics of agricultural and industrial production, world trade and international politics.

Demographers have delineated an intricate network of interactions among these factors. These involve complex circular relationships, in which, as in an ecological cycle, every step is connected to several others. Thus, while the rate of population growth is, of course, the result of the birth rate and the death rate, so that population size would tend to increase with birth rate and decrease with death rate, there is also an opposite effect mediated by social factors, in particular the desired family size. If death rate, especially infant mortality, is high, there may be an increased desire for children in order to make up for the expected loss as the family tries to achieve the desired number of surviving children. Because of this relationship, a drop in infant mortality can *reduce* population growth by reducing the birth rate. On the other hand, if the birth rate is high, the number of children born per woman is also high, a condition that tends to *increase* infant mortality.

Economic factors are also involved. If economic resources are limited, then a rising population reduces the resources available per capita, lowering the standard of living and tending thereby to raise the death rate. At the same time, a high standard of living may lower the age at marriage, which in turn raises the birth rate. On the other hand, if adequate resources are available, a rising population—by adding to the labor force —can lead to increased economic activity, which in turn elevates the standard of living and affects the influence of the latter on both birth rate and death rate. In addition, with a rising level of economic activity, educational level may improve, which in turn can increase the age at marriage, the employment of women, and the use of modern contraceptive techniques—and thereby reduce the birth rate. And added to all these relationships is the effect of deliberate government policies, which may increase the birth rate by propaganda or economic incentives or reduce it by similar means.

In view of these complexities, it is not surprising that demographers often differ in their views about the expected course of population growth or about the most effective ways of controlling it. Indeed, the network of effects may operate differently in each nation and within each cultural or economic group. One does, however, gain a general impression that most demographers agree that tendencies for self-regulation are characteristic of human population systems.

It is also generally recognized that the world population cannot grow indefinitely because there is some limit to crucial resources, such as food, available from the global ecosystem. However, the size of the world's ultimate food-producing capacity is also subject to disagreement and cannot be accurately estimated at this time. Hence, while it can be concluded that there is *some* limit to the possible size of the world population, where that limit might lie is only a more or less educated guess.

Demographers have learned a good deal about the connection between population growth and economic and social factors in industrialized countries. This is characterized by the "demographic transition," which was described in Chapter 7. Generally, in the industrialized nations, there is a tendency for population growth to level off, apparently as a natural social response to prosperity. This seems to be the way in which these societies have reacted to the acquisition of wealth, provided that this wealth is available in ways that improve their well-being and encourage confidence in the future.

The actual historical course of the demographic transition in the industrialized nations is particularly significant. With improved living conditions, over-all death rates and rates of infant mortality decline steadily over the years. At first, birth rates remain high, so that population growth is rapid. Later, birth rate and death rate decline more or less in concert, so that the population continues to grow, but less rapidly than before. In the final, most recent stages of the demographic transition, the birth rate drops particularly fast, narrowing the excess over death rate, and population growth becomes relatively slow. In nearly every advanced country, this rapid drop in birth rate occurs when death rates are from about 10 to 12 per thousand and infant mortality rates are about 20 per thousand. Thus, in industrialized countries, birth rates have been brought to the closest match with death rates only through a historical process—which may extend over a 50 to 100 year period—of achieving a minimal death rate largely as a result of improved living conditions. In other words, population balance has been approached through the material progress of the society.

When this course of events is compared to population trends in developing countries, certain important similarities and differences turn up. As a whole, the situation may be summed up as follows. Everywhere in the world where they have not yet reached the minimal rates characteristic of advanced countries, over-all death rates and rates of infant mortality have been dropping year by year. As it does in industrialized countries, the birth rate seems to decline particularly fast when the minimal death rate of from about 10 to 12 per thousand is approached. This situation can be seen in the demographic behavior of Taiwan, the Pacific Islands, Japan, Cyprus, Israel, and Singapore. In some Latin American countries, such as Venezuela and Costa Rica, the minimal death rates have been approached, but birth rates have *not* declined. However, in every country in which the *rate of infant mortality*— which has important effects on the desired family size— has approached the minimal value that is characteristic of industrialized countries (about 20 per thousand or less), birth rates also begin to approach the low rates now found in advanced countries (from about 14 to 18 per thousand). Wherever infant mortality rates, despite their decline, remain high, birth rates are also high. Thus, in India, infant mortality in the 1951–61 period was about 139 per thousand, and the birth rate was about 42 per thousand; the Latin American countries with persistent, high birth rates (45 to 50 per thousand) have infant mortality rates in the range of 50 to 90 per thousand. In most developing countries, birth rates are still well in excess of death rates and population growth is rapid.

The scientific evidence regarding the *future* course of world population growth is by no means unambiguous or conclusive. Any conclusion relevant to the future represents an extrapolation from past trends. Depending on the past data that are chosen as a base, strikingly different extrapolations can be made.

On the one hand, it is possible to conclude from extrapolations of present trends in birth rates and death rates that in many of the less developed nations of the world, the present high rates of population growth will continue until there are catastrophic disparities between population size and needed resources. In this case, the only possible means to bring these nations close to demographic balance would be a campaign to reduce fertility, although death rate and infant mortality remain high. On the other hand, if some of the more subtle social and economic factors that influence fertility are taken into account, and if credence is given to the evidence that societies that do successfully bring birth rate nearly into balance with death rate do so only when death rate and infant mortality are reduced to minimal levels, then a more optimistic outlook emerges. In particular, according to this view, the strongest effort should be made to eliminate overt and hidden hunger in developing countries, so powerfully described by the Brazilian nutritionist Josué de Castro. Taking *these* views into account, there is reason to expect that nations that now exhibit a high rate of population growth will reduce their birth rate much more rapidly than they have in the past when they reach the critically low levels of death rate and of infant mortality. In this case, demographic balance can be approached through efforts to improve living standards and, in particular, to reduce infant mortality.

A conservative view of the available demographic evidence would be that *neither* of these two alternative interpretations is as yet exclusively supported by the data. The two approaches are not mutually exclusive, and obviously *both* direct efforts to reduce birth rate and improvement in living standards and in infant mortality can contribute to reduction in population growth. This dual approach is exemplified by a recent proposal to develop, world-wide, clinics that simultaneously provide prenatal and child care and contraceptive services.

Every developing country favors efforts to improve living conditions and health. A few also favor efforts to widen the use of contraception. An example is the recent statement of the government of Ghana:

> The size of our present population does not pose immediate problems for us. However, the rate at which the population is increasing will very certainly create serious social, economic and political difficulties before the turn of the century. . . . The government will implement appropriate action programmes. . . . There will be no compulsion about these measures. They will be voluntary but . . . if the individual decides to plan the size of his family the Government will be ready to offer the necessary supporting services.

However, those in the United States who see in world population growth the single most powerful threat to survival are not content to permit each nation to choose its own balance between efforts to improve health and living conditions and efforts to control fertility. They urge the use of United States power to govern this decision from without:

> We [the United States] should: Withhold all aid from a country with an expanding population unless that nation convinces us that it is doing everything possible to limit its population. . . . Extreme political and economic pressure should be brought on any country or international organization impeding a solution to the world's most pressing problem. If some of these measures seem repressive, reflect on the alternatives.

Now a decision to campaign for the introduction of direct fertility control into developing countries carries with it, I believe, the conviction that it is morally right and politically sound for one society to persuade or to force another society to adopt such a program. However, one must then expect a response from these countries that is also political. On their part, they would be justified in pointing out that such direct reduction in birth rate, in the absence of a critically low death rate and infant mortality (and the requisite high standard of living), is not the course followed in the more advanced nations and has in fact never occurred in human history. They might be expected to question the morality of being singled out for such a gigantic and questionable experiment.

On the other hand, if one's moral convictions and political views regard the previous course as dictatorial and corrosive of human values, then one can adopt the view that population growth in the developing nations of the world ought to be brought into balance by the same means that have already succeeded elsewhere—improvement of living conditions, urgent efforts to reduce infant mortality, social security measures, and the resultant effects on desired family size, together with personal, voluntary contraceptive practice. It is this view with which I wish to associate myself.

That political outlook does indeed determine the interpretation of the population problem in developing nations is strikingly demonstrated by two reports on the problem, issued simultaneously in September 1966 by the same organization, the Committee for Economic Development (CED). One of these, which for the sake of simplicity I shall designate Report A, concluded:

> The experience of the past decade offers convincing evidence that if low income countries are to develop

rapidly they must avoid or extricate themselves from the "population trap," by which we mean rates of increase of population growth so large that they approach the feasible rates of increase in economic output, thereby preventing significant growth in per capita output. . . . To meet the population problem effectively, programs of family planning must play a part.

In contrast, Report B (which deals with problems in Latin America) asserts:

> Population is growing faster in Latin America than anywhere else in the world. Naturally, this slows the increase of per capita gross national product. Yet this fact should not be considered decisive. Much less can it be used to propose birth control, or, more euphemistically, family planning, as a solution. . . . Latin American experience demonstrates that this is not the main factor . . . the solution is not birth control but increased food production and economic development, which brings about higher productivity and therefore a higher standard of living.

Despite their origin, simultaneously, from the same organization, these reports take opposite views on the population control issues. What is significant about them is not merely their contradictory views but also their respective authorship. Report A, which urges "family planning" on developing countries, was prepared by the Resource and Policy Committee of the CED. This committee consists of forty-four North Americans, chiefly prominent businessmen. Report B, which emphasizes improved nutrition and reduction in infant mortality rather than birth control, was prepared by the CED Inter-American Council for Commerce and Production, which is composed of a representative from each of the following countries: Peru, Chile, Brazil, Argentina, Uruguay, Mexico, Colombia, Ecuador, Venezuela, and the United States. And, to make matters perfectly clear, the single representative from the United States found it necessary to add to this report a strong dissent to the effect that "the paper has overstated its case against birth control or family planning."

In the terms described earlier, the Latin Americans wish to pursue, for themselves, the course toward population balance that the advanced nations have followed—increased living standards, reduced mortality, followed by the commonly experienced reduction in birth rate. For their part, the North Americans are urging on the poorer nations a path toward demographic balance that no society in human history, certainly not their own, has ever followed—deliberate limitation of population to a size compatible with "feasible" resources —at a time when living conditions, as reflected in high death rates and infant mortality, are well below the levels attained by the more advanced nations. The problem of controlling world population growth is clearly a subsidiary part of a larger, political question —the relationships between the rich, technologically advanced nations and the poorer ones that are struggling, against enormous odds, to improve their living conditions. To understand this issue we need to look at the links between the historical development of the two groups of nations.

One of the most important links is established by the two issues that have been under discussion here —the impact of modern technology on the environment in advanced nations, and the effects of poverty and rapid population growth in the developing nations. The wealth of the advanced nations is largely a result of the application of modern science and technology to the exploitation of natural resources. As we have seen, before World War II this was heavily based on the use of natural products. The availability of these materials—such as rubber, fats and oils, and cotton—in undeveloped areas of the world led to their exploitation by the more advanced nations during the colonial period. There is evidence that colonialism had a great deal to do with the development of the rapid rates of population growth that now characterize so much of the world.

This is the conclusion reached by Nathan Keyfitz of the University of California from an analysis of the effects of colonialism on the present population explosion in the developing nations. He argues that the growth of industrial capitalism in western nations in the period 1800–1950 resulted in the development of a one-billion excess world population, largely in the tropics, as a result of the exploitation of these areas for raw materials (with the resultant need for labor) during the period of colonialism. He argues further that after World War II modern technology replaced tropical raw materials with synthetic ones so that the technologically developed world, "again with no one's intention, rendered functionless in relation to its further self-enrichment almost all the populations of the tropics."

Thus, the Dutch brought into their Indonesian colonies modern techniques that improved living conditions and reduced the mortality rate in the native population. And, according to the anthropologist Clifford Geertz, who has made a careful demographic study of the colonial period in Indonesia, the Dutch apparently fostered the growth of the Indonesian population in order to increase the labor force that they needed to exploit the colony's natural resources. However, much of the wealth acquired as a result of the increased productivity did not remain in Indonesia. Rather, it was acquired by the Netherlands where it supported the Dutch through their own demographic transition. In effect, the first, or population-stimulating, stage of the demographic transition in Indonesia became coupled to the second, or population-limiting phase of the demographic transition in the Netherlands—a kind of demographic parasitism. Then, in a final irony, with the postwar development of synthetic chemicals, Indonesia's natural rubber trade declined, further depleting the opportunities for the economic advancement that might support their own motivation for population control.

In this way, modern technology becomes a crucial link between the environmental crisis in the advanced nations and the population problem in the developing ones. The post war trend to replace natural products with synthetic ones has exacerbated ecological stresses in the advanced countries and has hindered the efforts of developing nations to meet the needs of their growing populations. We in the advanced nations like to think that the rest of the world depends on our technological charity. It may soon become clear that help will need to flow the other way. If the world is to return to environmental balance, the advanced countries will need to rely less on ecologically costly synthetics and more on goods produced from natural products— a process which, on both ecological and economic grounds, ought to be concentrated in the developing regions of the world.

Meanwhile, many of the environmental calamities generated by advanced technology are being exported to the developing nations. At a conference organized by the Washington University Center for the Biology of Natural Systems and the Conservation Foundation observers reported case after case in which new technologies, introduced into developing countries, led to unexpected ecological backlash. The most famous example, the Aswan Dam, was referred to earlier; here, against the power and irrigation which the dam produces, must be balanced the spread of a serious disease, schistosomiasis, by the snails which live in the irrigation ditches. The Kariba Dam, also in Africa, spread a fly-borne disease and disrupted the agriculture of peoples living along the riverbanks. In Latin America and Asia, introduction of DDT and other synthetic pesticides has often caused new *outbreaks* of insect pests by killing off their natural predators, while the pests themselves become resistant. In Guatemala, some twelve years after the start of a malaria "eradication program" based on intensive use of insecticides, the malarial mosquitoes have become resistant and the incidence of the disease is higher than it was before the campaign. The levels of DDT in the milk of Guatemalan women are by far the highest reported anywhere in the world thus far. Nor should we forget, in this connection, that the United States defoliation campaign has imposed on Vietnam concentrations of various herbicides—of still unknown toxicity to human beings—never achieved anywhere in the world on such a scale. Thus, the developing nations, which so desperately need the benefits of technology, are receiving more than their share of some of its calamities.

Both the environmental and population crises are the largely unintended result of the exploitation of technological, economic, and political power. Their solutions must also be found in this same difficult arena. This task is unprecedented in human history, in its size, complexity, and urgency.

It is natural to seek for easier solutions. Since the basic problems are themselves biological—limitation of population growth and the maintenance of ecological balance—there is a temptation to short-circuit the complex web of economic, social, and political issues and to seek direct biological solutions, particularly for the population crisis. I am persuaded that such reductionist attempts would fail.

Suppose, for example, we were to adopt the solution to the world population problem urged on us by the agriculturists William and Paul Paddock. They propose the application to famine-threatened nations of "triage" —a practice in military medicine that divides the wounded into three groups: those too seriously wounded to be saved, those who can be saved by immediate treatment, and those who can survive without treatment regardless of their suffering. The United States, for example, would decide which nations are too far gone down the road to famine to be saved and which would respond to rescue by American aid. Apart from its abhorrent moral and political features, this scheme is a certain road to biological disaster. Famine breeds disease, and in the modern world, epidemics are rarely confined by national boundaries; the Paddock scheme would condemn the earth to a kind of biological warfare. Nor can we ignore the political consequences. What nation, condemned to death by the very society that has, albeit blindly, brought it to its tragic condition, would willingly refrain from retribution? The Paddock scheme would condemn not merely the "hopeless" nations, but the whole world to political chaos and war. And the first victim of this political degradation might be the United States itself, for to quote the authors of the triage scheme: "The weakness of triage lies in its implementation by a democratic government like that of the United States." How long would this "weakness" last if the scheme were to be adopted?

There is a curious parallel between the import of an overinflated view of the power of technology and that of the pressure of population growth. Both technology and population growth take on the aspect of an autonomous, uncontrollable juggernaut, threatening to crush humanity beneath its weight. Understandably, the reaction is fear and panic; self-preservation becomes paramount; humanism is an early victim. One moves from a "war on crime" and a "war on poverty" to a war on people.

Throughout recorded history, mankind has been struggling to cope with conflicts that arise within the family of man. It has been one of the virtues of civilization that we have learned, increasingly, how to resolve these conflicts by creating new social relationships rather than by the stronger party annihilating the weaker one. War is in this sense a means of solving a social issue, not by social means but by a biological process—death. The same is true, I believe, of enforced population control.

This, it seems to me, is the main lesson to be learned from both the environmental crisis and the population problem—that if we would survive and preserve both our natural heritage and our own humanity, we must at last discover how to solve, by social means, the social evils that threaten both.

12

THE ECONOMIC
MEANING
OF ECOLOGY

It should be clear, at this point, that the environmental crisis is neither an innocuous "motherhood" issue, nor a passing fad for a new life-style, nor a means of evading basic economic, social, and political conflicts. On the contrary, environmental problems seem to have an uncanny way of penetrating to the core of those issues that most gravely burden the modern world. There are powerful links between the environmental crisis and the troublesome, conflicting demands on the earth's resources and on the wealth created from them by society.

Here, the environmentalist's concerns, which already range from the physical sciences, through biology, to engineering, technology, and demography, enter the even more controversial reaches of economics and political economy. If the environmentalist shrinks from intruding upon the complex domain of the economist and the political scientist, then *they* will need to find their own way into the equally difficult terrain of the environmental sciences. On the other hand, if the environmentalist plunges headlong into economic matters, he may quickly lose his way in a maze of unfamiliar theory and poorly understood controversies, finally to be swamped in a flood of professional disdain. Nevertheless, it seems to me that given the urgency of the situation, both economist and environmentalist are obliged to take the risk of reaching across the boundaries of their disciplines and to accept the consequent criticism as something to be borne, cheerfully if possible, as a social duty. I do not propose, however, that the environmentalist should reinvent economics or that the economist should rediscover the environment. Rather, each should rely on the other's knowledge, searching in it for links between the environmental crisis and social processes. Herewith, then, my own effort.

During the last few years, the environmental crisis has become sufficiently public to attract the interest of a number of relevant but previously aloof professions, including economics and political science. There now exists a small but valuable body of writings on the economic and political aspects of environmental issues to which the environmentalist can turn. However, to an outside observer it becomes quickly apparent that environmental concerns have until recently been far removed from the central problems of conventional economics.

Conventional economic science, as presently construed in professional academic circles, conceives of the production and distribution of wealth as a vastly elaborated development of the market place: in Robert L. Heilbroner's terms, the "ubiquitous market network, where both factors of production and goods and services are bought and sold." Goods are produced and services performed in order to be exchanged for other goods and services; values are determined, at least as a first approximation, by the interplay of supply and demand. This comprises the "private" sector of the economy. On this basic structure is superimposed the "public" sector: expenditures by government agencies carried out for a variety of social purposes, ranging from the construction of hospitals to the bombing of "enemy villages" in Vietnam. Finally, there is the complex interaction between government action and the operation of the private sector. This includes government regulation of productive activities (for example, to safeguard health and the environment), of some large-scale economic operations, and of national fiscal policy. This is a highly complex area which is sufficiently controversial to support, with apparently equal theoretical validity, the quite contradictory policies of successive political regimes in the United States.

Until recently, the role of environmental factors has been given only slight consideration in such conventional economic theory. For example, most U.S. textbooks contain only a few pages which discuss these issues, referring to them as "external economies and diseconomies." The more general term "externality" was introduced into economic theory in order to express what once appeared to be a rather rare departure from the basic economic process—exchange. In its simple form, an exchange is necessarily both mutual and voluntary; it takes place because both parties hope to gain from it and therefore undertake it voluntarily. In contrast, an externality is neither mutually beneficial nor voluntary: mercury benefits the chloralkali producer but harms the commercial fisherman; it is used voluntarily by one party and is involuntarily inflicted upon the other. This is an example of a negative externality or external diseconomy. In theory, but less commonly in practice, an externality may be economically positive. An example of such an external economy is the pleasant ambiance enjoyed by a householder living next to a well-kept golf course or farm. Since conventional economics is based on a market place for mutually beneficial, voluntary exchanges, it is not surprising that externalities should find little room in it, thus far. In one sense, we might regard such an externality as an economic transaction which, being essentially social in nature, is difficult to accommodate within the context of an economic theory much more concerned with private transactions than with social ones. But, with the recent advent of environmental problems, which generate very large negative externalities, economists have begun to pay much more attention to this hitherto minor facet of economic theory.

The task they face has been described earlier: how can the social costs of environmental deterioration be evaluated and met by the operation of the economic system? Recent efforts to answer this question are often guided by an earlier one by the British economist, A. G. Pigou, who proposed to "internalize" externalities by taxing operations that generate external diseconomies and subsidizing the rare ones that generate external values. A tax on an external diseconomy would, of course, lead to an increased price for the product— which could then express its "true" cost, including the cost of environmental deterioration or of the controls needed to prevent it. Some economists believe that, by this and similar means, the market system can readily adjust to the costs of environmental protection. No basic change in the economic system is then needed, for there is now a mutual, voluntary exchange. The producer meets the cost of pollution control or pays a fee for the benefit of using the environment as a dumping ground; the previously external process becomes internalized and thereby subject to the influence of the market place. Faced with the cost of pollution control or of a tax, the producer will endeavor to pass the added cost along to the consumer in a price increase. Where a tax is paid, it can be used by the government to protect and restore the environment.

Some relatively minor objections can be made to this approach. One is that a complex system of regulations, licensing, taxation, and monitoring would be needed—all of which violate the "free enterprise" spirit and add new constraints to the free exchange that is supposed to make the market system work. Another is that some producers might be willing to buy the right to pollute by paying a tax and then damage the environment in ways that no taxes can repair.

Far more serious than such objections is the question of whether a conventional "market place" economy is fundamentally incompatible with the integrity of the environment. A strong hint in this direction comes from E. L. Dale, Jr., a financial writer for *The New York Times*. He asserts that the private enterprise economic system operates according to "iron laws," dominated by the law of accelerating growth in productivity and output, which cannot be halted because "the profit motive will almost always propel individual daily decisions in the direction of higher productivity." Applying these iron laws to the demands for environmental integrity, Dale concludes that "our technology, which has given

253

us the rising GNP, might find the way out of one pollution problem after another. . . . But in the end we cannot be sure that the job will be done. Growth of the total output and output per capita will continue. . . . The long-term relief is perfectly obvious: fewer 'capita.' "

This view, which has been echoed in the environmental writings of industrialists (see, for example, page 3) asserts that the economic system is driven by its iron laws to increase productivity and therefore output. But since more output means more pollution (and in any event cannot be sustained indefinitely in view of the natural limits of the ecosystem and limited natural resources), the only means left to limit output is to reduce the population. For reasons that have been described earlier, so long as total resources appear to be sufficient to support the population, this approach, it seems to me, is equivalent to attempting to save a leaking ship by lightening the load and forcing passengers overboard. One is constrained to ask if there isn't something radically wrong with the ship.

Thus, once more, the environmental crisis demonstrates its proclivity for confronting a basic social issue. Here it raises the fundamental question of whether the basic operational requirements of the private enterprise economic system are compatible with ecological imperatives. Indeed, the same question exists in relation to the other major economic system in the world today, socialism, a matter that is considered later on.

The most complete study of the fundamental relationship between environmental externalities and the private enterprise economic system has been made by K. W. Kapp. In 1950 Kapp, an economist then at Wesleyan University, published a remarkable and, unfortunately, often neglected book, *The Social Costs of*

Private Enterprise. It is remarkable, first, for its detailed description of the seriousness of environmental pollution long before this issue became so popular. It is also remarkable as the first and apparently still unique attempt to show, from a consideration of these externalities, that, to quote one of Kapp's economist admirers, "economic growth renders many things obsolete, and one of the main things is economic theory."

In this book, and in a revised 1963 version, Kapp makes the following key observations about environmental externalities: they are substantial relevant to the conventional costs of doing business, ranging up to about 15 per cent for some industries. Indeed, he believes that when the cost of environmental externalities is included in the total business cost, in some cases "production may take place at total costs in excess of total benefits." Finally, the inclusion of such externalities within the range of economic analysis requires "a re-formation of the classical and neo-classical concept of wealth and productivity."

On such grounds, Kapp advances the following basic critique of private enterprise economics:

> As soon as one passes beyond the traditional abstractions of neo-classical price analysis and begins to consider the neglected aspects of unpaid social costs it becomes evident that the social efficiency of private investment criteria, and hence the alleged beneficial outcome of the allocation process under conditions of private enterprise, is largely an illusion. For, if entrepreneurial outlays fail to measure the actual total costs of production because part of the latter tend to be shifted to the shoulders of others, then the traditional cost-benefit calculus is not simply

misleading but actually serves as an institutionalized cloak for large-scale spoliation which exceeds everything which the early utopian socialists and even their Marxian successors had in mind when they denounced the exploitation of man by man under the emerging system of business enterprise.

In sum, Kapp suggests that conventional private enterprise economic theory is incapable of accommodating the powerful externalities generated by the very source of present economic strength—modern technology.

This raises two fundamental questions:

1. To what extent are the fundamental properties of the private enterprise system incompatible with the maintenance of ecological stability, which is essential to the success of *any* productive system?

2. To what extent is the private enterprise system, at least in its present form, inherently incapable of the massive undertakings required to "pay the debt to nature" already incurred by the environmental crisis —a debt which must soon be repaid if ecological collapse is to be avoided?

What follows is a tentative effort to consider these questions.

It is useful to begin with a basic feature of the private enterprise system that, according to conventional economists, is one of its chief motivating forces—private profit. What is the connection between pollution and profit in a private enterprise economic system such as the United States? Let us recall from the earlier chapters that in the United States intense environmental pollution is closely associated with the technological transformation of the productive system since World War II. Much of our pollution problem can be traced to a series of large scale technological displacements in industry and agriculture since 1946. A number of the new, rapidly growing productive activities are much more prone to pollute than the older ones they have displaced.

Thus, since World War II, in the United States, private business has chosen to invest its capital preferentially in a series of new productive enterprises that are closely related to the intensification of environmental pollution. What has motivated this pattern of investment? According to Heilbroner:

> Whether the investment is for the replacement of old capital or for the installation of new capital, the ruling consideration is virtually never the personal use or satisfaction that the investment yields to the owners of the firm. Instead, the touchstone of investment decisions is *profit*.

The introduction of new technology has clearly played an important role in the profitability of postwar business enterprise. The economic factor that links profit to technology is *productivity*, which is usually defined as the output of product per unit input of labor. Productivity has grown rapidly since World War II and, according to Heilbroner, this is largely due to the introduction of new technologies in that period of time. The following relationship seems to be at work: new investment in the postwar economy, as expected, has moved in directions that appeared to promise, and in fact yielded, increased profit; these investments have been heavily based on the introduction of new technology, which is a major factor in the notable increase in productivity, the major source of profit.

If these relationships have been operative in the technological displacements that, as we have seen, have played such an important role in generating the environmental crisis in the United States, then we would expect to find, in the appropriate statistics, that production based on the new technology has been more profitable than production based on the old technology it has replaced. That is, the new, more polluting technologies should yield higher profits than the older, less polluting technologies they have displaced.

The available data seem to bear out this expectation. A good example is the pervasive displacement of soap by synthetic detergents. As it happens, United States government statistics report economic data on the combined soap and detergent industry. In 1947, when the industry produced essentially no detergents, the profit was 30 per cent of sales. In 1967, when the industry produced about one-third per cent soap and two-thirds per cent detergents, the profit from sales was 42 per cent. From the data for intervening years it can be computed that the profit on pure detergent sales is about 52 per cent, considerably higher than that of pure soap sales. Significantly, the industry has experienced a considerable increase in productivity, labor input relative to output in sales having declined by about 25 per cent. Clearly, if profitability is a powerful motivation, the rapid displacement of soap by detergents—and the resultant environmental pollution —has a rational explanation. This helps to explain why, despite its continued usefulness for most cleaning purposes, soap has been driven off the market by detergents. It has benefitted the investor, if not society.

The synthetic chemical industry is another example that illustrates some of the reasons for the profitability of such technological innovations. This is readily docu-

mented from an informative volume on the economics
of the chemical industry published by the Manufacturing Chemists' Association. The chemical industry, particularly the manufacturers of synthetic organic chemicals, during the 1946–66 period recorded an unusually
high rate of profit. During that period, while the average
return on net worth for all manufacturing industries
was 13.1 per cent, the chemical industry averaged 14.7
per cent. The MCA volume offers an explanation for
this exceptionally high rate of profit. This is largely
based on the introduction of newly developed materials,
especially synthetic ones. For about from four to five
years after a new, innovative chemical product reaches
the market, profits are well above the average (innovative firms enjoy about twice the rate of profit of non-
innovative firms). This is due to the effective monopoly
enjoyed by the firm that developed the material, that
permits the establishment of a high sales price. After
four to five years, smaller competitors are able to develop their own methods of manufacture; as they enter
the market, the supply increases, competition intensifies,
the price drops, and profits decline. At this point the
large innovative firm, through its extensive research and
development effort, is ready to introduce a new synthetic substance and can recover a high rate of profit.
And so on. As the MCA volume points out: "The
maintenance of above average profit margins requires
the continuous discovery of new products and special-
ties on which high profit margins may be earned while
the former products in that category evolve into com-
modity chemicals with lower margins." It is therefore
no accident that the synthetic organic chemical industry
has one of the highest rates of investment in research
and development (in 1967, 3.7 per cent of sales, as

259

compared with an average of 2.1 per cent for all manufacturing industries).

Thus, the extraordinarily high rate of profit of this industry appears to be a direct result of the development and production at rapid intervals of new, usually unnatural, synthetic materials—which, entering the environment, for reasons already given, often pollute it. This situation is an ecologist's nightmare, for in the four to five year period in which a new synthetic substance, such as a detergent or pesticide, is massively moved into the market—and into the environment—there is literally not enough time to work out its ecological effects. Inevitably, by the time the effects are known, the damage is done and the inertia of the heavy investment in a new productive technology makes a retreat extraordinarily difficult. The very system of enhancing profit in this industry is precisely the cause of its intense, detrimental impact on the environment.

It is significant that since 1966, the profit position of the chemical industry has declined sharply. Industry spokesmen have themselves described environmental concern as an important reason for this decline. For example, at recent congressional hearings, an industry official pointed out that a number of chemical companies had found pesticide manufacturing decreasingly profitable because of the need to meet new environmental demands. Because of these demands, costs of developing new pesticides and of testing their environmental effects have risen sharply. At the same time, cancellation or suspension of official pesticide registrations increased from 25 in 1967 to 123 in 1970. As a result, a number of companies have abandoned production of pesticides, although over-all production continues to increase. One company reported that it had dropped pesticide production "because investments in other areas promised better business."

Another explicit example of the impact of environmental concern on the profitability of new chemicals is NTA, a supposedly nonpolluting substitute for phosphate in detergents. Under the pressure of intense public concern over water pollution due to detergent phosphates, the industry developed NTA as a replacement. Two large firms then proceeded to construct plans for the manufacture of NTA—at a cost of about $100 million each. When the plants were partially built, the United States Public Health Service advised against the use of NTA, because of evidence that birth defects occur in laboratory animals exposed to NTA. The new plants had to be abandoned, at considerable cost to these firms. As a result of such hazards, research and development expenditures in the chemical industry have recently declined—a process which is likely to reduce the industry's profit position even more.

Nitrogen fertilizer provides another informative example of the link between pollution and profits. In a typical United States Corn Belt farm, a yield that is more than from 25 to 30 bushels per acre below present averages may mean no profit for the farmer. Now as indicated earlier (Chapter 5), present corn yields depend on a high rate of nitrogen application. Under these conditions, the uptake of nitrogen by the crop is approaching saturation, so that an appreciable fraction of the fertilizer drains from the land and pollutes surface waters. In other words, under present conditions, it appears that the farmer *must* use sufficient fertilizer to pollute the water if he is to make a profit. Perhaps the simplest way to exemplify this tragic connection between economic survival and environmental pollution is in the words of one thoughtful farmer in recent testimony before the Illinois State Pollution Control Board:

> Money spent on fertilizer year in and year out is the best investment a farmer can make. It is one of our production tools that hasn't nearly priced itself out of all realm of possibility as is the case with machinery and other farm inputs. Fertilizer expense in my case exceeds $20 per acre, but I feel I get back one to three dollars for every dollar spent on fertilizer. . . . I doubt that I could operate if I lost the use of fertilizers and chemicals as I know them today. I hope adequate substitutes are developed and researched if the government decides our production tools are a danger to society.

National statistics support this farmer's view of the economic importance of fertilizers or pesticides. These statistics show that whereas such chemicals yield three or four dollars per dollar spent, other inputs—labor and machinery, for example—yield much lower returns.

This is evidence that a high rate of profit is associated with practices that are particularly stressful toward the environment and that when these practices are restricted, profits decline.

Another important example is provided by the auto industry where the displacement of small, low-powered cars by large, high-powered ones is a major cause of environmental pollution. Although specific data on the relationship between profitability and crucial engineering factors such as horsepower do not appear to be available, some more general evidence is at hand. According to a recent article in *Fortune* magazine:

262

As the size and selling price of a car are reduced, then, the profit margin tends to drop even faster. A standard United States sedan with a basic price of $3,000, for example, yields something like $250 to $300 in profit to its manufacturer. But when the price falls by a third, to $2,000, the factory profit drops by about half. Below $2,000, the decline grows even more precipitous.

Clearly, the introduction of a car of reduced environmental impact, which would necessarily have a relatively low-powered, low-compression engine and a low over-all weight, would sell at a relatively low price. It would therefore yield a smaller profit relative to sales price than the standard heavy, high-powered, high-polluting vehicle. This may explain the recent remark by Henry Ford II, that "minicars make miniprofits."

It will be recalled from Chapter 9 that prominent among the large-scale technological displacements that have increased environmental impacts are certain construction materials: steel, aluminum, lumber, cement, and plastics. In construction and other uses, steel and lumber have been increasingly displaced by aluminum, cement (in the form of concrete), and plastics. In 1969 the profits (in terms of profit as per cent of total sales) from steel production (by blast furnaces) and lumber production were 12.5 per cent and 15.4 per cent respectively. In contrast, the products that have displaced steel and lumber yielded significantly higher profits: aluminum, 25.7 per cent; cement, 37.4 per cent; plastics and resins, 21.4 per cent. Again, displacement of technologies with relatively weak environmental impacts by technologies with more intensive impacts is accompanied by a significant increase in profitability.

A similar situation is evident in the displacement of

263

railroad freight haulage (relatively weak environmental impact) and truck freight haulage (intense environmental impact). In this case, economic data are somewhat equivocal because of the relatively large capital investment in railroads as compared to trucks (the trucks' right-of-way being provided by government-supported roads). Nevertheless, truck freight appears to yield significantly more profit than railroad freight; the ratio of net income to shareholders' and proprietors' equity in the case of railroads is 2.61 per cent, and for trucks, 8.84 per cent (in 1969).

In connection with the foregoing examples, in which profitability appears to increase when a new, more environmentally intense technology displaces an older one, it should be noted that not all new technologies share this characteristic. For example, the displacement of coal-burning locomotives by diesel engines *improved* the environmental impact of railroads between 1946 and 1950, for diesel engines burn considerably less fuel per ton-mile of freight than do coal-burning engines. Unfortunately, this improvement has been vitiated by the subsequent displacement of railroad freight haulage by truck freight, and at the same time made no lasting improvement in the railroads' economic position. It is also evident that certain new technologies, which are wholly novel, rather than displacing older ones—for example, television sets and other consumer electronics —may well be highly profitable without incurring an unusually intense environmental impact. The point of the foregoing observations is not that they establish the rule that increased profitability inevitably means increased pollution, but only that many of the heavily polluting new technologies have brought with them a higher rate of profit than the less polluting technologies they have displaced.

Nor is this to say that the relationship is intentional on the part of the entrepreneur. Indeed, there is considerable evidence, some of which has been cited earlier, that the producers are typically unaware of the potential environmental effects of their operation until the effects become manifest, after the limits of biological accommodation have been exceeded, in ecological collapse or human illness. Nevertheless, despite these limitations, these examples of the relationship between pollution and profit-taking in a private enterprise economic system need to be taken seriously, I believe, because they relate to important segments of the economic system of the world's largest capitalist power.

In response to such evidence, some will argue that such a connection between pollution and profit-taking is irrational because pollution degrades the quality of the environment on which the future success of even the most voracious capitalist enterprise depends. In general, this argument has a considerable force, for it is certainly true that industrial pollution tends to destroy the very "biological capital" that the ecosystem provides and on which production depends. A good example is the potential effect of mercury pollution from chloralkali plants on the successful operation of these plants. Every ton of chlorine produced by such a plant requires about 15,000 gallons of water, which must meet rigorous standards of purity. This water is obtained from nearby rivers or lakes, in which purity is achieved by ecological cycles, driven by the metabolic activities of a number of microorganisms. Since mercury compounds are highly toxic to most living organisms, the release of mercury by chloralkali plants must be regarded as a serious threat to the sources of pure water on which these plants depend. Nevertheless, it is a fact that in this and other instances, the industrial operation—until constrained by outside forces—has proceeded on the seemingly irrational, self-destructive course of polluting the environment on which it depends.

A statistician, Daniel Fife, has recently made an interesting observation that helps to explain this paradoxical relationship between the profitability of a business and its tendency to destroy its own environmental base. His example is the whaling industry, which has been driving itself out of business by killing whales so fast as to ensure that they will soon become extinct. Fife refers to this kind of business operation as "irresponsible," in contrast with a "responsible" operation, which would only kill whales as fast as they can reproduce. He points out that even though the irresponsible business will eventually wipe itself out, it *may be profitable to do so*—at least for the entrepreneur, if not for society—if the extra profit derived from the irresponsible operation is high enough to yield a return on investment elsewhere that outweighs the ultimate effect of killing off the whaling business. To paraphrase Fife, the "irresponsible" entrepreneur finds it profitable to kill the goose that lays the golden eggs, so long as the goose lives long enough to provide him with sufficient eggs to pay for the purchase of a new goose. Ecological irresponsibility can pay—for the entrepeneur, but not for society as a whole.

The crucial link between pollution and profits appears to be modern technology, which is both the main source of recent increases in productivity—and therefore of profits—and of recent assaults on the environment. Driven by an inherent tendency to maximize profits, modern private enterprise has seized upon those massive tecnological innovations that promise to gratify this need, usually unaware that these same innovations are often also instruments of environmental destruction. Nor is this surprising, for, as shown earlier (Chapter 10), technologies tend to be designed at present as single-purpose instruments. Apparently, this purpose is unfortunately, too often dominated by the desire to enhance productivity—and therefore profit.

Obviously, we need to know a great deal more about the connection between pollution and profits in private enterprise economies. Meanwhile, it would be prudent to give some thought to the meaning of the functional connection between pollution and profits, which is at least suggested by the present information.

The general proposition that emerges from these considerations is that environmental pollution is connected to the economics of the private enterprise system in two ways. First, pollution tends to become intensified by the displacement of older productive techniques by new, ecologically faulty, but more profitable technologies. Thus, in these cases, pollution is an unintended concomitant of the natural drive of the economic system to introduce new technologies that increase productivity. Second, the cost of environmental degradation are chiefly borne not by the producer, but by society as a whole, in the form of "externalities." A business enterprise that pollutes the environment is therefore being subsidized by society; to this extent, the enterprise, though free, is not wholly private.

If the course of environmental degradation is to be reversed, these relationships need to be changed. To begin with, the environmental costs must be met by introducing the needed changes in the processes of production. In a private enterprise system this means, necessarily, that costs, however they are ultimately met, must be introduced into the system through the producer's enterprise. The new, highly polluting technologies will, of course, be more seriously affected by these changes than the relatively low-impact technologies they have displaced. Thus, the added costs would have a larger effect on producers of detergents than on soap manufacturers, and on trucks more than on railroads.

Now, the new, highly polluting technologies also represent a greater source of the over-all growth in productivity of the economic system than do the technologies they displace, as shown by their higher profits and rates of growth. However, when environmentally required changes in technology are imposed upon these highly productive enterprises, these activities do *not* thereby gain in productivity. This is in contrast to the effect of introducing *conventional* new productive technology, which is always motivated by, and usually achieves, an increase in productivity. Thus, no matter how pollution costs are ultimately met, if they are imposed initially through the producer they will not contribute to the over-all growth of productivity. This has been pointed out by the economist G. F. Bloom, who finds, in a study of productivity:

> Pollution controls . . . will add millions of dollars to industry's costs of production and will pour additional purchasing power into the income stream without increasing productivity, as conventionally measured. Indeed, carrying on production without fouling the air and polluting the water may require

an actual reduction in man-hour output [and therefore a reduction in productivity] in some industries.

The economics seem clear: the technology required for pollution controls, unlike ordinary technology, does not *add* to the value of the output of saleable goods. Hence, the extensive technological reform of agricultural and industrial production that is now demanded by the environmental crisis cannot contribute to the growth of productivity—to the continued expansion of the GNP. Bloom concludes that in part due to heightened environmental concern, the "prospect for increased productivity is therefore not bright." Since continued increase in productivity is closely linked to profitability, it is essential to the health of a private enterprise economy. Therefore there appears to be a basic conflict between pollution control and what is often regarded as a fundamental requirement of the private enterprise system—the continued maximization of productivity. Bloom sees a grave, underappreciated danger to the economic system in all this and concludes, pessimistically: "As far as productivity is concerned, there seems to be little awareness of the urgency of this problem. . . . Business underestimated the power of consumerism; likewise, it discounted the drive against pollution."

Another difficulty is that in certain important ways the stress on the environment due to ecologically faulty productive technology, so long as it is tolerated, seems to operate, for a time, to the advantage of the producer and to the disadvantage of the population as a whole. This situation arises out of certain time-dependent characteristics of ecological degradation and relates to a crucial feature of the private enterprise economic system—the competition between the entrepreneur's drive for maximal profit and the wage earner's interest in increased wages.

Thus, let us say, if through government regulations, the producer is prevented from passing the added costs of environmental control along to the consumer, he will need to find an alternative means of cutting general production costs in order to maintain profits. The obvious recourse is to reduce wages; this would, of course, exacerbate the conflict between entrepreneur and wage earner. On the other hand, if the added costs are met by raising prices, then the wage earner is confronted with a rising cost of living which will naturally lead him to demand higher wages; again the conflict is intensified. Moreover, increased prices would inevitably burden the poor most heavily. For example, given that present agricultural practice has heavily mortgaged soil and water ecosystems, their ecological reform would result in a very sharp increase in food prices. Inevitably, the poor would suffer most. Thus, the attempt to meet the real, social costs of environmental degradation, either through increased prices or reduced wages, would appear to intensify the long-standing competition between capital and labor over the division of the wealth produced by the private enterprise system and worsen the already intolerable incidence of poverty.

That the productive system as a whole "borrows" from the ecosystem and incurs the "debt to nature" represented by pollution is an immediate saving for the producer. At the same time, pollution often adds to the living costs of the population as a whole, most of whom are wage earners rather than entrepreneurs. Thus, when the workers in the vicinity of a power plant find their laundry bills increased because of soot emitted by its stacks, their wages are thereby reduced. In a sense, the workers' extra laundry bill subsidizes part of the cost of operating the power plant. In this hidden way, environmental deterioration erodes the wage earners' real wages.

However, some of these effects do not occur concurrently. For example, it may take from fifteen to twenty years of environmental pollution from, say, industrial plants along the shore of Lake Erie before the burden of waste reduces the water's oxygen content to zero, halts the self-purification process, and fouls the beaches —so that to continue to enjoy summer recreation, the plants' workers need to add to the cost of living the price of admission to a swimming pool. Similarly, chronic, low-level exposure to radiation, mercury, or DDT may shorten a wage earner's life without reducing his income or even incurring extra medical costs during his lifetime. In this case, the cost of pollution is not met by anyone for a long time; the bill is finally paid by exacting the wage earner's premature death, which—apart from the incalculable human anguish—can be reckoned in terms of some number of years of lost income. In this situation, then, during the "free" period, pollutants accumulate in the ecosystem or in a victim's body, but not all the result costs are immediately felt. Part of the value represented by the free abuse of the environment is then available to mitigate the economic conflict between capital and labor. The benefit *appears* to accrue to both parties and the conflict between them is reduced. Later, however, when the environmental bill is paid, it is met by labor more than by capital; the buffer is suddenly removed and the conflict between these two economic sectors is revealed in its full force.

Another way to look at this situation relates to the

271

value of the capital created by the operation of the private enterprise system. In the creation of this capital, certain goods are regarded as freely and continuously available from nature: the fertility of the soil, oxygen, water—in general, nature, or the biological capital represented by the ecosphere. However, the environmental crisis tells us that these goods are no longer freely available, and that when they are treated as though they were, they are progressively degraded.

This suggests that we need to reconsider the true value of the conventional capital accumulated by the operation of the economic system. The effect of the operation of the system on the value of its *biological* capital needs to be taken into account in order to obtain a true estimate of the over-all wealth-producing capability of the system. The course of environmental deterioration shows that as conventional capital has accumulated, for example in the United States since 1946, the value of the biological capital has *declined*. Indeed, if the process continues, the biological capital may eventually be driven to the point of total destruction. Since the usefulness of conventional capital in turn depends on the existence of the biological capital—the ecosystem—when the latter is destroyed, the usefulness of the former is also destroyed. Thus despite its apparent prosperity, in reality the system is being driven into bankruptcy. Environmental degradation represents a crucial, potentially fatal, *hidden* factor in the operation of the economic system.

It should be evident, from nearly everything that has been said in this book, that no economic system can be regarded as stable if its operation strongly violates the principles of ecology. To what extent is this true of present economic systems?

In the case of the private enterprise system, this question has already been answered in part, for there does seem to be a tendency for that system to enhance productivity—and therefore profits—by means of technologies that also intensify environmental stress. A more theoretical basis for the incompatibility between the private enterprise system and the ecosystem relates to the matter of growth.

The total rate of exploitation of the earth's ecosystem has some upper limit, which reflects the intrinsic limit of the ecosystem's turnover rate. If this rate is exceeded, the system is eventually driven to collapse. This is firmly established by everything that we know about ecosystems. Hence it follows that there is an upper limit to the rate of exploitation of the biological capital on which any productive system depends. Since the rate of use of this biological capital cannot be exceeded without destroying it, it also follows that the actual rate of use of *total* capital (i.e., biological capital plus conventional capital, or the means of production) is also limited. Thus there must be some limit to the growth of total capital, and the productive system *must* eventually reach a "no-growth" condition, at least with respect to the accumulation of capital goods designed to exploit the ecosystem, and the products which they yield.

In a private enterprise system, the no-growth condition means no further accumulation of capital. If, as seems to be the case, accumulation of capital, through profit, is the basic driving force of this system, it is difficult to see how it can continue to operate under conditions of no growth. At this point, it can be argued that some new form of growth can be introduced, such as increases in services. However, nearly all services

273

represent the resultant of human labor expended through the agency of some form of capital goods. Any increase of services designed to achieve economic growth would have to be accomplished without increasing the amount of these service-oriented capital goods, if the ecological requirements are to be met.

The ecosystem poses another problem for the private enterprise system. Different ecological cycles vary considerably in their natural, intrinsic rates—which cannot be exceeded if breakdown is to be avoided. Thus, the natural turnover rate of the soil system is considerably lower than the intrinsic rate of an aquatic system (e.g., a fish farm). It follows, then, that if these different ecosystems are to be exploited concurrently by the private enterprise system without inducing ecological breakdown, they must operate at differential rates of economic return. However, the free operation of the private enterprise system tends to maximize rates of return from different enterprises. If a given enterprise yields a return less than that available from another one, investment funds will tend to be transferred to the latter. "Marginal" enterprises, i.e., operations that yield a profit significantly below that available elsewhere in the economic system, are eventually dropped. However, in ecological terms an enterprise which is based on an ecosystem with a relatively slow turnover rate is *necessarily* economically "marginal"—if it is to operate without degrading the environment. Such enterprises are of obvious *social* value, but, given the profit-maximizing tendency of the private enterprise system, are not likely to be operated for long. A corrective expedient is the provision of subsidies; but in some cases these may need to be large enough to amount to nationalization—a contradiction of private enterprise.

All this does appear to justify Kapp's pessimism regarding the ability of the private enterprise system to adapt successfully to the demand for ecologically sound operation. More recently, a similar view has been expressed by Heilbroner, following a discussion of the impact of environmental demands on the capitalist system:

> But there is no doubt that the main avenue of capitalist accumulation would have to be considerably constrained; that net investment in mining and manufacturing would likely decline; that the rate and kind of technological change would need to be supervised and probably greatly reduced; and that, as a consequence, the flow of profits would almost certainly fall.

Heilbroner's conclusion is based on a single, very general ecological requirement—an essentially no-growth economy—and is reached in response to an inquiry as to the validity of two contrasting views of the nature of capitalism. One, originating with John Stuart Mill, holds that capitalism need not grow incessantly and could evolve into a balanced, stationary state. The second view, originating with Karl Marx, is very different. In Heilbroner's words:

> The very essence of capitalism, according to Marx, is expansion—which is to say, the capitalist, as a historical "type," finds his raison d'être in the insatiable search for additional money-wealth gained through the constant growth of the economic system. The idea of a "stationary" capitalism is, in Marxian eyes, a contradiction in terms.

275

If, on these grounds, it is concluded that the private enterprise system *must* continue to grow, while its ecological base will not tolerate unlimited exploitation, then there is a serious incompatibility between the two. Moreover, apart from the problem of growth, the preceding discussion adds more specific hurdles that the ecological imperative places before the private enterprise system: the need for ecologically grounded differential rates of return from different productive enterprises; the conflict between pollution control and the productivity of new technological enterprises; the exacerbation of poverty and of conflict between entrepreneur and wage earner that appears to be an inherent outcome of any effort, within the limits of the private enterprise system, to meet the social costs of environmental degradation; the temporary cushioning effect of the "debt to nature" represented by environmental degradation on the conflict between entrepreneur and wage earner, which, as it now reaches its limits, may reveal this conflict in its full force. Indeed, on these more detailed grounds, the environmental crisis not only reveals serious incompatibilities between the private enterprise system and the ecological base on which it depends, but may also help to explain why—as the crisis silently matured within the fabric of the ecosystem— these inherent faults in the economic system were covered over and could be tolerated. In this sense, the emergence of a full-blown crisis in the ecosystem can be regarded, as well, as the signal of an emerging crisis in the economic system.

What can be said about the compatibility of a socialist economic system with the ecosystem is very seriously hindered, at least in my own case, by a lack of information. What little I have been able to learn from available reports indicates that the *practical* problems of environmental pollution in industrialized socialist nations are not basically different from those typical of an industrialized private enterprise economy such as the United States.

Thus from an account by P. R. Pryde, an American geographer, based on Soviet reports, we learn that wastes dumped into surface waters in the USSR increased about twentyfold between the 1920's and 1962. He reports that water pollution problems became particularly intense after World War II "when the need to reconstruct quickly the country's war-damaged industrial capacity precluded building costly purification installations at new plants." The pollutants encountered in Soviet Union waters are similar to those that trouble the United States and other developed countries, both in their types and origins. They include organic wastes from municipalities and food processing plants; wastes from pulp and paper plants; industrial chemicals and metals; oil spills; and drainage of fertilizer. A report on the state of the Dniester River by a *Pravda* correspondent from the city of Kishinev, in the Moldavian region of the Soviet Union, tells a tale reminiscent of Lake Erie:

Many scenic places along the river's banks are no longer suitable for purposes of relaxation and are a menace to health. The fish are disappearing. The numbers of zherekh and pike-perch are falling sharply. Sterlet, at one time the pride of the river, has become a rarity. Beluga virtually don't appear. But concern is not only over fish. Above all, it is to preserve the water's purity for people and for industry, primarily for the foodstuffs industry.

It seems likely that environmental pollution in the USSR is following about the same course that it has taken in capitalist countries. In particular, there is no evidence that the new postwar technologies introduced in the USSR are very different from those that dominate United States production. Gasoline-driven automobiles are increasing in number, although it seems probable that average horsepower and compression ratio is less than that typical in the United States. The production of synthetic organic chemicals is on the rise and fertilizer production is being encouraged. In general, the modern technologies of the Soviet Union appear to be as counterecological as those introduced into the United States economy. Similar ecological effects are to be expected.

Finally, just as it is in the United States, inattention to pollution problems is a consequence of a heavy emphasis on productivity:

> The problem seems to be a lack of sufficient concern on the part of plant managers and an inefficient system of enforcing regulations, all of which is nourished by the familiar catalyst of economic expediency. Plan fulfillment [i.e., of production] is clearly understood to be paramount. If the plan is fulfilled, almost all else can be overlooked. An editorial in the government newspaper [*Izvestia*] succinctly summarized the industrial pollution problem in the USSR with the terse phrase "Victors are not judged."—Quoted from Pryde

This attitude, which is confirmed by the report of the *Pravda* correspondent from Kishinev, shows that despite pollution regulations—which certainly exist in the USSR —industrial productivity in the Soviet Union, as in the

United States, "borrows" some of the costs of production from the ecosystem in the form of pollution. Apparently, in the USSR's socialist system, the drive for "plan fulfillment," like the profit-motivated drive for productivity in the United States private enterprise system, takes its toll on the ecosystem. The American economist Marshall Goldman, who has made a special study of environmental problems in the USSR, reports observations similar to those summarized above.

In response to these difficulties, a strong ecological movement seems to be developing in the USSR; members of the scientific community have criticized industrial developments that ignore or underemphasize environmental effects, and citizens, as everywhere, complain of the resulting pollution. Recent government actions appear to presage a more vigorous ecologically oriented control over industrial planning. Here, of course, the socialist system in the Soviet Union does have an important practical advantage over the private enterprise system. Nationwide, all-encompassing plans for industrial and agricultural development—indeed, for nearly every aspect of economic life—are an intrinsic feature of the Soviet system. The advantage of such planning in any effort to alleviate environmental problems hardly needs to be demonstrated to anyone familiar with the chaotic environmental situation in the United States—where AEC atomic safety regulations have been challenged by several states; where government officials are engaged in a long, frustrating battle with the auto industry over pollution standards; where the need for ecologically sound agriculture comes in conflict with the economic interests of the producers of fertilizers and synthetic pesticides.

Finally, the socialist system may have an advantage

over the private enterprise system with respect to the basic relationship between economic processes and ecological imperatives. While it is true that the Soviet Union and other socialist states, just like capitalist states, have emphasized continued growth of the productive system, the *theory* of socialist economics does not appear to require that growth should continue indefinitely. Moreover, there is no inherent reason in socialist economic theory why it should not be possible to enforce ecologically required differential rates of return from productive activities that are based on different sectors of the ecosystem. On the other hand, the intrinsic role of ecological imperatives as necessarily *governing* economic processes does not appear to be an explicit part of socialist economic theory, although an early comment by Marx in *Das Kapital* does point out that agricultural exploitation in the capitalist system is, in part, based on its destructive effects on the cyclical ecological process that links man to the soil.

In any case, both socialist and capitalist economic theory have apparently developed without taking into account the limited capacity of the biological capital represented by the ecosystem. As a result, neither system has as yet developed a means of accommodating its economic operation to environmental imperatives. Neither system is well prepared to confront the environmental crisis; both will be severely tested by the urgent need to solve it.

It remains a fact, then, that no present economic system is immune to sweeping change if it is to come to grips with the environmental crisis. Whatever stands in the way of the necessary accommodation to the ecological imperative, whether private profit or "plan fulfillment," will need to abdicate its immunity from change.

It is impossible to predict how either the capitalist or socialist system will respond to these ecological imperatives. In response to the serious difficulties that raise the question of whether the private enterprise system can survive the environmental crisis without basic change, Robert Heilbroner states:

> Ordinarily I do not see how such a question could be answered in any way but negatively, for it is tantamount to asking a dominant class to acquiesce in the elimination of the very activities that sustain it. But this is an extraordinary challenge that may evoke an extraordinary response. Like the challenge posed by war, the ecological challenge affects all classes, and therefore may be sufficient to induce sociological changes that would be unthinkable in ordinary circumstances. The capitalist and managerial classes may see—perhaps even more clearly than the consuming masses—the nature and nearness of the ecological crisis, and may recognize that their only salvation (as human beings, let alone privileged human beings) is an occupational migration into governmental or other posts of power, or they may come to accept a smaller share of the national surplus simply because they realize that there is no alternative. When the enemy is nature, in other words, rather than another social class, it is at least imaginable that adjustments could be made that would be impossible in ordinary circumstances.

However, nature is not "the enemy" but our essential ally. The real question is to discover what kind of economic and social order is best adapted to serve as a partner in the alliance with nature.

281

It will be recognized that most of the foregoing discussion is rather theoretical, dealing with the relationships between the general properties of economic systems and the general features of the environmental crisis. However, the environmental crisis is not a theoretical danger, but a real and present one; it demands immediate social action. In the face of this immediate need, the previous theoretical discussion might be regarded as an irrelevant and, possibly, even dangerous diversion from the present task.

However, there is, in fact, a close connection between the immediate practical problems of environmental improvement and the apparently remote, theoretical questions regarding the design of present economic systems. Perhaps in making this remark I am only reflecting a personal faith that in the long run effective social action must be based on an understanding of the origin of the problem which it intends to solve. On these grounds there ought to be a close connection between theory and effective practice, and I believe that there is.

What are the practical steps that need to be taken in a country such as the United States, which is in the grip of the environmental crisis? Here I do not have in mind legislated environmental standards or restrictions, but rather the actions that such legislation are supposed to induce—the changes in the productive system that are needed to bring it into harmony with the ecosystem. If we are to survive economically as well as biologically, industry, agriculture, and transportation will have to meet the inescapable demands of the ecosystem. This will require the development of major new technologies, including: systems to return sewage and garbage directly to the soil; the replacement of many synthetic materials

by natural ones; the reversal of the present trend to re-
tire land from cultivation and to elevate the yield per
acre by heavy fertilization; replacement of synthetic
pesticides, as rapidly as possible, by biological ones;
the discouragement of power-consuming industries; the
development of land transport that operates with maximal fuel efficiency at low combustion temperatures and
with minimal land use; essentially complete contain-
ment and reclamation of wastes from combustion processes, smelting, and chemical operations (smokestacks must become rarities); essentially complete
recycling of all reusable metal, glass, and paper products; ecologically sound planning to govern land use
including urban areas.

As already noted, the economic burden will be heavi-
est on those enterprises which are based on ecologically
faulty postwar technology. However, there is a kind of
justice here, for it is precisely these enterprises which
have enjoyed an unusually high rate of profit. One can
argue, therefore, that these enterprises can well afford
the extra burden that will be imposed on them in an
environmental recovery program.

In sum, present productive technologies need to be
redesigned to conform as closely as possible to ecological requirements, and most of the present industrial,
agricultural, and transportation enterprises reorganized
in accordance with these new designs. In effect, a major
part of the new productive enterprises constructed on
the basis of postwar, ecologically faulty technology
simply has to be rebuilt along ecologically sound lines.

What might all this cost? Some very rough but
useful approximations can be made. For example, it is
generally reckoned that the total stock of capital
equipment in the United States is about three times

the annual GNP, or about two thousand four hundred billion dollars at the present time. (This and all following numbers are expressed as 1958 dollars to compensate for inflation.) A very rough estimate of the existing capital equipment that would need to be replaced in order to remedy major ecological faults might be about one-fourth, or about six hundred billion dollars worth. In comparison, the expenditures for structures and producers' durable equipment by private investors during the period 1946 to 1968 when, as we have seen, most of the ecologically faulty enterprises were built, amounts to roughly one thousand billion dollars. Accordingly, on the basis of the first estimates, something like one half of the postwar productive enterprises would need to be replaced by ecologically sounder ones.

Rough as they are, these figures give us some sense of the magnitude of the task of ecological reconstruction of the national productive system. To this estimate must be added the costs of efforts to restore damaged sectors of the ecosystem, which would range in the area of hundreds of billion dollars. This cost need not, and of course cannot, be met at once. If we accept as the period of grace—the time available before serious large-scale ecological catastrophes overtake us—let us say twenty-five years, then the cost of survival becomes about forty billion dollars annually over that period of time (again in 1958 dollars). Perhaps the simplest way to summarize all this is that most of the nation's resources for capital investment would need to be engaged in the task of ecological reconstruction for at least a generation. This means that new investments in agricultural and industrial production and in transportation would need to be governed chiefly by ecological considerations, so that the over-all pattern of investment would have to come under the guidance of ecological rather than conventional economic imperatives.

What are the practical problems that will be confronted in this huge undertaking and how will they be affected by the behavior of an economic system governed by the principles of private enterprise? In the first place, pervasive and complex dislocations will need to be accommodated by the economic system. Consider a rather small example. If the problem of sulfur dioxide pollution of the air is to be solved, essentially all the sulfur present in fuels will need to be recovered from them, either before or after combustion. The sulfur recovered in this way would probably be about sufficient to meet the total commercial need for this substance—so that the present sulfur industry would be wiped out, with the resultant loss of investments and jobs. Add to this relatively small problem the economic dislocations involved in transforming the technological base of agriculture, of the automotive industry and transportation generally, of power production and use, of the chemical industry and of packaging, and it becomes clear that on these grounds alone the process of environmental recovery will be an unprecedented challenge to the flexibility and strength of the economic system.

However, the most serious effect of an environmental recovery program on the economic system would be generated by the rather simple requirement for the rational social use of productive capacity. This is best illustrated by the role of power production, which is an essential requirement for almost every economic activity. On ecological grounds it is obvious that we cannot afford unrestrained growth of power production. Its use must be closely governed by over-all social needs rather than by the private interests of the producers or users of power. This means that the allocation of power to a given productive activity, in turn, would need to be governed by a judgment of the expected social values to be derived per unit of power consumption invested in that particular product. Applied, let us say, to two automobile factories, this principle would favor the manufacturer who produced the more durable vehicle—since that would enhance the social value (such as potential miles of use) achieved per unit of power expended in the manufacturing process. This same principle would favor the production of returnable bottles over nonreturnable ones, of a sparsely packaged product over one heavily encased in plastic, of natural products over synthetic ones. The general outcome would be a strong tendency to govern production according to the rational-use value of the final product rather than by the value added in the course of production, i.e., by productivity. In other words, the ecological imperative calls for the governance of productive processes by social thrift—a criterion which is likely to conflict with private gain. Thus, once it is recognized—under the force of the environmental crisis—that no productive system can operate without either fitting into the ecosystem or destroying it, and that the ecosystem is necessarily a social rather than a private good, then the logic of governing production by social criteria rather than by private ones becomes equally evident.

It is pertinent here to recall that in economic terms environmental "externalities" are, unlike private economic transactions, a burden on society as a whole. In effect, then, we now know that modern technology which is *privately* owned cannot long survive if it destroys the *social* good on which it depends—the ecosphere. Hence an economic system which is fundamentally based on private transactions rather than social ones is no longer appropriate and increasingly ineffective in managing this vital social good. The system is therefore in need of change.

Such an economic transformation would, of course, profoundly affect the rest of the culture. If factories are to operate according to principles of social thrift and ecological soundness, we can expect engineers to become impatient with narrowly conceived, single-purpose productivity- (and profit-) enhancing technologies and to invent new ones that are more appropriate to these new social goals. If such new technologies, which would necessarily cut across the narrow lines of present scientific disciplines, are in demand, we might expect scientists to overcome their reductionist bias and to develop new areas of knowledge which more closely than present ones match the structure of the real world and more readily illuminate actual human problems. As they became thus transformed, science and technology would in turn hasten the transformation of the system of production. Thus, once begun, ecological recovery could become an expanding, self-accelerating process. Moreover, we can expect that in an ecologically sound economy, meaningful employment would become universally available. For once the principle is established —as demanded by the ecological imperative—that production is for social use rather than private profit or "plan fulfillment," it would be clear that social good must begin with the welfare of the people who make up society.

These considerations apply to all industrialized nations; all of them need to reorganize their economies along ecologically sound lines. This huge task will place an unprecedented strain on world capital and human resources and may steadily overwhelm them unless these resources are carefully husbanded and employed according to ecologically determined priorities.

However, if this huge transformation is to be guided by ecological wisdom, the economic readjustment must rapidly spread beyond the industrial nations to the rest of the world. One major requirement for the ecological reconstruction of modern industry is to reduce the present reliance on synthetic materials and power-consumptive processes and, wherever possible, to substitute for them natural materials and processes that rely relatively more on labor than on power. Some natural raw materials, such as rubber, which have been displaced by synthetic materials, are exclusively produced in specific regions of the world—usually developing nations. Others, such as cotton and other plant fibers, wool, plant oils, and lumber, are derived from natural ecological niches that are more readily found in developing nations, especially in the tropics, than in most industrialized areas. Ecological widsom, then, would require that industrialized nations give up as much as possible of their synthetic production in favor of reliance on natural materials. And for this they will require the friendly cooperation of the developing nations of the world. For, to meet the need for natural fiber, rubber, and soap, production of the necessary raw materials in the developing nations will need to be increased—an undertaking they might be unwilling to accept in the absence of appropriate reciprocity.

Such reciprocity might well include assistance, on

the part of the industrialized nations, to help establish in the developing nations (if they so desire), in association with their own natural raw materials, industries for converting them to finished manufactured products for the world trade. Thus Malaysia, for example, may wish to supply the industrialized nations not with natural rubber, but with tires; India supply not cotton, but finished fabrics and even clothes; West Africa supply the world not with palm oil, but with soap. And I would emphasize, of course, that these enterprises ought to be developed not on the basis of the ecologically faulty productive technologies now available from the industrialized nations—such as monoculture-agriculture heavily burdened with inorganic fertilizers and synthetic insecticides and herbicides, high-powered lead- and nitrogen oxide-disseminating gasoline engines, power plants that pollute the air. Rather these nations should share with all others in the benefits of the new ecologically sound technologies that must now be developed.

Moreover, harmony with the ecosystem may often be enhanced by the use of new processes which, while taking advantage of the best available scientific knowledge and technological skills, are relatively labor-intensive rather than demanding intensive use of capital equipment and power. Here the developing nations, with their large and growing labor supply, will have a special advantage and, given effective economic and social organization, could enjoy an opportunity to meet their urgent need for generating productive employment.

If, for the sake of the world's ecological survival, such a global reconstruction of both the economy of the industrialized nations and of the developing ones is undertaken, clearly we are faced, as well, with equally sweeping political changes. Thus, it is inconceivable that the United States could find the huge capital resources for the needed reconstruction of industry and agriculture along ecologically sound lines unless we give up our preoccupation with large-scale military activities —which since World War II have preempted most of the nation's disposable income. The postwar experience of Japan and West Germany shows that a modern industrial economy can produce the resources needed for large-scale capital construction, if, as in these nations, military commitments are held to a very low level. In any case, if in keeping with ecological wisdom a nation such as the United States were to become seriously dependent on natural products manufactured in foreign countries, it could not do so without undertaking— at last—to live in peace with the rest of the world.

While the solution of the environmental crisis is necessarily global in scale, it remains true, I believe, that the United States holds the key to its success. One reason is that the United States does, after all, control— and wastefully consume—so much of the world's resources. If the United States were to embark on a program of ecological reconstruction, for the reasons set forth earlier, it would be possible to meet present United States requirements for food, clothing, housing, and other basic needs at a much lower expenditure of nonrenewable resources and of power than at present. If, in order to survive the environmental crisis, the United States were to establish the necessary ecologically sound, socially thrifty productive economy, it would have an impact on the availability of resources to the rest of the world in proportion to the huge share of these resources which the country now consumes. Similarly, if the United States fails to take this course, there is little hope that the developing nations could gain a sufficient share of the world's resources to achieve living standards compatible with a stabilized population. Finally, unless the United States becomes committed to peaceful fraternization with the rest of the world, it will have neither the productive resources for its own ecological restoration, nor the world's cooperation needed to carry it out.

The lesson of the environmental crisis is, then, clear. If we are to survive, ecological considerations must guide economic and political ones. And if we are to take the course of ecological wisdom, we must accept at last the even greater wisdom of placing our faith not in arms that threaten world catastrophe, but in the desire that is shared everywhere in the world—for harmony with the environment and for peace among the peoples who live in it. Like the ecosphere itself, the peoples of the world are linked through their separate but interconnected needs to a common fate. The world will survive the environmental crisis as a whole, or not at all.

13

THE
CLOSING
CIRCLE

In this book I have been concerned with the links between the environmental crisis and the social systems of which it is a part. The book shows, I believe, that the logic of ecology sheds considerable light on many of the troubles which afflict the earth and its inhabitants. An understanding of the environmental crisis illuminates the need for social changes which contain, in their broader sweep, the solution of the environmental crisis as well.

But there is a sharp contrast between the logic of ecology and the state of the real world in which environmental problems are embedded. Despite the constant reference to palpable, everyday life experiences—foul air, polluted water, and rubbish heaps—there is an air of unreality about the environmental crisis. The complex chemistry of smog and fertilizers and their even more elaborate connections to economic, social, and political problems are concepts that deal with real features of modern life, but they remain *concepts*. What is real in our lives and, in contrast to the reasonable logic of ecology, chaotic and intractable, is the apparently hopeless inertia of the economic and political system; its fantastic agility in sliding away from the basic issues which logic reveals; the selfish maneuvering of those in power, and their willingness to use, often unwittingly, and sometimes cynically, even environmental deterioration as a step toward more political power; the frustration of the individual citizen confronted by this power and evasion; the confusion that we all feel in seeking a way out of the environmental morass. To bring environmental logic into contact with the real world we need to relate it to the over-all social, political, and economic forces that govern both our daily lives and the course of history.

We live in a time that is dominated by enormous technical power and extreme human need. The power is painfully self-evident in the megawattage of power plants, and in the megotonnage of nuclear bombs. The human need is evident in the sheer numbers of people now and soon to be living, in the deterioration of their habitat, the earth, and in the tragic world-wide epidemic of hunger and want. The gap between brute power and human need continues to grow, as the power fattens on the same faulty technology that intensifies the need.

Everywhere in the world there is evidence of a deep-seated failure in the effort to use the competence, the wealth, the power at human disposal for the maximum good of human beings. The environmental crisis is a major example of this failure. For we are in an environmental crisis because the means by which we use the ecosphere to produce wealth are destructive of the ecosphere itself. The present system of production is self-destructive; the present course of human civilization is suicidal.

The environmental crisis is somber evidence of an insidious fraud hidden in the vaunted productivity and wealth of modern, technology-based society. This wealth has been gained by rapid short-term exploitation of the environmental system, but it has blindly accumulated a debt to nature (in the form of environmental destruction in developed countries and of population pressure in developing ones)—a debt so large and so pervasive that in the next generation it may, if unpaid, wipe out most of the wealth it has gained us. In effect, the account books of modern society are drastically out of balance, so that, largely unconsciously, a huge fraud has been perpetrated on the people of the world. The rapidly worsening course of environmental pollution is a warning that the bubble is about to burst, that the demand to pay the global debt may find the world bankrupt.

This does *not* necessarily mean that to survive the environmental crisis, the people of industrialized nations will need to give up their "affluent" way of life. For as shown earlier, this "affluence," as judged by conventional measures—such as GNP, power consumption, and production of metals—is itself an illusion. To a considerable extent it reflects ecologically faulty, socially wasteful types of production rather than the actual welfare of individual human beings. Therefore, the needed productive reforms can be carried out without seriously reducing the present level of *useful* goods available to the individual; and, at the same time, by controlling pollution the quality of life can be improved significantly.

There are, however, certain luxuries which the environmental crisis, and the approaching bankruptcy that it signifies, will, I believe, force us to give up. These are the *political* luxuries which have so long been enjoyed by those who can benefit from them: the luxury of allowing the wealth of the nation to serve preferentially the interests of so few of its citizens; of failing fully to inform citizens of what they need to know in order to exercise their right of political governance; of condemning as anathema any suggestion which re-examines basic economic values; of burying the issues revealed by logic in a morass of self-serving propaganda.

To resolve the environmental crisis, we shall need to forego, at last, the luxury of tolerating poverty, racial discrimination, and war. In our unwitting march toward ecological suicide we have run out of options. Now that the bill for the environmental debt has been presented, our options have become reduced to two: either the rational, social organization of the use and distribution of the earth's resources, or a new barbarism.

This iron logic has recently been made explicit by one of the most insistent proponents of population control, Garrett Hardin. Over recent years he has expounded on the "tragedy of the commons"—the view that the world ecosystem is like a common pasture where each individual, guided by a desire for personal gain, increases his herd until the pasture is ruined for all. Until recently, Hardin drew two rather general conclusions from this analogy: first, that "freedom in a commons brings ruin to all," and second, that the freedom which must be constrained if ruin is to be avoided is not the derivation of private gain from a social good (the commons), but rather "the freedom to breed."

Hardin's logic is clear, and follows the course outlined earlier: if we accept as unchangeable the present governance of a social good (the commons, or the ecosphere) by private need, then survival requires the immediate, drastic limitation of population. Very recently, Hardin has carried this course of reasoning to its logical conclusion; in an editorial in *Science,* he asserts:

> Every day we [i.e., Americans] are a smaller minority. We are increasing at only one per cent a year; the rest of the world increases twice as fast. By the year 2000, one person in twenty-four will be an American; in one hundred years only one in forty-six. . . . If the world is one great commons, in which all food is shared equally, then we are lost. Those who breed faster will replace the rest. . . . In the absence of breeding control a policy of "one mouth one meal" ultimately produces one totally miserable world. In a less than perfect world, the allocation of rights based on territory must be defended if a ruinous breeding race is to be avoided. It is unlikely that civilization and dignity can survive everywhere; but better in a few places than in none. Fortunate minorities must act as the trustees of a civilization that is threatened by uninformed good intentions.

Here, only faintly masked, is barbarism. It denies the equal right of all the human inhabitants of the earth to a humane life. It would condemn most of the people of the world to the material level of the barbarian, and the rest, the "fortunate minorities," to the moral level of the barbarian. Neither within Hardin's tiny enclaves of "civilization," nor in the larger world around them, would anything that we seek to preserve—the dignity and the humaneness of man, the grace of civilization—survive.

In the narrow options that are possible in a world gripped by environmental crisis, there is no apparent alternative between barbarism and the acceptance of the economic consequence of the ecological imperative—that the social, global nature of the ecosphere must determine a corresponding organization of the productive enterprises that depend on it.

One of the common responses to a recitation of the world's environmental ills is a deep pessimism, which is perhaps the natural aftermath to the shock of recognizing that the vaunted "progress" of modern civilization is only a thin cloak for global catastrophe. I am convinced, however, that once we pass beyond the mere awareness of impending disaster and begin to understand *why* we have come to the present predicament, and where the alternative paths ahead can lead, there is reason to find in the very depths of the environmental crisis itself a source of optimism.

There is, for example, cause for optimism in the very complexity of the issues generated by the environmental crisis; once the links between the separate parts of the problem are perceived, it becomes possible to see new means of solving the whole. Thus, confronted separately, the need of developing nations for new productive enterprises, and the need of industrialized countries to reorganize theirs along ecologically sound lines, may seem hopelessly difficult. However, when the link between the two—the ecological significance of the introduction of synthetic substitutes for natural products—is recognized, ways of solving both can be seen. In the same way, we despair over releasing the grip of the United States on so much of the world's resources until it becomes clear how much of this "affluence" stresses the environment rather than contributes to human welfare. Then the very magnitude of the present United States share of the world's resources is a source of hope —for its reduction through ecological reform can then have a large and favorable impact on the desperate needs of the developing nations.

I find another source of optimism in the very nature of the environmental crisis. It is not the product of man's *biological* capabilities, which could not change in time to save us, but of his *social* actions—which are subject to much more rapid change. Since the environmental crisis is the result of the social mismanagement of the world's resources, then it can be resolved and man can survive in a humane condition when the social organization of man is brought into harmony with the ecosphere.

Here we can learn a basic lesson from nature: that nothing can survive on the planet unless it is a cooperative part of a larger, global whole. Life itself learned that lesson on the primitive earth. For it will be recalled that the earth's first living things, like modern man, consumed their nutritive base as they grew, converting the geochemical store of organic matter into wastes which could no longer serve their needs. Life, as it first appeared on the earth, was embarked on a linear, self-destructive course.

What saved life from extinction was the invention, in the course of evolution, of a new life-form which reconverted the waste of the primitive organisms into fresh, organic matter. The first photosynthetic organisms transformed the rapacious, linear course of life into the earth's first great ecological cycle. By closing the circle, they achieved what no living organism, alone, can accomplish—survival.

Human beings have broken out of the circle of life,

driven not by biological need, but by the social organization which they have devised to "conquer" nature: means of gaining wealth that are governed by requirements conflicting with those which govern nature. The end result is the environmental crisis, a crisis of survival. Once more, to survive, we must close the circle. We must learn how to restore to nature the wealth that we borrow from it.

In our progress-minded society, anyone who presumes to explain a serious problem is expected to offer to solve it as well. But none of us—singly or sitting in committee—can possibly blueprint a specific "plan" for resolving the environmental crisis. To pretend otherwise is only to evade the real meaning of the environmental crisis: that the world is being carried to the brink of ecological disaster not by a singular fault, which some clever scheme can correct, but by the phalanx of powerful economic, political, and social forces that constitute the march of history. Anyone who proposes to cure the environmental crisis undertakes thereby to change the course of history.

But this is a competence reserved to history itself, for sweeping social change can be designed only in the workshop of rational, informed, collective social action. That we must act is now clear. The question which we face is how.

**NOTES
ACKNOWLEDGMENTS
INDEX**

NOTES

Chapter 1
THE ENVIRONMENTAL CRISIS

Page 6: Unruh, quotation: Mr. Unruh's statement is quoted from an article in *Newsweek,* January 26, 1970, p. 31.

Page 6: FBI report, quotation: The report quoted here was entered into the Congressional Record (for April 14, 1971, pp. S-4744–5) by Senator Muskie in the course of a speech in which he protested the surveillance of Earth Week activities by the FBI.

Page 6: Hardin, quotation: This quotation will be found in Garrett Hardin's well-known article "The Tragedy of the Commons," *Science,* vol. 162, pp. 1243–8.

Pages 6–7: Ehrlich, quotation: From Paul R. Ehrlich: *The Population Bomb* (New York: Ballantine; 1968), pp. 66–7. Ehrlich's emphasis. This widely read book offers a full exposition of the view that "overpopulation" is the chief cause of our environmental ills. The book, however, carries the argument rather beyond the limits of the scientific evidence, providing, for example, detailed instructions on how to persuade very diverse people (called "targets") of the virtues of population control. Thus, the reader is advised on how to handle, presumably with equal effectiveness, situations in

303

which "target is extreme conservative" and "target is extreme liberal."

Page 7: Howard, quotation: From Walter Howard: "Man's Population-Environment Crisis," *Natural Resources Lawyer,* 4 (January 1971), p. 106.

Page 7: Davis, quotation: From Wayne Davis: "Overpopulated America," *The New Republic,* January 10, 1970, pp. 13–15.

Page 7: Wiley, quotation: George Wiley, a former professor of chemistry, is now chairman of the National Welfare Rights Organization. The quotation is from "Ecology and the Poor," a speech delivered at the Harvard University Earth Day meeting, April 21, 1970, reprinted in *Earth Day—The Beginning* (New York: Bantam Books; 1970), compiled and edited by the national staff of Environmental Action, pp. 213–16.

Page 7: Knapp quotation: From the pamphlet by Sherman Knapp: *Nuclear Industry and the Public,* published by Atomic Industrial Forum, 1970.

Page 8: Roth, quotation: From his closing remarks delivered to the "Conference on Man and His Environment: A View Toward Survival," San Francisco, November, 1969, reprinted in H. D. Johnson, ed.: *No Deposit—No Return* (Reading, Mass.: Addison-Wesley; 1970), pp. 317–18.

Page 8: Sandoval, quotation: From "La Raza," a speech delivered at the Albuquerque, New Mexico, Earth Day rally, April 22, 1970, reprinted in *Earth Day,* p. 224.

Page 8: Phillips, quotation: From his speech "Unity," delivered at the Earth Day rally in Washington, D.C., April 22, 1970, reprinted in *Earth Day,* p. 74.

Page 8: White, quotation: From his widely quoted article "The Historic Roots of Our Ecologic Crisis," *Science,* vol. 155, pp. 1203–7.

Page 8: Hartke, quotation: From his speech delivered at an Earth Day meeting at Concordia Senior College, Fort Wayne, Indiana, April 22, 1970, reprinted in *Earth Day,* p. 134.

Page 9: Cameron, quotation: From his speech delivered at an Earth Day meeting, State University of New York, April 22, 1970, reprinted in *Earth Day,* p. 173

Page 9: Davis, quotation: From his speech delivered at the Earth Day rally, Washington, D.C., April 22, 1970, reprinted in *Earth Day,* pp. 87–8.

Pages 9–10: Shepard, quotation: From a pamphlet widely distributed by the Soap and Detergent Association, *The Disaster*

Lobby, which is the text of a speech delivered by Thomas Shepard, Jr., at the Forty-fourth Annual Meeting of the Soap and Detergent Association, New York, January 28, 1971. Shepard's emphasis.

Chapter 2
THE ECOSPHERE

Page 15: African Bushmen: For a highly enlightening account of the life of the Bushmen and their relationship to their environment, see Elizabeth M. Thomas: *The Harmless People* (New York: Alfred A. Knopf; 1959).

Page 18: The "organic soup" and the origin of life: Oparin's *The Origin of Life on the Earth* (New York: Macmillan; 1938) is the classic work on this subject, and well worth reading. For a more up-to-date discussion, see A. I. Oparin: *The Origin of Life on Earth* (New York: Academic Press: 1957). See also, Barry Commoner: "Biochemical, Biological and Atmospheric Evolution," *Proceedings, National Academy of Science,* vol. 53, pp. 1183–94.

Pages 23–4: Nitrogen cycle: For a more detailed account of the nitrogen cycle, see Barry Commoner: "Nature Unbalanced: How Man Interferes with the Nitrogen Cycle," *Scientist and Citizen,* 10:1 (January 1968), p. 12.

Pages 31–2: Ecology generally: Readers interested in becoming acquainted with the science of ecology might start with Eugene P. Odum: *Ecology* (New York: Holt, Rinehart and Winston; 1963).

Page 35: Rabbit–lynx cycle: For a discussion of some similar natural cycles, see Lloyd B. Keith: *Wildlife's Ten-Year Cycle* (University of Wisconsin Press; 1963), pp. 64–6.

Page 47: Leo Marx, quotation: This quotation and a later one are from Leo Marx: "American Institutions and Ecological Ideals," *Science,* vol. 170, pp. 945–52.

Chapter 3
NUCLEAR FIRE

Pages 50–1: The fallout problem: For a general description of the scientific background of the fallout problem and of key fallout data, see the following issues of *Nuclear Information* (1958–August 1964), later known as *Scientist and Citizen*

(September 1964–December 1968), and since January 1969 as *Environment:* October 1959, November 1959, April 1960, October 1960, January 1961, April 1962, September 1962, March 1963, August 1963, November 1963, and September 1964. The last issue is a comprehensive review of the problem. See also the following reference. (This is a good place to suggest to the reader that a subscription to *Environment* is perhaps the best way to keep up with environmental problems; the address is: 438 North Skinker Blvd., St. Louis, Mo. 63130.)

Page 52: The Lucky Dragon: For an excellent discussion of the March 1954 weapons test, see Ralph Lapp: *The Voyage of the Lucky Dragon* (New York: Harper & Row; 1958).

Page 52: Ingestion of strontium 90 from bone splinters: see AEC Thirteenth Semi-Annual Report, Washington, D.C., January 1, 1953.

Pages 54–5: Radiation standards: For a general discussion of this problem, see *Scientist and Citizen,* September 1965, p. 5.

Page 57: Estimates of defective births due to fallout: For the first of these estimates, see *Scientist and Citizen,* September 1964; for the second, see "Report of the UN Scientific Committee on the Effects of Atomic Radiation," New York, 1969; for the third, see Ernest J. Sternglass: *Stillborn Future* (New York: Alfred A. Knopf; 1970); for the fourth, see John Gofman and Arthur Tamplin: *Population Control Through Nuclear Pollution* (Chicago: Nelson-Hall; 1971) and an article by these same authors, "Radiation: The Invisible Casualties," *Environment,* 12:3 (April 1970), p. 12.

Page 58: Ecological aspects of nuclear war, quotation: see Rand Corporation: *Ecological Problems and Post-War Recovery: A Preliminary Study from the Civil Defense Viewpoint,* Santa Monica, Calif., August 1961. Also see September 1963 issue of *Nuclear Information.*

Pages 58–9: Plowshare Proposals: News items describing Dr. Johnson's proposals will be found in St. Louis *Post-Dispatch,* February 9, 1965, and Memphis *Commercial Observer,* April 19, 1964.

Page 59: Report of Panama Canal Commission: For a description of the Commission's report, see *New York Times,* December 1, 1970, p. 92.

Page 59: Practical value of Plowshare, quotation: The exchange quoted here was reported in *National Observer,* April 20, 1964.

Page 60: Radioactive gas: See Colorado Committee for Environmental Information and St. Louis Committee for Environmental Information: *Nuclear Explosives in Peacetime,* a Scientists' Institute for Public Information Workbook (SIPI), 30 East 68th Street, New York, 1970, pp. 4–5.

Page 60: General data on nuclear power production: See Bureau of the Census: *Statistical Abstract of the United States* (Washington, D.C., 1970), p. 529; and Hubert Risser: "Power and the Environment: A Potential Crisis in Energy Supply," *Environmental Geology Notes,* 40, Illinois State Geological Survey, Urbana, Illinois (December 1970), pp. 3, 16, 35.

Page 61: Pollution from nuclear power plants: What very few people realize, and—to my knowledge—has never been pointed out by the AEC, is that although nuclear power plants do not themselves produce nonradioactive pollutants, such pollution is, nevertheless, associated with the production of nuclear power. For example, in order to produce fuel for nuclear power plants, a considerable amount of electricity is needed. This electricity is produced by conventional coal-burning plants, which are of course responsible for chemical pollution of the air. The coal burned to produce nuclear fuel represents at least five per cent of the power ultimately yielded by that fuel. Therefore, nuclear power production involves at least five per cent of the *chemical* air pollution due to the production of an equivalent amount of power from coal.

Page 61: Public opposition to reactor siting: For a balanced view of this problem by an experienced science writer, see the Washington *Post* article cited below. For an industry view, see *Electrical World,* December 17, 1969, p. 35.

Page 61: Seaborg, quotation: Dr. Seaborg's statement is quoted from the Washington *Post,* October 19, 1969.

Pages 61–2: Livermore Laboratory research group: A lively account of Gofman and Tamplin's experiences in evaluating environmental contamination from weapons and reactors will be found in their book *Population Control Through Nuclear Pollution* (Chicago: Nelson-Hall; 1971). The quotation is from an AEC press release cited on p. 60 of their book.

Page 62: Estimates of the effects of radiation: For Thompson's estimate, see T. J. Thompson and W. R. Bibb: "Response to Gofman and Tamplin: The AEC Position," *Bulletin of the Atomic Scientists* (September 1970), vol. 26, p. 9; for Morgan's, see K. Z. Morgan and E. G. Struxness: "Criteria for the Control of Radioactive Effluents," *Environmental Aspects of Nuclear Power* (Vienna: International Atomic Energy Agency; 1971).

Chapter 4
LOS ANGELES AIR

Page 66: Air pollution in general: For a good, simple introduction to the air pollution problem and a useful list of readings, see A. A. Nadler *et al.: Air Pollution,* a Scientists' Institute for Public Information Workbook (SIPI), 30 East 68th Street, New York, 1970. For a more detailed survey, see J. P. Dixon *et al.: Air Conservation* (Washington, D.C.: American Association for the Advancement of Science; 1965). See also, Virginia Brodine: *Air Pollution* (New York: Harcourt, Brace & World; in press 1972).

Pages 66 ff: Levels of various air pollutants in Los Angeles air: Unless otherwise noted, all of the data regarding changes in levels of air pollution in Los Angeles are from the excellent summary prepared by local officials—L. J. Fuller *et al.: Profile of Air Pollution Control in Los Angeles County* (Los Angeles County Air Pollution Control District; 1967). See especially pp. 8, 9, 11, and 59.

Pages 66–7: Dust-fall in Los Angeles: These data are from: J B. Taylor: *Dustfall Trends in the Los Angeles Basin, 1947–60* (Los Angeles County Air Pollution Control District; 1961).

Pages 69–71: Kenneth Hahn's correspondence: Mr. Hahn thoughtfully supplied a file of his correspondence at the U. S. Senate hearings on air pollution in 1967. See *Air Pollution—1967,* Part 1, Hearings Before the Subcommittee on Air and Water Pollution, Committee on Public Works, U.S. Senate, February 13–14 and 20–1, 1967, Washington, D.C., pp. 155–207.

Pages 71–2: Toxicity of nitrogen oxides: The data referred to here, together with a good deal of additional relevant information about nitrogen oxides and photochemical smog, is presented in a paper by I. R. Tabershaw, F. Ottoboni, and W. C. Cooper, which is reprinted in *Air Pollution—1968,* Part 3, Hearings Before the Subcommittee on Air and Water Pollution, Committee on Public Works, U. S. Senate, 1968, p. 968. Effects of air pollution on vegetation and crops are discussed in an accompanying paper by O. C. Taylor (p.

959). In the same volume of these hearings useful papers will also be found on the effects of carbon monoxide, sulfur dioxide, lead, and dust.

Page 74: Environmental effects of lead: For the data referred to here, and for general information about lead in the environment, see a series of articles in *Scientist and Citizen,* 10:3 (April 1968).

Page 76: U. S. Public Health Service survey of urban air: The data referred to here are reported in E. Sawicki, *Archives of Environmental Health,* 14 (1967), pp. 524–30. Related data are summarized in *Air Pollution—1967,* Part 3, Hearings Before the Subcommittee on Air and Water Pollution, Committee on Public Works, U. S. Senate, Washington, D.C., 1967, pp. 1284–1308.

Pages 76–7: Interactions among air pollutants and other factors: A good general source of information on this and related issues is: *Inhalation Carcinogenesis,* proceedings of a conference sponsored by the National Cancer Institute and the United States Atomic Energy Commission (Washington, D.C.: U. S. Atomic Energy Commission, Division of Technical Information; 1970). See especially papers by N. Nelson, H. L. Falk, and U. Saffiatti.

Pages 76–8: Health effects of air pollution: Readers interested in a comprehensive, current review of the effects of air pollution on health, might consult S. M. Ayers and M. E. Buehler: *Clinical Pharmacology and Therapeutics,* 11 (1970), p. 337.

Page 78: Complexity of air pollution effects: Although their training compels most scientists to seek persistently for single cause-and-effect relationships, in a situation as complex as air pollution, it eventually becomes clear that this approach is futile. Air pollution has been imposed upon us not one pollutant at a time, but as a complex whole; since it cannot be successfully analyzed piecemeal, there is no really effective way to control air pollution except as a whole. This view is now becoming accepted by specialists who are concerned with air pollution as a *comprehensive* problem. Thus, the paper by Tabershaw *et al.* referred to above concludes with regard to photochemical smog that "There are so many factors—peaks, duration, acute and chronic effects, etc.—that adequate summation in one or several numerical standards is almost impossible. The dose oxidant and the biological mechanisms are so interdependent and difficult to unravel, and coupled with potential unbalance caused by changing any factor in the

309

system, [as to] suggest that the prudent long-range approach should be control of pollutants at the source."

Chapter 5
ILLINOIS EARTH

Pages 81–2; The nitrate problem generally: For a summary of recent changes in the nitrogen cycle and their effects on nitrate levels in the environment, see Barry Commoner: "Nature Unbalanced," *Scientist and Citizen*, 10:1 (January 1968), pp. 9–19. A more technical treatment will be found in Barry Commoner: "Threats to the Integrity of the Nitrogen Cycle: Nitrogen Compounds in Soil, Water, Atmosphere," in S. F. Singer, ed.: *Global Effects of Environmental Pollution* (Dordrecht, Holland: D. Reidel; 1970).

Pages 83–4: Corn production and fertilizer use in Illinois: The data are from a paper by J. H. Dawes *et al.* in *Proceedings, Twenty-fourth Annual Meeting, Soil Conservation Society of America*, Fort Collins, Colorado, 1968, pp. 94–102.

Page 85: Nitrate levels in Illinois rivers: The data referred to here are from an article that summarizes the extensive and valuable studies of the Illinois State Water Survey: R. H. Harmeson, F. W. Sollo, and T. E. Larson: "The Nitrate Situation in Illinois," the Ninetieth Annual Conference of the American Water Works Association, Washington, D.C., 1970.

Page 89: Nitrogen isotope studies at Cerro Gordo: A brief account of our studies can be found in *CBNS Notes*, September 1970, published by the Center for the Biology of Natural Systems, Washington University, St. Louis, Missouri. An account of the meeting at Cerro Gordo can be found in *CBNS Notes*, January 1971.

Page 93: Dr. Gelperin's observations: These were presented verbally at a meeting of the American Medical Association in June 1971; the quotation from Dr. Gelperin is from a report of his presentation in the Chicago *Tribune*, June 22, 1971.

Chapter 6
LAKE ERIE WATER

Page 94: Lake Erie, generally: Most of this chapter is adapted from Barry Commoner: "The Killing of a Great Lake," *The*

1968 World Book Year Book (Chicago: Field Enterprises Educational Corporation; 1968). Data regarding changes in the conditions of Lake Erie are available in this article. For a detailed survey of most, though not all, of the lake's pollution problems, see *Lake Erie Report,* United States Department of Interior, Federal Water Pollution Control Administration, Great Lakes Region, 1968. This report is based on a five-year study. While it is an excellent source of data regarding the general features of lake sources of pollution, it does not adequately explain the ecology of lake pollution.

Page 95: Water pollution, generally: For a brief introduction, see George L. Berg: *Water Pollution,* a Scientists' Institute for Public Information Workbook (SIPI), 30 East 68th Street, New York, 1970.

Page 96: Lake Erie fish catches: These data are from *Report on Commercial Fisheries Resources of the Lake Erie Basin,* United States Department of Interior, Fish and Wildlife Service, Bureau of Commercial Fishing, Washington, D.C., 1968.

Page 96: Buffalo Society of Natural Science study: See *Preliminary Report on the Cooperative Survey of Lake Erie— Season of 1928, Bulletin,* Buffalo Society of Natural Sciences, 14:3 (1929).

Page 98: Dr. Britt's survey: See his paper, "Stratification in Western Lake Erie in Summer of 1953: Effects on *Hexagenia* (Ephemeroptera) population," *Ecology,* 36 (1955), pp. 239–44.

Pages 100–1: Changes in May fly nymph population and in oxygen levels, 1930–61: These data are from *Report on Commercial Fisheries Resources of the Lake Erie Basin* (cited above), pp. 22, 25.

Page 102: Oxygen deficit: See *Lake Erie Report* (cited above), p. 34.

Page 104: Lake Erie phosphate budget: The computations that are the basis of the estimated phosphate budget are reported in *Proceedings, in the Matter of the Pollution of Lake Erie and Its Tributaries,* vol. 1, United States Department of Interior, Federal Water Pollution Control Administration, Great Lakes Region, 1966, pp. 59–60.

Page 105: Studies of iron II and III in English lakes: The work referred to here is an important series of studies by C. H. Mortimer which are summarized in two articles by him in *Journal of Ecology,* 29 (1941), p. 280, and 30 (1942), p. 147.

Page 107: Chemical changes in Lake Erie and Lake Superior: See A. M. Beeton: "Changes in the Environment and Biota of the Great Lakes," in *Eutrophication: Consequences, Correctives,* Symposium, National Academy of Sciences, Washington, D.C., 1969. This volume is a good general source of technical information on eutrophication.

Page 107: Algal counts in Lake Erie: These data are from C. C. Davis' article in *Limnology and Oceanography,* 9 (1964), p. 275.

Page 108: Evidence on "aging" of lakes from sediment analysis: This very important study, which unfortunately is rarely taken into account in popular discussions of eutrophication, was carried out by F. J. H. Mackereth, and is reported in *Philosophical Transactions of the Royal Society of London,* Series B, 250 (1966), p. 165. Dr. Mackereth's research made ingenious use of the differences in the behavior of two metals, iron and manganese, in different concentrations of oxygen. From the ratio between the contents of iron and manganese in samples of sediments from a lake bottom, it is possible to deduce the relative oxygen level at the time the sediment was laid down. Standard geological techniques are used to date different sediment samples. The result is a graph of oxygen level as a function of geological time since the lake's initial formation. If eutrophication were indeed a gradual process of aging, these graphs should show a gradual decrease in oxygen levels. They do not; rather, lakes become eutrophic either very soon after their formation or not until affected by human activity.

Page 109: The causes of eutrophication: For examples of the detergent industry's approach, consult the industry's newsletter *Water in the News* published by the Soap and Detergent Association. Thus, the front page of the April 1971 issue is taken up with two articles. One, headlined "Nitrogen Is Limiting, *Science* Paper Says," reports that eutrophication in coastal waters is in response to nitrogen rather than phosphorus addition; the second, headlined "Panelists See Role of Phosphates in Eutrophication Is Misjudged," reports similar information from other sources. An example of the fertilizer-booster's approach is the following: "The Dept. of Agriculture's views can be summarized thus. . . . Nitrates can indeed promote growth of algae, but phosphorus is more likely to be the culprit"—*Chemical Engineering,* April 21, 1969, p. 53. The possibility that carbon dioxide concentration may control eutrophication is taken up in L. E. Kuentzel:

"Bacteria, Carbon Dioxide, and Algal Blooms," *Journal of Water Pollution Control Federation*, 41 (1969), p. 1739.

Page 110: Lake Erie study: See conclusions reported on p. 69 of *Lake Erie Report* (cited above).

Chapter 7
MAN IN THE ECOSPHERE

Page 114: Growth of world population: For these data see, for example, John McHale: *The Ecological Context* (New York: Braziller; 1970), p. 95.

Page 116: Role of technology in modern industry: For comprehensive treatment of this important issue, see John Kenneth Galbraith: *The New Industrial State* (New York: New American Library; 1967).

Page 118: The demographic transition: An excellent survey of the complex factors governing population is E. A. Wrigley: *Population and History* (New York: McGraw-Hill; 1969).

Chapter 8
POPULATION AND "AFFLUENCE"

Page 128: Increased emissions of pollutants since 1946: For the sources of these data and related computations, see Barry Commoner: "The Environmental Cost of Economic Growth," in *Energy, Economic Growth, and the Environment* (Washington, D.C.: Resources for the Future; in press 1971).

Page 133: Increase in United States population: Statistical Abstracts (cited above), 1970, p. 5.

Page 134: Productivity in chemical industry: J. Backman: *The Economics of the Chemical Industry* (Washington, D.C.; Manufacturing Chemists' Association; 1970), p. 172.

Page 135: Incidence of lung cancer: Department of Health, Education and Welfare: *A Strategy for a Livable Environment* (Washington, D.C.: United States Government Printing Office; 1967), p. 11.

Page 135: Urban automobile travel: Automobile Manufacturers Association: *Automobile Facts and Figures* (Washington, D.C.; 1970), p. 57.

Page 136: GNP per capita: United States Department of Commerce: *The National Income and Product Accounts of the*

United States, 1929–1965 (Washington, D.C.: United States Government Printing Office; 1966), pp. 4–5.

Page 137: Per capita food intake: These data are summarized in *Agricultural Statistics* (cited above), 1967, p. 6974; 1970, p. 576.

Page 138: Data on clothing and fiber production: These are taken from *Statistical Abstracts*, 1947, p. 854; 1948, pp. 811, 865; 1953, p. 97; 1962, p. 798; 1970, pp. 83, 685, 713, 717. Graphs describing the changes in production year by year will be found in Barry Commoner, Michael Corr, and Paul J. Stamler: *Data on the United States Economy of Relevance to Environmental Problems,* prepared for Committee on Environmental Alterations, American Association for the Advancement of Science, Washington, D.C., 1971 (in press). It will be noted that here and elsewhere in the book emphasis is on data for *production* of goods, so that the influence of exports and imports on consumption is neglected. This approach reflects the facts that pollution levels are most directly related to domestic production and that in most cases imports and exports are relatively small compared to domestic production. A possible exception is textiles, which, especially in recent years, have been increasingly imported into the United States. Thus, actual use of textiles per capita, especially in the last few years, is probably somewhat higher than indicated by domestic production data.

Page 138: Housing per capita: See *Statistical Abstracts*, 1948, p. 811; 1970, p. 685.

Chapter 9

THE TECHNOLOGICAL FLAW

Page 141: Nitrates in the Missouri River: See reference for Chapter 5, *pages 81–2.*

Page 142: Rates of growth of various productive activities: The full range of computations described here and elsewhere in this chapter and the relevant references are contained in Barry Commoner, Michael Corr, and Paul J. Stamler: *Data on the United States Economy of Relevance to Environmental Problems* (cited above). Relevant references and a graphical presentation of some of the key data will also be found in Barry Commoner: "The Environmental Cost of Economic Growth" (cited above). See also, Barry Commoner, Michael Corr, and Paul J. Stamler: "The Causes of

Pollution," *Environment*, 13:3 (April 1971), p. 2. With these and related data reported in this chapter, an effort was made, wherever possible, to describe changes between the first postwar year, 1946, and the most recent year for which statistics are available, usually 1968. However, in some instances, data are available only for a shorter span, as noted.

Page 148: Cattle in feedlots: For the relevant statistics, see *Agricultural Statistics*, 1958, pp. 309–10; 1970, p. 306.

Pages 149–50: Relationships among acreage, crop production, and annual use of nitrogen fertilizer: The relevant computations will be found in Barry Commoner: "The Origins of the Environmental Crisis," address before Council of Europe, Second Symposium of Members of Parliament Specialists in Public Health, Stockholm, Sweden, July 1, 1971; and in Barry Commoner: "The Environmental Cost of Economic Growth" (cited above).

Page 150: Illinois corn yields: The figures given here are estimates provided by agricultural agents in the Decatur area. The exact figures vary from place to place, but the general principle remains the same: under present economic conditions, so much fertilizer must be used to obtain a profitable yield that the corn plant is close to saturation and a considerable fraction of the fertilizer leaches into the water.

Page 151: Pesticide use per unit crop yielded: For these computations, see references given in the note for *pages 149–50*.

Page 156: Toxicity of biodegradable detergents: J. A. Edmisten: "Hard and soft Detergents," *Scientist and Citizen*, 8:10 (October 1966), p. 4.

Page 156: Usefulness of soap, quotation: Quoted from R. M. Stephenson: *Introduction to the Chemical Process Industries* (New York: Reinhold; 1966), p. 365.

Page 157: Advertising and detergent sales: These and other relevant data can be found in a very interesting book about the British detergent industry, P. A. R. Puplett: *Synthetic Detergents* (London: Sidgwick and Jackson; 1957), p. 219.

Page 158: Phosphorus content of cleaners: See references given in note for *page 142*.

Page 158: Fiber consumption statistics: See references given in note for *page 142*.

Page 160: Energetic comparison of cotton and nylon: Here we find a good example of what we need to know, and as yet do not, about the social value of alternative means of meeting human needs. For a rational decision about the need for displacing cotton with nylon, we should compare the two materials with respect to: energy requirements for production, and the resultant air pollution; environmental impacts due to production wastes such as pesticides, fertilizer, and chemical plant effluents; durability of the products, and the environmental impacts incident to maintaining them (e.g., laundering, ironing). From such an assemblage of facts, a rational strategy for using these alternative products could be worked out. For example, if the analysis were to show that cotton is generally more socially valuable than nylon, except that cotton requires ironing while nylon does not, it might prove useful to design nonironing cotton fabrics, or even to develop and encourage clothing fashions that no longer call for ironed fabrics. What is important is that the relative benefits and costs associated with the alternative products be made explicit, so that a rational social choice can be made.

Page 163: Plastic fragments in the sea: The report is described in *Marine Pollution Bulletin,* vol. 2 (1971), p. 23. More poignant evidence that plastic fibers are not biodegradable comes to us from Africa's Bushman country. A conservationist reports: "Once the Africans wore animal skins, and when they were discarded the ants disposed of them. Now the people here are starting to wear nylons, and the ants can no longer cope. As a result, fragments of discarded clothes now dot the landscape" (*New York Times,* June 27, 1971).

Page 165: Biochemical effects of DDT: See D. L. Dahlsten et al.: *Pesticides,* a Scientists' Institute for Public Information Workbook, New York, 1970; and J. Frost: "Earth, Air, Water," *Environment,* 11:6 (July 1969), p. 14.

Page 165: Consequences of herbicidal warfare in Vietnam: After several years of persistent effort by a number of scientists and by the American Association for the Advancement of Science, the effects of herbicide spraying in Vietnam began to be aired publicly. The most extensive observations were made by an AAAS survey team led by Dr. Matthew Meselson of Harvard University. For reviews of the most recent information, see Terri Aaronson: "A Tour of Vietnam," *Environment,* 13:2 (March 1971), p. 34; and P. Boffey: "Herbicides in Vietnam; AAAS Study Finds Widespread Devastation," *Science,* 171 (1971), p. 3966.

Page 166: Mercury pollution from chloralkali plants: A detailed summary of this problem will be found in R. A. Wallace et al.: *Mercury in the Environment* (Oak Ridge, Tenn.: Oak

Ridge National Laboratory; 1971), p. 5. See also Barry Commoner: "A Current Problem in the Environmental Crisis: Mercury Pollution and Its Legal Implications," *Natural Resources Lawyer*, 4 (1971), p. 112.

Page 167: Automobile statistics: See references given in note for *page 142.*

Page 168: Automobile engine characteristics: These data are from *Brief Passenger Car Data* (New York: Ethyl Corporation; 1951 and 1970).

Pages 169–70: Nitrogen oxides and lead emissions: See references given in note for *page 142.*

Page 171: Comparison of trucks and railroad freight: These figures were computed by Michael Corr from data provided by the Missouri Pacific Railroad and the Missouri Department of Highways, and from statistics available in Interstate Commerce Commission: *Transportation Statistics in the United States,* 1968, Part 1, Release 2, pp. 19 and 172; and Automobile Manufacturers Association: *Motor Trade Facts,* 1962, p. 52.

Page 172: Per capita power consumption: See *Statistical Abstracts,* 1970, pp. 821–2.

Page 173: Power consumption by different industries: See references given in note for *page 142.*

Pages 173–4: Beer bottles: See references given in note for *page 142.* As noted earlier, in comparing two alternative goods, such as beer delivered in returnable bottles and in nonreturnable ones, it is necessary to compare the relative environmental impacts as fully as possible. In such a comparison the amount of energy involved is important, since energy production invariably generates serious environmental impacts. Such a comparison, for returnable and nonreturnable bottles, has recently been made by three students, Jim Benten, John Hrivnak, and George Voss, working with Dr. Bruce Hannon of the Center for Advanced Computation of the University of Illinois, Urbana. They find that, taking into account all the uses of energy involved in producing and handling the two types of bottles (e.g., in manufacture, transportation, and, in the case of returnable bottles, washing and sterilizing), nonreturnable bottles require the expenditure of about 4.7 times the energy as returnable ones, per unit of fluid reaching the consumer. Thus the use of the nonreturnable bottle generates considerably more air pollution from power production than does the use of the returnable bottle.

Page 176: Importance of relevant factors in postwar environmental impacts: For these computations, see Barry Commoner: "The Origins of the Environmental Crisis" (cited above).

Chapter 10
THE SOCIAL ISSUES

Page 179: Ramo, quotation: Quoted from Simon Ramo: *Century of Mismatch* (New York: David McKay; 1970), p. 152.

Page 179: Galbraith, quotation: Quoted from *The New Industrial State* (cited above), pp. 30–1.

Page 180: Ellul, quotation: Quoted from Jacques Ellul: *The Technological Society* (New York: Alfred A. Knopf; 1964), pp. 14, 227. Ellul's emphasis.

Page 180: Ramo, quotation: Quoted from *Century of Mismatch,* p. 12.

Pages 180–1: MacLeish, quotation: Quoted from his article in *Saturday Review,* October 14, 1967, p. 22.

Page 181: Nixon, quotation: Quoted from President Nixon's State of the Union address, January 22, 1970, *New York Times,* January 23, 1970.

Page 186: Galbraith, quotation: Quoted from *The New Industrial State,* pp. 24–5. Barry Commoner's emphasis.

Page 190: Holism: For an appreciation of this approach to biological problems and its significance for man's relationship to the environment, the reader is directed toward René Dubos' incisive writings. A good place to start is René Dubos: *Man Adapting* (New Haven: Yale University Press; 1965).

Page 195: Costs of air pollution: For current estimates, see First Annual Report of the Council on Environmental Quality, *Environmental Quality,* Washington, D.C., 1970, p. 72.

Page 195: United States radiation policy, quotation: Federal Radiation Council, Staff Report No. 2, 1961, p. 2.

Page 196: Hazard of thyroid cancer: C. W. Mays: "Thyroid Irradiation in Utah Infants Exposed to Iodine 131," *Scientist and Citizen,* 8:8 (August 1966), p. 3.

Page 197: Biological warfare arsenal at Pine Bluff: See *New York Times,* June 10, 1971.

Pages 199–203: Activities of SIPI information committees: For description of these and similar activities and the addresses of SIPI activities (for readers interested in participating in them) see *SIPI Report*, 1:1 (1970), SIPI, 30 East 68th Street, New York.

Page 202: Norvald Fimreite's exploit: Chemical and Engineering News, April 13, 1970, p. 9.

Page 205: Chauncey Starr's risk/benefit analysis: See his article in *Science*, 165 (1969), p. 1232.

Page 208: The Hilton Head controversy: St. Louis *Post-Dispatch*, January 17, 1971.

Page 210: Pentagon position on long-term ecological effects of herbicides in Vietnam: The statement given here is from a letter to the AAAS Board of Directors, from John S. Foster, Jr., Director of Defense Research and Engineering, Department of Defense, dated 29 September 1967. See statement of AAAS Board of Directors in *Science*, 161 (1967), p. 253, which describes one of the early skirmishes in the struggle between scientists and the military over herbicide spraying in Vietnam. The outcome was a Presidential order, in 1971, to halt spraying.

Pages 211–12: Alternative means of preventing postwar rise in pollution levels: The computation of the reduction in environmental impacts due to technology and population size that would have been needed to prevent the postwar rise in pollution levels is achieved as follows. First, recall that pollution level = population size × production/capita × pollution-emission/production. In this computation, it is assumed that the second ("affluence") factor remains unchanged, which is approximately the case for most pollutants (excepting those arising from automobiles). Then, suppose that in 1946 the pollution level = 1, population size = 1, and pollution-emission/production = 1, while in 1968, pollution = 10, population size = 1.4, and pollution-emission/production = 7. The foregoing approximates the actual changes for a number of pollutants. Now, if we were to set out in 1946 to keep the pollution level from rising (i.e., maintaining it at a value of 1), then, if the population size were allowed to increase to 1.4, the "technology" factor (pollution-emission/production) would need to be reduced to 0.7 if the pollution level were to remain at 1 (since 1.4 × 0.7 = approximately 1). This represents a 30 per cent improvement in technology with respect to pollution emission. On the other hand, if the technology factor were allowed to increase to 7, then in order to maintain the pollution level at a value of 1, the population would need to be *reduced* (between 1946 and 1968) from 1 to 0.14

(since $0.14 \times 7 =$ approximately 1). This represents an *86 per cent reduction* in population size.

Page 212: Unemployment and population, quotation: From an address by Willard Wirtz, former Secretary of Labor, "Optimum Population and Environment," in *Population, A Challenge to Environment,* Report No. 13, Victor-Bostrom Fund Report, Washington, D.C., 1970, p. 28.

Page 213: "The United States has more people than it can adequately maintain," quotation: Quoted from Paul R. Ehrlich: "The Population Explosion: Facts and Fiction," in H. D. Johnson, ed.: *No Deposit—No Return* (Reading, Mass.: Addison-Wesley; 1970), p. 39.

Page 213: Resources available to meet population's demands, quotation: Quoted from *Population Growth and America's Future,* interim report, United States Commission on Population Growth and the American Future, Washington, D.C., 1971, p. 5.

Page 214: Population control "by compulsion if voluntary methods fail," quotation: Quoted from Paul R. Ehrlich: *The Population Bomb* (New York: Ballantine; 1968), Prologue.

Page 214: "Mutual coercion," quotation: See Garrett Hardin: "The Tragedy of the Commons" (cited above). It is also relevant to note that in the United States at the present time, birth rate and death rate would be very close to the balance point if there were no "unwanted" children. This derives from a study by Larry Bumpass and Charles F. Westoff (*Science,* 169, 1970, p. 177), who determined from interviews whether births, after they occurred, were "wanted" by the parents. This kind of estimate is, of course, subject to a number of imponderable effects. Nevertheless, it is worth noting that the study showed that nearly twenty per cent of U.S. births were classified as "unwanted." This means that if contraception were perfect, birth rate and death rate would be nearly in balance (the birth rate under these circumstances would be 2.5 children for women in the 35–44 age group; at 2.25 the balance would be achieved).

Chapter 11
THE QUESTION OF SURVIVAL

Page 217: Too late in 1972: In an interview published in *Look* (April 21, 1970), Paul R. Ehrlich was quoted as follows: "When you reach a point where you realize further efforts will be futile, you may as well look after yourself and your friends and enjoy what little time you have left. That point for me is 1972."

Page 218: Mark Twain, quotation: From *Life on the Mississippi* (New York: Harper and Brothers; 1917), p. 156.

Page 219: Report on oxygen content of surface waters: Waste Management and Control, Publication 1400, National Academy of Sciences–National Research Council (Committee on Pollution), Washington, D.C., 1966. The computation is based on the seasonal (summer) low in river flow.

Page 222: Meningioencephalitis: For a summary of clinical cases, see J. H. Callicott: "Amebic Meningioencephalitis Due to Free-Living Amebas of the Hartmanella (acanthamoeba)-Naegleria Group," *American Journal of Clinical Pathology,* 49 (1968), p. 84.

Page 223: Soil molds in polluted water: The study referred to here is being carried out by John Noell, Junior Fellow of the Center for the Biology of Natural Systems.

Page 223: Infections at European beaches: Sheldon Novick: "Last Year at Deauville," *Environment,* 13:6 (July-August 1971), p. 36.

Page 224: NTA-metal synergism: For a recent summary of this problem, see *Medical World News,* January 22, 1971, pp. 47–57. It is important to note that the scientific basis of the present views of the NTA hazard is still rather weak. Only one, as yet inadequately reported study, has been completed thus far, although more are in progress. Much more information is needed before the hazard can be evaluated.

Page 225: Methylation of mercury and arsenic in polluted water: For a recent review of this problem, see *Chemical and Engineering News,* July 5, 1971, pp. 22–34.

Page 226: Acidity of rain in Sweden: See Eric Albone: "The Ailing Air," *Ecologist,* 1:3 (September 1970), p. 3.

Page 227: DDT in the ocean: See "Chlorinated Hydrocarbons in the Ocean Environment," National Academy of Sciences, Washington, D.C., 1971.

Pages 227–9: Polyvinyl plastics: For a general account of the development of the medical problems associated with the plasticizers used in these plastics, see the articles by Robert De Haan: *Nature,* 231 (1970), p. 85; and by R. J. Jaeger and R. J. Rubin in *Lancet,* 1970-II (1970), p. 151; and also *Chemical and Engineering News,* February 15, 1971, p. 12; Baltimore *Sun,* March 8, 1971; *Chemical and Engineering*

News, April 26, 1971, p. 3 (letter from Frederick C. Gross regarding NASA experience with volatile plasticizers in plastics).

Page 229: Organotin stabilizers, quotation: Quoted from W. C. Guess and S. Haberman: "Toxicity Profiles of Vinyl and Polyolefinic Plastics and Their Additives," *Journal of Biomedical Materials Research*, 2 (1968), p. 313.

Page 230: Fetal deformities from phthalic acid derivatives: Both quotations are from R. K. Bower *et al.*: "Teratogenic effects in the chick embryo caused by esters of phthalic acid," *Journal of Pharmacology and Applied Therapeutics*, vol. 171, p. 314. More recently and more ominously, similar effects have been detected in rats by A. R. Singh *et al.*: "Teratogenicity of a Group of Phthalate Esters in Rats," Abstracts, Tenth Annual Meeting, Society of Toxicology, 1971, p. 23.

Page 232: "The battle to feed all of humanity is over . . . ," quotation: From Paul R. Ehrlich: *The Population Bomb*, rev. ed. (New York: Ballantine; 1971), p. xi.

Pages 233–4: Newspaper advertisements on "overpopulation": Both quotations are from a series of advertisements reproduced in L. K. Lader: *Breeding Ourselves to Death* (New York: Ballantine; 1971), pp. 96–100. Original emphasis.

Page 236: Multiple factors affecting population size: E. A. Wrigley's *Population and History* (cited above) is well worth consulting for an excellent summary of the various factors that affect population size, their complex interactions, and the relevant data.

Pages 238–9: Birth rate and infant mortality trends in developing countries: For the relevant statistics, see Roger Revelle: "Population and Food Supplies: The Edge of the Knife," in *Prospects of the World Food Supply*, National Academy of Sciences, Washington, D.C., 1966.

Page 240: Hunger in developing countries: See Josué de Castro: *The Black Book of Hunger* (New York: Funk and Wagnalls; 1967), for a moving and enlightening account of hunger, its origins, effects, and recent efforts to combat it. For a brief account of the problem, see Margaret Mead: *Hunger*, a Scientists' Institute for Public Information Workbook (SIPI), 30 East 68th Street, New York, 1971.

Pages 240–1: Statement of government of Ghana, quotation: Quoted from *Studies in Family Planning*, Population Council Publication No. 44 (August 1969), p. 1. I wish to thank Dr. Thayer Scudder of the California Institute of Technology for calling this statement to my attention, and for valuable discussions of the problems of developing nations in general.

Page 241: Withholding aid is a means of enforcing fertility control, quotation: Quoted from Paul R. Ehrlich: "The Population Explosion: Facts and Fiction" (cited above), p. 44.

Pages 242–3: "Reports A and B" on population control: The two reports quoted here were published together under the title *How Low Income Countries Can Advance Their Own Growth,* by the Committee for Economic Development (New York; 1966).

Page 245: Keyfitz's analysis of the relationships between the population problem and colonialism: See Nathan Keyfitz: "National Population and the Technological Watershed," *Journal of Social Issues,* 23 (1967), p. 62.

Page 245: Colonialism in Indonesia: Clifford Geertz: *Agricultural Involution* (Berkeley: University of California Press; 1968). This is a fascinating account of the impact of Dutch colonialism on demographic and ecological processes in Indonesia.

Pages 246–7: Ecological backlash in developing countries: For a series of illuminating accounts of the untoward ecological effects of the introduction of modern technology into developing countries, see M. Taghi Farvar and John P. Milton, eds.: "The Careless Technology —Ecology and International Development," *Proceedings of the Conference on Ecological Aspects of International Development,* organized by the center for the Biology of Natural Systems and the Conservation Foundation (New York: Natural History Press; 1972).

Page 248: The "triage" proposal: See William and Paul Paddock: *Famine 1975* (Boston: Little, Brown; 1967). The statement quoted here is from p. 226.

Chapter 12
THE ECONOMIC MEANING OF ECOLOGY

Page 250: Economic considerations generally: I wish to thank Dr. Donna Allen for valuable comments on this chapter, and to express my deep appreciation to two good friends, Roy Battersby and Arthur Kinoy, for a series of perceptive discussions of the issues considered here.

Page 252: The market place economy, quotation: Robert L. Heilbroner: *Understanding Macroeconomics,* 2nd ed. (Englewood Cliffs, N.J.: Prentice-Hall; 1968), p. 12.

Page 253: Proposal to "internalize" externalities: A. G. Pigou: *The Economics of Welfare* (London: Macmillan; 1962).

Pages 254–5: E. L. Dale, Jr., quotations: From E. L. Dale, Jr.: "The Economics of Pollution," *New York Times Magazine,* April 19, 1970.

Page 256: "Economic growth renders many things obsolete . . . ," quotation: The quotation is from Alan Coddington's interesting article, "The Economics of Ecology," *New Society,* April 19, 1970, p. 596.

Pages 256–7: Kapp, quotations: These quotations are from the revised edition of the book by K. William Kapp: *Social Costs of Business Enterprise* (Bombay, London, New York: Asia Publishing House; 1963). The first quotation is from p. 272, the second from p. 290, and the third from p. 271.

Page 258: Heilbroner, quotation: From *Understanding Macroeconomics* (cited above), p. 89. Heilbroner's emphasis.

Page 259: Soap and detergent industry profits: See *Census of Manufactures* (1947), pp. 407–8; 1954, p. 28D-7; 1958, p. 28D-9; 1963, p. 28D-8; 1967, p. 28D-9 for original data. The profits for soap and detergents can be computed from the changes in the proportion of soap and detergent manufactured following 1947 and concurrent changes in profit (as per cent of sales).

Pages 260–1: Chemical industry, profits, and research expenditures: See, generally, J. Backman: *The Economics of the Chemical Industry* (cited above). The quotation is from p. 215.

Page 261: Pesticide hearings: The hearings were held before the House Agricultural Committee on March 8, 1971, and reported in *The New York Times,* July 11, 1971. The quotation is from the latter.

Page 262: NTA manufacturing plants abandoned: According to the *Wall Street Journal* (December 21, 1970), construction of NTA manufacturing plants was abandoned by the W. R. Grace Company and the Monsanto Chemical Company.

Page 263: Farmer's views on profits, quotation: Quoted from the testimony of W. G. Beeler before Illinois State Pollution Control Board, Normal, Illinois, March 17, 1971.

Page 263: National statistics on economic importance of fertilizers and pesticides: For a summary, see E. O. Heady and L. Auer: "Imputation of Production to Technologies," *Journal of Farm Economics,* 48 (1966), p. 309.

Page 264: Car manufacturing profits, quotation: Fortune (March 1969), p. 112.

Page 264: "Minicars make miniprofits," quotation: St. Louis *Globe-Democrat,* May 14, 1971.

Pages 264–5: Comparative profits of displaced and displacing product: Computed from data originating as follows: lumber, *Census of Manufactures* (cited above), 1967, pp. 24–8 and 24A-10; steel, ibid., p. 33A-14; aluminum, ibid., p. 33C-13; cement, ibid., p. 32-10; plastics, ibid., p. 28B-9; railroad and truck freight, Interstate Commerce Commission Annual Report, Washington, D.C., 1970.

Page 267: Profitability of "irresponsible" operations: Daniel Fife, "Killing the Goose," *Environment,* 13:3 (April 1971), p. 20.

Pages 269–70: Productivity and pollution controls, quotations: G. F. Bloom: "Productivity, Weak Link in Our Economy," *Harvard Business Review* (January 1971), p. 5.

Page 276: Capitalism and pollution control: The quotations are from Robert Heilbroner: *Between Capitalism and Socialism* (New York: Random House; 1970), pp. 282–3.

Pages 278–9: Environmental pollution in the USSR: The quotations and most of the observations reported here are from P. R. Pryde: "Victors Are Not Judged," *Environment,* 12:9 (November 1970), p. 30. See also Gil Jordan: "The Soviet Environment," *Clear Creek* (July 1971), p. 12.

Page 280: Goldman's study of environmental pollution in the USSR: See Marshall I. Goldman: "Environmental Disruption in the Soviet Union," in T. R. Detwyler: *Man's Impact on Environment* (New York: McGraw-Hill; 1971), p. 61.

Page 280: Divergent Soviet views on environmental pollution: See, for example, Bernard Gwertzman's dispatch, *New York Times,* March 2, 1970.

Page 281: Karl Marx on soil ecology: This perceptive statement, which appears to have been based on Marx's reading of the German agricultural chemist, Liebig, follows: "Capitalist production . . . disturbs the circulation of matter between man and the soil, i.e., prevents the return to the soil of its elements consumed by man in the form of food and clothing; it therefore violates conditions necessary to lasting fertility of the soil. . . . Moreover, all progress in capitalistic agriculture is a progress in the art, not only of robbing the laborer, but of robbing the soil; all progress in increasing the fertility of the soil for a given time is a progress toward ruining the lasting sources of that fertility. The more a country starts its development on the foundation of modern industry, like the United States, for example, the more rapid is this process of destruction. Capitalist production, therefore, develops technology, and the combining together of various processes into a social whole, only by sapping the original sources of all wealth—soil and the laborer." Karl Marx, *Capital*, vol. I (New York: International Publishers; 1967), pp. 505–6.

Page 282: The private enterprise system and the environmental crisis, quotation: Robert Heilbroner: *Between Capitalism and Socialism*, p. 283.

Pages 284–5: Cost of environmental reconstruction: For data regarding cost of United States capital stock, see *Economic Report of the President and Annual Report of Council of Economic Advisers*, Washington, D.C., 1970, p. 190.

Page 287: Ecologically rational economics: An economist who has given serious thought to the influence of ecological imperatives on the economic system is E. F. Schumacher, economic adviser to the British National Coal Board. His ideas are developed in a series of very interesting but unfortunately little-known articles: "Buddhist Economics," *Resurgence*, 1:11 (January 1968); "The New Economics," *Manas*, 32:14 (April 1969) and 22:25 (June 1969).

Page 290: International aid and ecological recovery: As indicated earlier, there are moral grounds for regarding the developing nations as major creditors of the developed ones. In recent years the United States and other wealthy nations have made a pitifully small effort to repay the debt through international aid. Now even this small repayment is in doubt. Aid declines, and we hear instead a new emphasis on population control. Thus a recent State Department briefing document for President Nixon offers the following reasons for "United States interest in helping LDC's [diplomatic jargon for 'less developed countries'] slow population growth": "The United States and other nations providing aid are disappointed because rapid population growth consumes and nullifies two-thirds of our aid. Improvements in standards of living we hoped to see in a reasonably few years are taking much longer. . . . More aid will be needed just to maintain the present slow rate of progress. Congress and the public will be more reluctant to increase aid when so much goes to maintain more people at the same levels of poverty which now prevail. The United States is in danger of losing mar-

kets, investments and sources of raw materials as LDC's seek
ways to increase their resources. Frustrated hopes among
the peoples of the LDC's, unemployment and underemploy-
ment will lead to civil unrest, political upheavals and in
some instances threaten the disintegration of nations."

Chapter 13
THE CLOSING CIRCLE

Page 297: Garrett Hardin, quotation: Quoted from an editorial, "The Survival of Nations and Civilizations," in
Science, vol. 172, p. 1297.

ACKNOWLEDGMENTS

In a number of crucial ways, this book is the outcome of my participation in several organizations that are deeply concerned with environmental problems: The St. Louis Committee for Environmental Information, The Scientists' Institute for Public Information, The Committee on Environmental Alterations of the American Association for the Advancement of Science, and The Center for the Biology of Natural Systems at Washington University. Most of the factual material presented in this book has been developed during the course of the activities of one or more of these organizations, and many of the ideas which it advances have emerged from discussions with colleagues in these groups. I owe a great debt to these colleagues, not only for information and ideas freely shared, but also for the simple hard work of creating and sustaining these important organizations.

Nearly all of the ideas presented in this book have been elucidated, tested, and modified—sometimes beyond recognition—in the course of numerous discussions with a number of close collaborators and friends, in particular: Dean E. Abrahamson, Walter Bogan, Virginia Brodine, Michael Corr, M. Taghi Farvar, Daniel H. Kohl, Julian McCall, Alan H. McGowan, Sheldon Novick, Max Pepper, Kevin P. Shea, Paul J. Stamler, and Wilbur Thomas. I am deeply grateful to all of them for their vigorous, insightful, and often enough, patient participation in these discussions.

329

Michael Corr and Paul J. Stamler, of the staff of the AAAS Committee on Environmental Alterations, have carried out most of the analysis of the statistical data on environmental impact that are reported here. They have made important contributions to the development of the concept itself and to the analysis of its relation to the environmental crisis. In addition, Mr. Stamler has been largely responsible for assembling the notes and references.

Finally, I wish to thank my administrative assistant, Mrs. Gladys Yandell, for her devoted and matchless work; Mrs. Corinne Clark and Mrs. Peggy Whitlow for very effective assistance in the typing of the manuscript; and Anita Hultenius, Kay Shehan, and Bernard Watts of the Washington University Library for their frequent aid in finding elusive references.

It is a pleasure, too, to express my appreciation for the superb efforts of my editor, Robert Gottlieb, his assistant, Toinette Rees, and the copy editor, Ann Close, in the preparation of this book; and my gratitude to Marie Rodell for very valuable assistance in this and related projects.

INDEX

A Letter from the Author

Dear Reader:

I would like to take another few moments of your time to ask you to consider ways in which you, yourself, may do something about the environmental crisis. As I said in the final paragraphs of this book, there is not, and cannot be, any simple or single solution to a problem that stems from the very nature of our modern industrial society. The crisis of the environment is not a problem which occurs in isolation; if it is to be resolved the solution will be found by all of us as we work, each in our fashion, toward a more just and less wasteful society.

The obligation is all the greater therefore, for each of us to learn the realities of environmental problems and to carry an awareness of the environmental imperative into all of our activities. I am thinking particularly about those activities, in which all of us engage, that in sum determine the course of social change: Your day-to-day involvement in community affairs, in your work, in political elections, church groups, unions, schools.

In all of those activities in which we engage as citizens, we will have to learn to understand how environmental improvement relates to the general betterment of our lives; as I have tried to explain, these are complementary and not conflicting goals. To do so, you will have to be fully and accurately informed. The scientist has a special responsibility to provide the information you need, and I and many of my colleagues have tried to discharge this responsibility, in part, through the activities of the scientists' information movement, which I have mentioned briefly in Chapters 3 and 10. If you would like to know more about the activities of these groups, or would like to assist in their work, you should write to the Scientists' Institute for Public Information (SIPI), 30 East 68th Street, New York, New York 10021.

An immediate and direct step you can take, which will put a great deal of valuable information in your hands and which will assist further efforts to inform the public, is to subscribe to *Environment* magazine, published by SIPI. I know of no better way to learn about environmental problems, their causes and their cures, than to read *Environment,* in which scientists, professional writers, and editors collaborate to make scientific information readable, useful, and even entertaining. The magazine is published ten times yearly, and subscriptions are $10.00 for one year, $18.50 for two years, and $27.00 for three years. For subscriptions outside the United States $2.00 per year should be added. Subscription orders should be addressed to *Environment,* Post Office Box 755, Bridgeton, Missouri 63044.

Sincerely yours,
Barry Commoner

ABOUT THE AUTHOR

BARRY COMMONER—biologist, ecologist, educator ("A professor with a class of millions," *Time* has called him) —is widely regarded as America's best informed and most articulate spokesman for the safeguarding of man's environment. "If America's policy makers take his central doctrine to heart," Stewart Udall wrote about Commoner's greatly acclaimed book, *Science and Survival*, "we can enjoy the fruits of science without destroying the tree of life."

A city boy, but always fascinated by nature, he was born in Brooklyn in 1917, was graduated from Columbia in 1937, and received his M.A. and Ph.D. degrees in biology from Harvard. He has been, since 1947, on the faculty of Washington University in St. Louis and is now Director of its Center for the Biology of Natural Systems. He is noted for his pioneering studies of fundamental problems on the physicochemical basis of biological process, has written over 120 scientific papers, and is the recipient of innumerable academic honors. Dr. Commoner is a member of the Board of Directors of the American Association for the Advancement of Science, Chairman of the Board of Directors of the Scientists' Institute for Public Information, and a founder of the St. Louis Committee for Environmental Information.